MARYAM ASLANY

PEASANTS

MARYAM ASLANY

PEASANTS

Makers of the Modern World

BLOOMSBURY PUBLISHING
LONDON • OXFORD • NEW YORK • NEW DELHI • SYDNEY

BLOOMSBURY PUBLISHING
Bloomsbury Publishing Plc
50 Bedford Square, London, WC1B 3DP, UK
Bloomsbury Publishing Ireland Limited
29 Earlsfort Terrace, Dublin 2, D02 AY28, Ireland

First published in Great Britain in 2026

A catalogue record for this book is available from the British Library

ISBN: HB: 978-1-5266-5477-9 ; TPB: 978-1-5266-5478-6; EBOOK: 978-1-5266-5480-9

2 4 6 8 10 9 7 5 3 1

Typeset by Six Red Marbles India
Printed and bound in Great Britain by Clays Ltd, Elcograf S.p.A

MIX
Paper | Supporting responsible forestry
FSC® C018072
FSC www.fsc.org

To find out more about our authors and books, visit www.bloomsbury.com and sign up for our newsletters
For product-safety-related questions, contact productsafety@bloomsbury.com

For Rana

Contents

Once upon a time – says the Persian tale[1] – a prince and his companions rode out for the hunt. 'The sun was bright,' says the poet, 'and the game was plentiful.'

After the day was finished, the aristocrats came upon the house of a peasant family, which they took over for their lodging. Filling the dwelling with wine and song, they gradually lost their senses. Staggering into the night to pick grapes from the vines, a drunken servant startled the prince's horse, which ran headlong into the darkness, trampling the fields and ruining the crops.

Surveying the devastation the next morning, the peasant was outraged. Soon, his complaints reached the court. Furious, the king summoned the prince and reminded him of the kingdom's most cherished principle: 'The rights of the ruled must always rule.' He stripped his son of his title, and transferred it to the aggrieved peasant. The man who had picked the grapes was given to the peasant as a slave; even the musician's harp was destroyed.

We can judge the quality of a society, the tale suggests, by examining the way it treats its peasants. After all it is they – and not the prince – who make the human community viable, and regulate its relationship to nature.

Preface

For millennia, peasants stood at the heart of human society. In Western lands, industrialisation pushed them into obscurity – and everywhere, modernisers came to regard them as relics of an undeveloped past.

Many city dwellers believe the urbanisation of our species is natural and inexorable. Extrapolating from past trends, they imagine a future in which the great majority have abandoned the land, leaving it bucolic, automated and sparsely inhabited. They assume that all agriculture will be consolidated under large capital and machinery, and cities will absorb the bulk of the population. They predict the imminent extinction of that ancient character: the peasant.

To date, that disappearance has not occurred. Nearly 42 per cent of humanity lives in the countryside, mostly in Asia, Africa and Latin America, where small family farms remain the economic backbone. After three centuries of 'modernisation', peasant households still make up roughly a quarter of the world's population.

Despite this, the global countryside continues to fade from public conversation. Most of us are therefore oblivious to the profound crisis it is in – even though symptoms of that crisis break into our news headlines under other names: food insecurity, inflation, mass migration, the spread of militancy. If we continue to ignore this crisis, we will all fall victim to it. Because of the sheer numbers involved, the collapse of peasant systems will reverberate across the world – destabilising food systems and supply chains, deepening political conflict and accelerating ecological breakdown.

To understand this crisis, this book first offers a history of the global peasantry – Part One – whose role in making our modern world is both astonishing and overlooked. Part Two takes us to the far-flung fields where four commodities central to the twenty-first-century economy are grown: sugarcane, rice, coca (cocaine) and cocoa (chocolate). Each of these is cultivated by small farmers and then absorbed into commercial networks, which are mostly dominated by corporations or cartels. While the corporations are often household names, few consumers know anything about the farmers.

To write *Peasants*, I spent four years travelling across remote regions of Asia, Africa and Latin America, living with peasant families, sharing daily life in their homes, farms and villages, speaking with them at length, and witnessing first hand the rhythms of cultivation, harvest, debt and survival. Alongside English, our conversations were conducted in local languages – primarily Marathi, Khmer, Twi and Spanish – often with the help of translators and interpreters from each region who accompanied me during my research trips.

As a rural sociologist who has devoted my academic life to this subject, I am aware that no single book can capture the full complexity of the global countryside, which is filled with a great variety of economies, societies, cultures and moral worlds. Moving across continents, centuries, political systems and academic disciplines necessitates omissions and simplifications. My aim here is not to provide an exhaustive account but rather to restore to the countryside the visibility it demands. And to show that the future of small farmers is the future of us all.

PART ONE

How We Forgot

I

The Peasant Within

> PEASANT. (1) A person who lives in the country and works on the land, esp. as a smallholder or a labourer; (chiefly Sociology) a member of an agricultural class dependent on subsistence farming. Now used esp. with reference to foreign countries (or to Britain and Ireland in earlier times), and often to denote members of the lowest and poorest rank of society (sometimes contrasted with prince or noble). (2) As a term of abuse: a person of low social status; an ignorant, stupid, unsophisticated, or (formerly esp.) unprincipled person; a boor, a lout; (also more generally) a person who is regarded with scorn or contempt, esp. by members of a particular social group.
>
> – OXFORD ENGLISH DICTIONARY

The word has an unusual bite. It is not anodyne – like 'baker', 'soldier' or 'merchant'. It has a negative edge; it produces embarrassment, discomfort, hostility. Like an obscene epithet, it is avoided in general conversation – but also serves, in English and many other languages, as an expression of anger and abuse.

The uncanny feelings associated with this word are a residue of the massive psychodrama which made us who we are. 'Modernisation' would be one name for it – for we became modern by expelling the peasant parts of ourselves. If 'modern' people are still so threatened by the word, it is because that expulsion was never complete, and the mention of 'peasants' returns them to the most uncomfortable and unresolved parts of their psyche. We will not be capable of any meaningful encounter with the global countryside, therefore, until we have first confronted our own persona – and the peculiar potency of the peasant we still carry within. That is the purpose of Part One.

Until just a couple of centuries ago, human beings were overwhelmingly dependent on what we might call the biological order. We have since grown accustomed to a rival, industrial order; but for most of history, human activity was powered almost exclusively by animals and plants. Populations derived their social structures, in fact, from the differing biological processes underlying their economies. Steppe societies, for instance – which depended on goats, sheep, cattle, horses, asses or camels to turn otherwise useless grassland into commodities (meat, milk, blood, leather, bone, wool) – were organised as nomadic tribes of herders, traders and soldiers. Moving in seasonal grazing loops, they were strangers to agriculture and therefore to peasants. In sedentary kingdoms and empires, however, whose economies were based on intensive cultivation of the land, peasants were always the largest social group. Of the three estates in Chaucer's England, the clergy and aristocracy together accounted for only 4 per cent of the population. The third, the labouring estate, was comprised overwhelmingly of peasants. Over the next four centuries, Britain would become one of the most urbanised societies in the world – and yet, even on the eve of the industrial revolution, no more than 30 per cent lived in cities. In France and China, meanwhile, whose structure was more typical of pre-industrial states, peasants made up at least 80 per cent of the population.

Peasants were not 'natural' creatures. They were not farmers in their raw condition; human societies had engaged in agriculture for several millennia, after all, before there was any fixed peasantry. During that period, farmers were usually mobile and seasonal, and they worked only to feed themselves. They minimised risk by maintaining access to diverse food sources, and avoided being tied to particular parcels of land. To protect this flexibility, they generally opposed hierarchy and domination. 'Peasants', then, emerged only with early states, whose purpose was to extract a surplus from a fixed territory and which required a subjugated class to farm the land; indeed, there were no states without peasants, and vice versa. In essence, peasants were farmers held captive by states – prevented from leaving the land or the territory and forced to give up much of their produce for the maintenance of the state.[1] Peasants emerged not from agriculture itself but from the loss of autonomy and mobility associated with early state power.[2]

Shaped by bondage to land, by debt and by tax obligations to rulers, the peasant condition was always, therefore, political (Figure 1). States and peasants were locked in a perennial tussle: states had to dominate peasants, but they also had to acknowledge their demands, dependent on them as they were for their existence. No state activity, whether warfare or worship, was possible without the agrarian contribution; if supplies from the countryside ceased, cities would starve and the social order would collapse. The manifold strategies for controlling peasants were implicit acknowledgement of this existential importance: peasants were enslaved and enserfed, regulated and punished, indoctrinated, reduced to the status of mere labouring bodies, surrounded by walls and soldiers and prevented from fleeing to the greater freedom of nomadic tribes or meritocratic cities.[3] But the need to extract a surplus could not be pushed so far that the peasantry collapsed. In order to fulfil their function, peasants needed certain political safeguards, which were respected by all the most successful agrarian states. They expected rulers to protect their relationship to the land, from malicious aristocrats, for instance, or landowners or moneylenders; to keep taxes and levies to a bearable level; and to provide food security in times of need. In general, peasants campaigned for states to punish aristocratic corruption and urban decadence and to enforce what they held to be sacred values: reciprocity between peasants and ruler, and respect for natural systems.

'Peasant power' was not economic alone. It was also moral. Living on the boundary between society and nature, peasants possessed a social vision quite distinct from that of the castle or the city. Their production was ultimately destined for those control centres, yes;

but it emerged from a more mysterious system of natural cycles, with which human beings could cooperate, but which they could not direct. Of course, peasants possessed deep botanical and zoological knowledge, and the emotional and moral intelligence for collaborative relationships with plants, animals and landscapes; of course, their social systems were well adapted to enable collective success in completing the fantastically arduous tasks of the agricultural year. But all this specialisation could not control the sun or the rain. Peasants lived in awe of nature, and their perennial fear of calamity – drought, flood, infestation, soil erosion and sedimentation – placed them in a fundamentally different cosmos from that of their urban cousins.

As a result of all this, peasants viewed themselves – and were often viewed by others – as the moral conscience of society. Peasant movements had a knack for distilling their vision of hard work and mutuality into proverbs whose moral authority was all the greater for their simplicity. 'When Adam delved and Eve span / Who was then the gentleman?' rhymed John Ball, a clergyman who joined the English Peasants' Revolt against corruption and taxes in 1381 – pointing out the social equality of God's original creation. Peasants often appeared in culture as sages and teachers. John Ball may himself have been influenced by the dream poem *Piers Plowman*, in which the eponymous peasant preaches the spiritual importance of tilling the soil and is eventually revealed to be the divine gardener – Christ himself. At the other end of the continent, where peasants were endowed with even greater spiritual authority, this mythology was more developed. China's great protagonists were the emperor and the peasantry; their harmonious co-production of well-tended irrigation systems, prolific harvests and peace demonstrated that the cosmos was in order. If the emperor should lose divine favour – the 'Mandate of Heaven' – the first indication would be the collapse of this harmony; in that event, the peasantry must act as guardians of Chinese history and rise up against the disfavoured ruler. From ancient times up to – and including – 1949, Chinese history was full of peasant revolts. In several cases, emperors were successfully removed, a peasant rebel took the throne and the empire's vitality was refreshed.

There was nothing meek about the peasant conscience. When agrarian orders were disturbed, peasants were usually the first to starve; their moral outrage was combined, therefore, with terror, and their retribution could be terrible.* City walls were often designed to repel not invading foreigners, but furious peasant armies. France's devastating Jacquerie of 1358 took place while the French king was in English custody, and peasants accused landowners and nobles of taking advantage of his absence to violate the sacred bargain between themselves and him. Descriptions from near-contemporaries show the enduring terror sown by their frenzied retribution:

> certain people assembled in the agricultural towns . . . and said that the nobles, knights and squires spoiled and shamed the kingdom and that it would be right if everyone destroyed them . . . They killed a knight and placed him on a spit and roasted him, in the presence of his lady and his children. After ten or twelve had violated the lady, they tried to force her to eat her husband, then they put her to a terrible death.[4]

This was the threat the modern world sought to suppress. From about the eighteenth century, as we shall see, the West set about destroying its peasantry as the precondition for becoming 'modern'. Intellectuals of every hue argued that peasants stood in the way of 'progress': Karl Marx believed the socialist future could not emerge while small-scale peasant farming persisted, while at the other end of the political spectrum, Adam Smith thought that the capitalist future would arrive only when peasants gave way to wealthy technocratic landlords. Both felt that the destruction of the peasantry was necessary to the progress of history, and such

* James C. Scott famously argued that peasant politics were shaped by a 'moral economy' centred on subsistence security. Unrest often broke out when there was a violation of those obligations and protections established to guarantee minimal levels of peasant survival, particularly as a result of commercialisation and agrarian disruption. See James C. Scott, *The Moral Economy of the Peasant: Rebellion and Subsistence in Southeast Asia* (New Haven, CT: Yale University Press, 1976).

destruction was built into the strategy of all the leading states. In keeping with the nature of peasant power, the destruction was not only physical – automating the countryside, turning peasants into industrial workers – but moral and spiritual too. The peasant no longer represented a social ideal. Rather, she became the incarnation of everything Western society was running away from – dirty, stupid, primitive, inefficient and stubbornly unchanging. Peasant sensibilities were determinedly stamped out: clock time replaced the rhythm of the seasons, modern states demanded the allegiance once offered to soil and sun and rain, plastic covered the stink of the field.

Of course, there were still people working the land, but they were given new, scientific names. 'Farmers' and 'agricultural labourers' now did all the work in England; the French *paysan* succumbed to the *agriculteur*, Italy's *paesano* became the *agrario*, and Germany's *Bauer* was replaced by the *Farmer* or *Landwirt*. There could be no 'peasants' in the modern world: that was its definition (Figure 2). Their only existence, now, was in the history books, or in those remote regions where (as far as Westerners were concerned) modernity had still to arrive. Even after the Second World War, Asia, Latin America and Africa were still full of peasants – and, as the Cold War gathered pace, this became a point of concern for the capitalist West. Mao's victory in China demonstrated the continuing power of peasant revolt, even in the twentieth century. After leading a successful peasant revolution in Cuba, Fidel Castro poured contempt on the West's blithe assumptions about history. 'Were Kennedy not a millionaire, illiterate and ignorant,' he claimed in 1960, 'then he would obviously understand you cannot revolt against the peasants.' President John F. Kennedy's successors became increasingly attuned to Castro's thinking: Washington during the Vietnam War years (1955–75) was fixated on the Third World peasant and her dangerous political ambitions.

Even when applied to the most 'underdeveloped' places, however, the word eventually felt awkward. As the decades of 'development' succumbed to those of markets, 'peasant' began to sound like a clumsy rich-world accusation: *we* are modern, *you* are not. Globalisation introduced a planetary 'now': 'backward' and 'advanced' were both subsumed into one, universal modern system, and by the 1990s peasants were dematerialising even in the poorest countries. The world filled up with 'cultivators' and 'smallholders'; economic reports quantified the output of so many 'cotton growers' or 'rice farmers'; there were millions of 'agriculturalists' and 'customers' for expanding agribusiness to sell to. 'Peasants', however, dropped out of the vocabulary.

In the heartlands of abstract capitalism, many imagined that the disappearance of the word meant the disappearance of the thing itself. In supermarkets, rice and chocolate sat alongside soft drinks and frozen pizza; wrapped and barcoded, every object seemed equivalent and immaterial – like data. If shoppers wondered at all where these commodities came from, they perhaps imagined vast robotic plantations monitored on screens by corporate administrators. Their newspapers told them that the global countryside was emptying. Statesmen in Third World countries told them, indeed, that this was the very definition of their development: India's finance minister, for instance – whose economics was absorbed from Harvard Business School – declared in 2008 that 'My vision of a poverty-free India will be an India where a vast majority, something like 85 percent, will eventually live in cities.'[5] Their own experience told them that agriculture, in time, is taken over by large capital and heavy machinery. Great intellectuals told them, explicitly, that peasants no longer existed. 'The most dramatic and far-reaching social change of the second half of [the twentieth] century,' wrote the historian Eric Hobsbawm, 'and the one which cuts us off for ever from the world of the past, is the death of the peasantry.'[6] Western consumers were extremely invested in this death, as we have said: they wanted to believe the world was becoming, like them, massified and urban – and so they did.

As we shall see, this story has become constitutive of who we are. It is also a fairy tale: the 'death of the peasantry' never happened. There are more peasants today than at any time in history, and this will not change in the decades to come. But the story is more than just false, it is also dangerous. Not only does it give rise to a political assault on the global countryside – whose consequences, if unchecked, will be economic and political breakdown, and waves of refugees on a scale never seen before. It also threatens to destroy the remaining social systems and knowledge formations which still insulate our planet from total corporate takeover.

Before we begin our tour of the peasant world, then, we need to understand the history of our own aversions.

2

Peasants in the Chinese System

The first stage in detaching ourselves from the story of the peasant's inevitable obsolescence is to remind ourselves of traditions where she held an altogether more grandiose position.

Across the relatively brief span of time we call history, the 'normal' mode of large-scale organisation was the agrarian empire – and the 'normal' human being was a peasant in such an empire. Agrarian empires sustained most of the planet's human population until modern times and produced most of its wealth. From 3000 BCE until the rise of industrial-era London, the biggest cities in the world were concentrated in the agrarian empires of Egypt, Mesopotamia and China. The remarkable calorific surplus produced by such empires was invested in some of the most massive building works ever undertaken: the Egyptian pyramids, the Mesopotamian ziggurats, the Cambodian temple complex at Angkor Wat, the Great Wall of China, the Mayan city of Chichén Itzá.

The last of the great agrarian empires collapsed in the nineteenth century, when the European superpowers began to dismantle their economies and incorporate their territories and peoples into global industrial networks. Having emerged on the back of this destruction, the West has tended to be rather disdainful, also, of agrarian empires – and to overlook, therefore, how extraordinarily successful and stable they were. Most of the states currently in existence are no more than eighty years old; several agrarian empires, by contrast, lasted for a millennium or more. One of the reasons for their stability was the powerful protection they offered to their peasant masses, who constituted their economic foundation. In their worldview, peasants were not primitive hangers-on. Peasants were the grand force of history, driving society forward, producing wealth, innovation – and, sometimes, revolution. Peasants were the heroes.

This was the case in many societies, but we will content ourselves with a consideration of just one: China. From classical times until the fall of the last emperor in 1911, the Chinese empire was built on a simple and enduring formula: high-intensity peasant agriculture, enabled by a vast irrigation system, administered by a dynamic and proactive state, staffed by the world's most educated bureaucrats. This formula was rolled out to the edges of imperial territory, turning it into an ecological as well as a political entity. China's land mass had remained largely uncovered during the last ice age, so its ecosystem, in 3000 BCE, was one of the most diverse. The relentless expansion of Chinese agriculture would ultimately destroy most forests and grasslands, resulting in the extinction of countless plant and animal species, including the megafauna which persisted elsewhere in Asia to the present day: elephants, rhinos and tigers.[1] For China's ideologues, however, this tidy, productive, managed landscape was the very definition of 'civilisation'; it was contrasted with the 'barbarian' lands to the north and west, where nomadic tribes roamed the steppe. Chinese writers noted that nomadic peoples did not acknowledge the basic principles of 'civilised' life – they did not farm the land, eat grain or even cook their food. Certainly, China was not averse to trading with these peoples, who supplied the resources that were foreign to their own agrarian system: woods and metals, furs and hides and, most famously, horses. China's economic success would come to depend very significantly, in fact, on its proximity to grand nomadic empires, which provided trade connectivity to India, Persia, Greece and Rome – the 'silk route'. But China was also terrified of its 'barbarian' neighbours, which, precisely because their populations were not occupied in the fields, were mobile and capable of devastating military raids. What we know as the Great Wall was only the last of many physical barriers designed to protect the peasant economy from easy destruction by lightning horseback armies. Despite such measures, China was obliged, until modern times, to pay enormous tributes to the nomads in order to avoid invasion – and even that did not prevent the capture of the empire by the Mongols in the thirteenth century or by the Manchu in the seventeenth.

Representing China's dominant ethnic group, and perpetuating the values established during the unifying Han dynasty (206 BCE–220 CE), the Han peasant was the main protagonist of Chinese history. A popular tale, told and retold since at least the second century BCE, shows a typical representation:

> A righteous peasant lived near the border. His horse ran off into barbarian territory. Everyone felt sorry for him. But his father said, 'This will quickly turn to good luck.'
>
> Several months later, the horse came back with a fine barbarian mate. Everyone congratulated him. But his father said, 'This will quickly turn to bad luck.'
>
> Now there were many fast barbarian horses, which the peasant loved to ride. He fell and broke his leg. Everyone felt sorry for him. But his father said, 'This will quickly turn to good luck.'
>
> Some time later, the barbarians invaded across the border. Able men strung up their bows and went into battle. Nine out of ten border residents were killed. But the peasant was saved because of his broken leg.
>
> Hence: bad luck brings good luck and good luck brings bad luck. This happens without end, and nobody can estimate it.[2]

This peasant lives in the border regions and is therefore exposed to the terrifying danger of barbarian raids. Despite his vulnerability, however, he does not run away from his labours, but remains true to his peasant purpose. He is incurably 'civilised': when he tries to imitate barbarian horsemanship, he falls off and breaks his leg. His father is not stupid or dull: he is in fact an amateur philosopher, possessed of a stoic wisdom which allows him to rise above the vagaries of existence. Just like his relationship to the land, his sense of fate takes the form of an eternal cycle which began before him and endures beyond his death; to quote John Berger's assessment of the peasant condition, '[The peasant's] determination is to hand on the means of survival (if possible made more secure, compared to what he inherited) to his children. His ideals are located in the past; his obligations are to the future, which he himself will not live to see.'[3] In the Chinese moral universe, the peasant is not a passive onlooker; he is in fact the fount of good sense and virtue.

Organised into nuclear families owning private plots of land, working hard and paying taxes to the emperor, it was the peasants who settled the empire's expanding territory and turned it into revenue. For much of history, China accounted for a quarter of global GDP; at its peak in the early nineteenth century, the figure may have approached one-third.[4] This stupendous economy was structured as a partnership between the peasantry and the state, without whose sustenance and protection rice cultivation would have been impossible. By 'state' we mean not only the emperor but also the bureaucracy. Sovereignty flowed, of course, from the emperor, but he was otherworldly; earthly, managerial power was wielded by bureaucrats. From the seventh century CE, China's bureaucrats were chosen by an imperial examination open to educated men of any social rank; thanks to an extensive system of government schools, there were significant numbers of such men.[5] The examination rewarded those who had mastered the ideological system named after the philosopher known as Confucius (Kongzi, *c.* 551–479 BCE), who, writing during the Warring States period which preceded China's unification in 221 BCE, had theorised an ideal empire, unified under an authoritarian emperor, whose virtue was animated by philosopher advisers. Successive emperors developed the bureaucracy into a formidable operational power – partly to neutralise the influence of military aristocrats, whose role in Chinese history was much less significant, as a result, than in Europe. Civilian bureaucrats contrived to maximise revenue and to minimise ruinous expenditure, especially war. Their continual innovation in economy, taxes and welfare concentrated financial and political power in the hands of the imperial state, which managed a vast economy and population with remarkably little internal competition or mediation.[6]

How did one increase revenues in an agrarian society? In Europe, the usual way was to raise taxes. This accounts for the abject condition of peasants in Europe's feudal societies, where they were tied to aristocratic land, produced nearly all food and wealth, and bore the burden also of most rents and taxes. Raising taxes did not necessarily produce the desired rewards, since grain yields were erratic; it did, however, produce peasant rebellion. More ecological in their thinking, China's anti-aristocratic bureaucrats were determined to keep taxes on the peasantry to a fraction of European levels and therefore to ensure fewer disruptions to the economic machine. China's approach to revenue generation, therefore, was continually to introduce new ways of augmenting the productive capacity of the nuclear peasant family. This was achieved by securing peasant health and nutrition with an extravagant welfare system, and by supplying the countryside with a constantly improving array of farming resources and techniques. The bureaucracy was above all *technological*: it solved social and economic problems with efficiency-enhancing innovations which were developed at the centre and dispersed across imperial territory.

Its most conspicuous production was the irrigation system. Early China was concentrated around the millet fields of the Yellow River; by the third or fourth century CE, the empire had expanded southwards into the Yangtze valley, which was conducive to rice cultivation. In terms of calories per hectare per year, rice was three times more fructiferous than wheat – the European staple – but 'flooded field' farming required constant access to fresh water. To extend rice fields hundreds of kilometres away from major rivers, therefore, required monumental earthworks. Over two centuries, the Yellow and Yangtze river valleys were connected by an extensive network of canals and irrigation channels, at the heart of which lay the Grand Canal. First completed in the seventh century, and stretching nearly 2,000 kilometres from Beijing to Hangzhou, the Grand Canal remains, even today, the longest artificial waterway in the world. The hydraulic network turned the Chinese empire into a single physical object, enabling water and resources to be directed according to the requirements of the agrarian system, and permitting the efficient transport of information, taxes and armies. For the ensuing thousand years and more, the peasantry judged imperial dynasties on their ability to maintain this system, whose power of transporting water to the remotest regions (even, in some cases, over mountains) seemed to provide evidence of the emperor's miraculous, life-giving paternity. At the same time, it made China dependent on engineering massive rivers, which were themselves transformed as a result – sometimes with catastrophic consequences.[7] Because of the continental deforestation associated with the creation of China's homogeneous agrarian landscape, silt was perennially washed off hills and fields, accumulating on riverbeds and raising them, over the centuries, by many metres. Walls and dykes were required to keep rivers from overflowing; whenever these were breached, there were floods. The violence of these floods would ultimately play a decisive role in Chinese history.

But the irrigation system was only one aspect of the imperial state's power over nature. Bureaucrats constantly inspected and documented farming practices and disseminated the more valuable innovations. In around 900 CE, for instance, an official travelling in Guangdong Province saw that local peasants introduced carp into their rice fields and noted that the fish both rid the fields of weeds and mosquito larvae and fertilised the rice with their faeces; this practice was later adopted across all rice-growing regions. By the thirteenth century, such knowledge would be collected into agricultural treatises such as the state-published *Essentials of Farming and Sericulture* (*Nung Sang Chi Yao*, 1285) or the privately issued *Book of Agriculture* (*Nong Shu*, 1313), written by the famous inventor and agronomist Wang Zhen. There was also continual development of new and better botanical stock. A great advance occurred, for instance, when fast-growing rice was brought from the Champa kingdom (in modern Vietnam) in the early eleventh century; this enabled two harvests a year in the lowlands, as well as terrace cultivation in the highlands.[8]

China's agrarian base supported spectacular achievements in other areas. So great was the nutritional surplus that by the time of the Song dynasty (960–1279), great quantities of labour were directed elsewhere – and the technological drive of the Chinese state was arriving at what many have called the first industrial revolution. Powered by coal mines and gas wells, eleventh-century China produced a great range of industrial goods, including quantities of iron that would be unmatched elsewhere until Britain's industrial explosion of the eighteenth century.[9] Iron was used, most conspicuously, in shipbuilding, which itself lay at the centre of a vast project of exploration, trade and technological innovation. Powered by rice and millet, therefore, Chinese power was felt as far away as Somalia and Egypt in the west and Java and Sumatra in the east.

In 1279, horseback armies from Central Asia completed their multi-decade conquest of China, and a new, Mongol dynasty took over the empire. Nomadic tribespeople, with a vision of society almost diametrically opposed to what we have just described, the Mongols did not possess the administrative knowledge necessary for maintaining China's agrarian system, which substantially collapsed during their one-century interregnum. The traditional obsession with state-led agrarian development came to an end. Replacing the directive power of China's bureaucracy with an entrepreneurial elite of merchants and financiers, the Mongols created what we might call a 'proto-capitalist' regime concentrated in the ports and cities (this was the era when such foreigners as the Venetian Polo family flocked to benefit from Mongol commerce). Without proper supervision, the neglected water system fell apart: the Yellow River broke its banks in 1344, dramatically shifting its course and producing widespread droughts and epidemics. The land split open, 'with cracks like the back of a tortoise'.[10]

Given the size of China's population, ecological disruption was necessarily catastrophic. By the mid-fourteenth century, the empire's population had fallen to slightly more than half the level of the Song period. The Mongols' dramatic financial achievements notwithstanding – theirs was the first successful paper currency in history – they destroyed the Chinese agrarian core and were remembered ever afterwards as a cautionary tale: theirs was the chaos to which the empire will be reduced whenever peasant agriculture is not protected.

The Mongols' incomprehension of the agrarian system made them one of the shortest lived of all major Chinese dynasties. In the 1360s, rebellions broke out among peasants forced into the impossible task of rebuilding the hydraulic system. The movement was driven by a millenarian brand of Buddhism which looked forward to the coming of Maitreya, an enlightened saviour who would reign as emperor and restore peace and harmony to the world. The leader was a peasant whose parents had died in the 1344 epidemics and who had lost most of his siblings to a failed harvest in the same year. 'The people in my village lacked food,' Zhu Yuanzhang remembered later, 'with grasses and bark serving as nourishment.'[11] Raising enormous popular forces, Zhu's armies drove their rulers far to the north and, in 1368, established a new dynasty: the Ming.

Invoking the glories of the Song dynasty, the new peasant emperor set about restoring China's 'classical' formula – lowering taxes, confiscating aristocratic lands, implementing laws to protect peasant property and restoring the irrigation system (Figure 3). From overpopulated areas, he organised great tides of peasant migrants to settle the fringes of the empire and subject it to traditional Han agriculture; this was designed both to increase agricultural output and to prevent the rise of large landowners. His dramatic rise to power – he came from abject poverty and received no education until, as an adult, he took refuge in a Buddhist monastery – cemented the peasant's place at the centre of Chinese history. The throne could always be captured by foreign elements, and even good emperors could lapse into decadence; it was up to the peasantry, in such moments, to preserve and restore the imperial conscience. Peasants and emperor were linked in an eternal circle, one protecting the virtue of the other.

A century after the fall of the Mongols, the Chinese system was restored; indeed it now entered its period of greatest glory. From the early sixteenth century, hardy new crops such as potatoes arrived from the Americas, with which peasants were able to settle regions previously abandoned to indigenous tribes. Central to Ming recovery was the restoration of China's dilapidated hydraulic works. In the 1570s, under the direction of the hydrological engineer Pan Jixun, millions of workers rebuilt the Yellow River basin. In undertaking 'the single engineering work that had the greatest environmental impact at any time anywhere in the premodern world', they enclosed the main channel within 'thread dykes' at the banks, which were themselves set within a system of 'set-back dykes' about a kilometre away from the river – which could contain any waters that broke over the thread dykes during the peak discharge period of late summer.[12] The canal network was also much expanded, allowing the Ming dynasty, and the subsequent Qing dynasty, to deliver welfare and famine relief more effectively to the peasant masses.

By that time, China also had immense international standing as the source of key global commodities – most visibly, tea and porcelain. As late as the eighteenth century, China's porcelain factories in Jingdezhen (located just inland of the major southern ports) were the largest industrial installations in the world. China in the seventeenth and eighteenth centuries was without a doubt the global economic hub. It was an imperial axiom, meanwhile, that the emperor never borrowed money, but ran the state only from the wealth he possessed in physical silver. China never developed, therefore, the elaborate debt mechanisms which lay behind the rise of modern Europe, and nor were there Chinese bankers equivalent to the Medici, Fuggers or Rothschilds. Merchants, landowners and financiers never enjoyed the prestige they did in Europe. Very often, in fact, they were viewed with suspicion (in this, Mao was not original). China's immense wealth and commercial power never displaced the fundamental truth: peasants were the archetypal citizens of the empire; everyone else was secondary.

There is no room here to describe the full complexity of the Chinese empire's decline and fall, which took about a century. We will focus on just one aspect – the breakdown of China's agrarian base and the consequent collapse of peasant life – which was at least as consequential as the better-known invasions by European powers.

Already by 1800, the water system was overwhelmed by silt run-off. Between 1800 and 1850, the population increased by over 40 per cent to 430 million; as land use became more intense, inundations became more frequent and dangerous. Floods of the Yellow River in 1851, 1852 and 1853 caused damage too great for the state to repair; in 1855 the river finally smashed the dykes, surged out across the plain and cut a new course 400 kilometres to the north, killing 200,000 peasants and displacing millions.[13] Other rivers, meanwhile, were choked up completely with silt, their buried bridges were the only remembrance of what had been – and whole regions were cut off, as a result, from both water and supplies.

By that time, self-evidently, the emperor had become unable to fulfil his primary, hydraulic responsibility. His claim to the 'Mandate of Heaven' therefore expired. Peasant rebellions erupted everywhere. The most monumental was the Taiping revolution, led by a frustrated southern peasant named Hong Xiuquan, who developed a millenarian vision based on biblical teachings. These verses from the Prophet Isaiah seemed particularly poignant to Hong: 'Your country is desolate, your cities burned with fire; your fields are being stripped by foreigners right before you, laid waste as when overthrown by strangers.'[14] In the 1840s, he headed to the remote hill country of Guangxi Province, where he began to preach a new age of justice and plenty to the impoverished countryfolk. He would lead an uprising against China's 'foreign' Manchu rulers and establish God's kingdom on earth.

In the rapidly declining economic and ecological conditions of mid-nineteenth-century China, his cause rallied peasants in their millions. By the time hostilities were stamped out in 1864, as many as 30 million Chinese had died.[15] The imperial state nearly collapsed in the process – and it never recovered. The canal system was so compromised that relief efforts and tax collection were now impossible. A *New York Times* correspondent wrote, 'The most extensive and important canal in the world, [the Grand Canal] is now for hundreds of miles unnavigable, its old channel grass-grown and incumbered with the rotting hulks of hundreds of . . . imperial junks.'[16] The granaries, anyway, had been emptied by hungry armies. With all these safety nets removed, failed harvests in the mid-1870s and then the mid-1890s produced famines which may have killed 50 million people.[17] Another major rebellion erupted in the late 1890s, which the state was too weak to quell without foreign assistance: the Chinese destiny was contested by armies dispatched by the great European powers plus Russia, Japan and the USA, and in 1911 the last imperial dynasty collapsed.

The next, modern phase of Chinese history would also be crucially shaped by the peasantry – not just because the central character in China's modernisation, Mao Zedong, was himself of peasant stock, though that was of course essential to his success. More particularly, the titanic struggles between warlords and Nationalists, and Nationalists and Communists, *were ultimately decided by the peasant question*: which movement could most authentically present itself as a 'peasant rebellion'? Unlike his US-supported rival, Chiang Kai-shek, whose Nationalist Party extended a one-party, authoritarian regime over mainland China between 1928 and 1949, Mao understood that the peasantry was the decisive force for Chinese transformation. This force had to be galvanised with promises that the traditional relationship between peasant and state would be revived. Mao promised an authoritarian state committed to peasant land ownership and to the restoration of the irrigation system; he opposed landowners and moneylenders and foreigners. Throughout the 1920s and 1930s, peasant brigades such as the Red Spears resisted the Nationalists' political reforms with chants of 'Restore the Ming' – and they would eventually rally behind him rather as they had rallied behind the new peasant emperor in the fourteenth century. Ruthless and violent though Mao's campaign was, it was cannily designed to respond to the perennial peasant expectations of sublime imperial rule. As one peasant manifesto cried out, invoking the mythical emperor who, according to legend, centralised Chinese rule and inaugurated Han civilisation: 'We can no longer endure the scourge of bandits, soldiers, and evil government. The present warlords and politicians are not the rightful rulers of China; we wait expectantly for the true Yellow Emperor to appear.'[18]

The Nationalists could not fulfil such expectations. Their party emerged from an American vision of parliamentary democracy and, faced with the turbulent realities of 1930s China, turned inexorably towards fascism. Chiang Kai-shek depended on the support of landlords, businessmen and mafia leaders, and he sought to instil a militaristic nationalism which bore little relation to the aspirations of the vast peasant majority. The Nationalist administration was much concerned, therefore, with changing those aspirations: enormous education and propaganda campaigns were unleashed on the peasantry. These campaigns were highly unpopular. Rebel brigades such as the Red Spears marched to cries of 'Eliminate the Party Headquarters', 'Use the Lunar Calendar', 'Root Out the New Schools' and 'Repair the Temples'.[19] What peasant communities most wanted was a leadership capable of protecting their agrarian way of life, which the Nationalists were clearly failing to do. The peasantry was particularly aroused by the Nationalists' inadequate attempts to renovate the hydraulic infrastructure: dykes were collapsing under the watch of corrupt officials and landlords. The Yangtze River flood of 1931 was one of the most devastating in Chinese history, killing hundreds of thousands and affecting twenty-five million.[20] In 1938, Chiang Kai-shek blew up the Yellow River embankments in order to slow the Japanese invasion; this caused the river to move southwards to its pre-1855 channel, destroying everything in between; at least half a million died.[21] Psychologically scarred by the disaster, northern peasants could not excuse Chiang's fundamental betrayal of the ancient political bargain. This would play directly into Mao's hands.

Mao's ability to attract peasant recruits was not accidental, but the result of his patient study of village communities. In March 1927, he wrote a 'Report on an Investigation of the Peasant Movement in Hunan', in which he celebrated the Hunan peasantry's innate instinct for revolution. Peasants were overthrowing 'local bullies, the bad gentry and the lawless landlords, and in passing they also hit out against patriarchal ideas and institutions of all kinds'.[22] They also wished to be modern: of their own accord they were attempting to leave behind the old vices of the countryside: gambling, opium smoking, superstition and banditry. 'The lesson

Mao learned in Hunan was that the violence he believed necessary to bring about revolution could be found most easily in the countryside. He did not want to turn farmers into citizens but peasants into revolutionaries.'[23]

The news was encouraging. Communist strategists decided they would easily be able to recruit village defence leagues such as the Red Spears to their cause. Li Dazhao and Chen Duxiu, who had co-founded the Chinese Communist Party in 1921, believed that the Red Spears were 'the latest episode in a glorious two-thousand-year history of Chinese peasant uprisings',[24] and therefore essential partners for the Communists, whose own revolution was only the final and perfect instalment of this venerable tradition. Though the peasantry's parochialism and superstition were jarring, they had no doubt that its cause, ultimately, was the same as their own – and that these primitive vestiges would quickly fall away when confronted by the true and universal insights of Communism.

In the short term, they were wrong. The peasant societies were set up to hold society together, not to break it further; and after detailed discussions the Communists concluded that they were too irremediably conservative in their instincts. Japanese occupation, however, radicalised the peasants, and many threw in their lot with the Communists; Party membership expanded from 40,000 in 1928 to 1.2 million in 1945.[25] In this, they were heavily influenced by the markedly different treatment they received at the hands of the Nationalists and Communists respectively. Mao was determined that his guerrilla forces should not mistreat or steal from the people but rather move among them like 'fish in water' (such peasant imagery was itself a hallmark of his political discourse). In 1937, he attributed his army's success to:

> a code known as Three Rules and Eight Remarks, which we list here.
>
> *Rules*
>
> All actions are subject to command.
>
> Do not steal from the people.
>
> Be neither selfish nor unjust.

Remarks
Replace the door when you leave the house.
Roll up the bedding on which you have slept.
Be courteous.
Be honest in your transactions.
Return what you borrow.
Replace what you break.
Do not bathe in the presence of women.
Do not without authority search those you arrest.[26]

The Japanese were defeated; Mao won the Civil War. As premier, he devoted himself first to the restoration of 'normal' Chinese ecological relations. The ruling Communist Party embarked on a furious programme involving the clearing of forests for agriculture and the damming of rivers for electricity. Most importantly, the irrigation system was revived and modernised, which for many peasants signalled the restoration of the traditional political contract. Controlling the Yellow River – China's perennial lifegiver and -taker – was Mao's personal challenge and obsession: like the emperors of the past, he imagined himself as a leader endowed with epic powers of water management. His engineers proposed not just to rebuild the dykes, but also to install a staircase of forty-six dams that would hold back the floodwaters and silt and so finally defuse the river's destructive power.[27] (In the hope of bringing great floods to an end, some 80,000 dams and reservoirs were built across China between 1949 and 1990, though the quality of the construction was often poor.)[28]

Despite all this, the experience of the peasantry under Mao was of course traumatic in the extreme. Even during his campaigns, Mao's interest in land reform had never been purely idealistic: yes, he had wished to 'give China's peasants pieces of land and so make them beneficiaries of the revolution', but since 'the Communists retained the money confiscated from large landowners and rich peasants', reform had also been a way of funding the Communist war machine – which explains the almost psychopathic nature of village reorganisation in the final phases of the Civil War, when hundreds of thousands of landlords and wealthier peasants were killed.[29] Mao's 'reforms' were anyway short-lived, since farm collectivisation began in 1955, which progressively dispossessed peasants in favour of the state. Collectivisation displaced the family dynamics of traditional agriculture and introduced serious new conflicts and inefficiencies; since the collectives were also expected to produce enormous grain surpluses for sale to the state, mass famine quickly ensued.

But it is important we understand that Mao's approach to the peasantry, despite all this, remained essentially true to tradition. What was the purpose of collectivisation, after all? The first objective was to fuel rapid industrial development in order to close the gap between China and the rest of the world – a gap which had caused overwhelming suffering during the preceding century. Collectivisation was supposed to allow Chinese agriculture to operate on a much larger scale and therefore to become more efficient; the resulting surplus would allow China to keep its meagre foreign currency reserves for buying industrial goods. Things did not work out like that at all, of course, but the basic conception – a dynamic industrial system sitting atop intensive peasant agriculture – was well known from the past. Like many of China's previous rulers, also, Mao was anxious to keep peasants from leaving the land: in 1955 he introduced the internal 'passport' to prevent famine-afflicted villagers from fleeing to the cities. The peasant foundation was essential to him and, like the imperial dynasties before him, Mao used the technologies of his own age dramatically to increase both the extent and the intensity of Chinese cultivation. By 1949, agricultural land was terribly depleted of nitrogen and, since China had almost no chemical fertiliser production, expansion was imperative. Between 1949 and 1980, China's cultivated land increased from about 80 million hectares to nearly 130 million.[30]

The other objective of collectivisation was ideological: Mao wished to incorporate peasant nuclear families into bigger, state-run structures so that they might be more fully indoctrinated.[31] By banning practices of the nuclear family and requiring peasants to serve the collective, he hoped to instil a sense of Communist belonging. This too was absolutely traditional: for Mao's primary fear, of course, was that peasants would do exactly what he had previously encouraged them to do, and what they had done since time immemorial – rebel.

3

Why Britain Destroyed the Peasant

Unlike China, Europe was a patchwork of competing states, and European kings were obliged to maintain their position through constant warfare. This consumed gold and silver in quantities rulers could usually not raise from their own resources. For long periods, England's monarchs, whose access to taxation was restricted by parliament, lagged behind in this contest. They therefore became particularly dependent on loans and investments from financial elites and promoted the accumulation of private wealth on a massive scale. One of their strategies was to develop powerful legal protections for private property in order to permit its maximum commercial exploitation.[1] Britain's emergence as a world power can be traced, in fact, to the moment when land ceased to function as an ecological entity and was turned into a financial asset. This required the extinguishing of peasant claims, legal and moral – and it would ultimately destroy the British peasantry. Since Britain then took over the world with its model of capitalist modernity, this destruction subsequently became normative: peasants went down in textbooks as the primitive residue which must be sacrificed in order for an economy to become modern. This accounts for technocrats' continuing contempt.

England did not begin like that. Medieval customary law, as enshrined in the royal charters of 1215–17, was profoundly ecological. The welfare of the population was guaranteed not with coin but with access to natural systems, and property rights, as a result, could never be asserted beyond certain limits. Substantial areas of land – close to 40 per cent of the total in the high medieval period[2] – were set aside for common use. This land was mostly used for grazing animals, which were more fundamental to the English economy than to the Chinese. But it was also used for poverty relief, for which – unlike in China – there was no formal provision. Before hunger drove them to seek the charity of monasteries – which usually required migration to an urban centre – peasants could scour the commons 'for useful and saleable produce such as fuel, fruits and nuts, small birds, rushes, and bracken'.[3] The medieval economy was only sustainable, in short, because of the availability of common land.

Even private land was not exclusive to the proprietor in the modern way. Landowners were subject to superior and overlapping claims: sovereignty was the only absolute form of ownership, so all land was held from the king; the church, meanwhile, retained a claim on 10 per cent of agricultural produce. More crucially, commoners enjoyed legally enshrined rights of access to the aristocratic estates. The Little Charter of 1217 – a codicil to the Magna Carta of 1215 – laid out a long list of the uses they were permitted to make of private land: widows, for instance, could not be prevented from entering to collect estovers (wood for fuel, fencing and building).[4] In addition, the feudal system itself created bonds of reciprocal responsibility that often required landlords, in the interests of social harmony, to house poor and weak members of the peasant community. Property, in other words, was not a parcel: it was a mesh of interdependencies.

Despite all this, peasants struggled enormously. This was principally the consequence of onerous taxes, which could be imposed arbitrarily and simultaneously by several overlapping ecclesiastical and aristocratic powers. Most resented was the talle or tallage (from the French verb *tailler*, 'to cut'), which was a changing percentage of produce due, potentially, to numerous authorities, which competed to extract the maximum possible benefit. In China, we remember, imperial authority suppressed aristocratic profiteering in order to ensure the security of the masses and the durability of the agrarian system itself. In England, things were less rational. The system of grand houses, churches and war was sustained by relentless tax demands, and, since peasants themselves enjoyed few of the property rights or legal protections available to their Chinese counterparts, landlords could continue introducing new levies beyond the limits of sustainability.

English peasants therefore needed far more land than Chinese. In fourteenth-century England, both peasants and landlords considered four hectares to be the minimum viable plot size – and yet most Chinese families subsisted on plots one-fifth as large.[5] Some of this discrepancy was botanical: rice delivered 50 per cent more calories per land unit than wheat or barley, which were the English staples, and 100 per cent more than oats. More English land was given over, also, to animals. But the differences between England and China were especially political and economic. English peasants needed to produce a greater surplus to cover their much higher taxation. Not only that, but the absence of a Chinese-style granary-and-waterway system, which might deliver poor relief directly to the countryside, meant that English plots had to be big enough to support peasants even in a bad year.

In a small and populous island state, this placed pressures on the land mass from early times. Between 1000 and 1300, English rulers not only expanded into Wales, Scotland and Ireland, but also cleared woods and forests and drained swamps, fens and marshes. Many rural dwellers had to leave the land all the same: since plots were passed undivided from fathers to first sons, widows, younger sons and unmarried daughters had no guaranteed place in the agrarian system. Not all could be absorbed into urban trades, domestic service or charitable foundations, and almshouses and hospitals were overwhelmed with beggars and vagabonds arriving from the countryside.

In the fourteenth century, this fragile balance collapsed. The population was catastrophically reduced by disease and famine – most especially during the 1340s, when plague wiped out between one-third and one-half of the workforce.[6] Great swathes of agricultural land went untilled; many villages were left completely uninhabited. Landlords sold land they could not exploit or transferred arable land to pasture. With labour so scarce, peasants pressed their advantage, bargaining for high wages and enhanced freedoms; some also bought cheap land in this period and eventually joined the ranks of the gentry. But no institutions or processes existed to allow landlords and peasants to arrive at negotiated settlements; the system was built on peasants' near-total disenfranchisement. Faced with increasing peasant demands, landlords responded with the only tools they possessed, which were repressive: wages were capped under law, and penalties made harsher for peasants who abandoned their estates. Since this coincided with the increased tax demands of the Hundred Years' War with France, peasant communities were bound to explode.

It is difficult for urban dwellers in industrial societies to imagine the insurrectionary power that peasants could exert in medieval Europe. During England's Peasants' Revolt of 1381, they broke into the city of London, killing and destroying, and striking terror into the souls of urban elites. The rebellion threatened the very basis of the kingdom, and chroniclers could not find expression enough for its horrors. Despite their descriptions of carnage and chaos, however, the movement was not in fact anarchic. The peasants burned the palaces of those who were in control of the feudal system, and they burned the tax and property records by which that system was sustained; they avoided wanton destruction, however, and even went so far as to execute those found guilty of looting.[7] They sought not to sow chaos but to destroy the institutions of their subjugation and establish a rival legal order of 'king and commons' – as the chronicler Thomas Walsingham made clear in his account:

> For when they were not far from London near the estate of the master of the Hospital of St John called Highbury, they saw there a huge crowd of about twenty thousand peasants and common folk. They had just set fire to some very tall houses, and, as the blaze was now past all control, they were also trying to raze to the ground with various tools the parts that could not be destroyed

> by fire. The people from St Albans were seen by a rebel leader called Jack Straw. He at once summoned and called them over and they gave him their pledge that they would support King Richard and the commons.[8]

Of course the rebels believed, as so many medieval peasants did, that the crown would be their saviour – that all their problems derived from evil aristocrats who deceived the king and corrupted his goodly laws (Figure 4). In reality, King Richard was as terrorised by the uprising as the rest of his class. When his armies had taken back control of the cities, he cursed their envoys to their face:

> 'You miserable people, hated on land and sea, who do not deserve to live, you are asking to be made the equals of your lords . . . [Give your comrades] this message from the king: "Peasants you were and peasants you are. You will remain in bondage, not as before, but in an incomparably worse state." '[9]

This revolt had struck a terrifying blow at the heart of the state, and, for centuries afterwards, elites would fear a resurgence. European history makes no sense, in fact, if we do not understand the dread with which rulers contemplated peasant power. For the uprising of 1381 was by no means an isolated affair. England saw more large-scale peasant rebellions in the fifteenth, sixteenth and seventeenth centuries. France's terrifying Jacquerie of 1358, during which peasants stormed aristocratic strongholds in and around Paris, was similarly repeated up to the time of the 1789 revolution. The Peasants' War which consumed much of the Holy Roman empire in the 1520s grew out of decades of rural resistance in south-western Germany. That conflict illustrates well the nature of aristocratic fears. Not only did they face a formidable military campaign, which saw tens of thousands of peasants burning and occupying castles, monasteries and towns, but they were also confronted by a moral vision that was in many respects more developed than their own. German peasants used the language of reformed Christianity to rationalise a coherent defence of the commons: in response to the illegitimate seizure of 'God's gifts' by aristocratic powers, peasants proposed an ethos of Christian brotherhood and mutual ownership, which was summarised in a clear political manifesto (the Twelve Articles of 1525).[10] Typically, European elites tried to dismiss their peasant antagonists as ignorant, uncouth and immoral, but this was implicit acknowledgement of the more uncomfortable truth: the peasant account of society and ecology was sufficiently brilliant and profound to undermine the entire intellectual scaffolding of feudal power. Throughout history, in fact, and even today, the insistence on peasant stupidity has always been more strategic than it appears – an attempt to defuse an alternative conception of social and ecological arrangements which, precisely because of its superior sustainability, threatens the very basis of extractive state power.

When the dust had settled following England's fourteenth-century cataclysm, things began to change. Landlords realised they were no longer able to manage the complex interrelations of peasant society, land ecology and food markets. They accepted reduced rents in return for a predictable income whose generation, now, was the responsibility of professional managers. Tenant farmers began to take over larger and larger estates; typical lease terms also increased from about a decade in the early 1400s to sixty years or more two centuries later.[11] Many of these tenant farmers demonstrated considerable skill and vision: they would eventually become one of England's dominant classes, credited by later agrarian historians with the technological advances of the early modern period. As far as the landlords were concerned, however, the implications were very different. Over the next two centuries – and more quickly than in most other European countries – their connection to agriculture would wither. Land would become a purely *financial* asset, whose ecological and social dimensions were secondary or irrelevant.

This created new incentives, especially as the English economy became more complex. Large estates did not *have* to be given over to agriculture; they could be diverted to any activity which promised a higher return. From the early sixteenth century, indeed, mines and factories began to appear on aristocratic estates, as well as commercial canal routes and turnpikes. But such innovations required landowners to possess absolute control over their estates, allowing them to deny all other claims, and indeed to physically 'enclose' their land to prevent unauthorised entry. And that required a more far-reaching conception of property – not only as legal theory but also as political project.

By the seventeenth century, that project had become the central purpose of England's commercial elite, and it brought them into direct conflict with the king. Their principal problem with Charles I (r. 1625–49), after all, was that he refused to respect their property rights, resorting to stealing gold and commodities from London merchants to fund his wars. To mount a successful offensive against the king, however, they needed the support of ordinary people, who clearly did not share their political agenda. Peasants signed up willingly to the English Civil War (1642–51), but often for opposite reasons to their commanders: they believed the war offered the hope of a genuine revolution, which would restore the commons and reverse the programme of enclosure. Deploying the Bible as a manifesto for the rule of the commons, so-called Leveller intellectuals such as Gerrard Winstanley rallied the rural masses not only against the king but also against the commercial aristocracy and their property regime:

> The Earth (which was made to be a Common Treasury of relief for all, both Beasts and Men) . . . is bought and sold, and kept in the hands of a few, whereby the great Creator is mightily dishonoured . . . O thou Powers of England, though thou hast promised to make this People a Free People, yet thou hast . . . wrapped us up more in bondage, and oppression lies heavier upon us . . .[12]

But it was not to be. When the war was won, and rank-and-file soldiers pressed for the settlement they believed they had fought for, it became clear that the army's grandees were committed to a more absolute rule of property than anything seen hitherto. Such a programme had no room for democracy and, notwithstanding the great sacrifices made by ordinary people, the new rulers reserved the political franchise to men with property. In 1649, Oliver Cromwell, victorious commander and now lord protector of England, executed Leveller leaders in his New Model Army, and the movement's power base collapsed.

But Cromwell too fell foul of the commercial elite – England's true power brokers – who ultimately found his regime too authoritarian for their 'free-market' interests. In 1660, the monarchy was restored – but Charles II resumed the profligate ways of his father, invading property rights once again. The oligarchs needed a definitive solution, for which they turned to a state already ruled by businesspeople and bankers like them, and where property rights were prized above all else: the Dutch Republic. On the invitation of English grandees, William of Orange and his wife Mary sailed across the sea and took the throne without opposition or bloodshed.

Over the following century, commercial elites completed their political takeover. This was the period, also, of dramatic territorial expansion in North America, where English landowners, having no prior history, were forced to develop new arguments to support their property claims.[13] Those arguments were based on the distinction between, on the one hand, their own intensive cultivation of grain and tobacco and, on the other, the more varied farming techniques of American 'savages' which, in the eyes of English colonialists, left the land 'waste'. Their superior property claim rested on their ability to pour capital, technology and labour (often enslaved) into an enclosed plot and so to generate its maximum yield. This logic was now brought back to England, where it was used to defeat those who continued to defend the commons against private enclosure. In 1773, 'enclosure' was solemnised in 'An Act for the better Cultivation, Improvement, and Regulation of the Common Arable Fields, Wastes, and Commons of Pasture in this Kingdom'.[14] In Scotland, the decades either side of 1800 saw waves of so-called Highland Clearances, when tenant farmers were evicted from the lairds' estates, which were turned over to wool production. In the most extreme cases, villagers were physically turned out of their houses, which were then burned behind them so they could not return. Many were resettled in coastal crofts where the land was almost uncultivable and where they subsisted by collecting kelp (Figure 5).

This sustained assault on the countryside produced a constant tide of refugees. It is often imagined that these uprooted people were seamlessly absorbed by new urban factories – as if there were a necessary equivalence between the waste of one process and the need of the other. Most migrants, however, simply became part of a roving underclass: eighteenth-century factories were small, and it would take decades – or more – before the British population was primarily occupied by industry. Crime, vagrancy and addiction were the fate of most former peasants, who were therefore subjected to the full terror of the state: eighteenth-century law prescribed mutilation or death for even minor offences against the property regime.

London's slum world was the horror of all the generations from Hogarth and Thackeray through Dickens to Jack London and George Orwell. It is easy to understand, therefore, why the most obvious experience of British peasants from the 1640s onwards was exodus. Britain's transition to the industrial era would have been even more violent and conflicted, indeed, had it not been able to transport felons to the American colonies and Botany Bay – and had millions of British people not decided to flee poverty and authoritarianism for a better existence overseas.[15]

Those emigrants took with them the memory of their ancestral peasant society. The ones left behind became part of a turbulent imperial machine which ultimately, from the end of the nineteenth century onwards, began to employ the greater part of the British population in the industrial system, and to share rewards with the lowliest members of society. Even factory workers could afford to purchase the agricultural produce of peasants in much poorer countries. They began to receive education and healthcare from the imperial state; by the twentieth century they could vote and retire secure.

The ecological conception of society faded into the past, and there was nothing tragic about that. It was the proud accomplishment, rather, of a modern superpower.

4

Revolution: Are Peasants Modern?

England's attitude was commercial: peasants were incompatible with a modern *economy*. Elsewhere in Europe, the approach was philosophical: peasants were incompatible with the modern *spirit*. The philosophical assault has been just as consequential – since the eighteenth century, countless countries have, in their attempt to become modern, declared war on the peasant personality, which is assumed to be the repository of everything retrograde. The discomfort of our present-day relationship with the peasant carries this spirit: she represents everything we have been educated to flee, abhor and reject.

In 1765, as French thinkers poured scorn on the 'savage' societies of Africa and America, the philosopher Voltaire dissented.

> We must agree above all that that peoples of Canada and of southern Africa, whom we are pleased to call 'savages', are infinitely superior to our own. The Huron, the Algonquin, the Illinois, the African: they possess the art of making for themselves everything they need, which our peasants do not. The peoples of America and Africa are free, while our savages do not even have an idea of freedom. The so-called savages of America . . . know honour, of which the savages of Europe have never heard.[1]

The real savages, he argued, were at home. The peasants of France were the lowest of the low; they knew nothing:

> Except the land which feeds them and the market where they sometimes go to sell their produce and buy a few rude garments; speaking a jargon never heard in towns; having few ideas and consequently few expressions; subjected, without knowing why, to a man in an office to whom they carry every year the half of what they have produced by the sweat of their brow; gathering on certain days in a kind of barn to celebrate ceremonies about which they know nothing, and to listen to a man with unfamiliar clothes whose words they do not understand.[2]

Peasants were culturally and socially removed from the French nation; most spoke languages other than French. An influential urban writer could therefore represent them any way he liked without fear of contradiction.[3] Voltaire conceptualised the peasant in such a way as to vindicate his own system of ideas. Incapable of reflection or innovation, his dim-witted figure was unable to understand or change her pitiful condition, which was precisely why his 'Enlightenment' was so important (Figure 6). This burst of eighteenth-century philosophical brilliance found its ultimate justification in Voltaire's empty and tragic peasant: it would redeem that character and save the world from everything she represented.

Voltaire's was only one kind of peasant fantasy. His younger contemporary, Jean-Jacques Rousseau, imagined a more likeable figure – an untouched peasant living in pastoral purity. This honest character offered a refreshing contrast to urban life, and Rousseau felt she should be maintained in her innocence, which must not be corrupted by education, mobility or politics. Rousseau's portrait of an immaculate and unchanging rural spirit appealed to many urban elites, not least to the queen, Marie-Antoinette, who was eager to shield herself from a world that was changing too quickly. She went so far as to turn the Palace of Versailles over to that fantasy: building a bucolic hamlet in the grounds, dressing up in haute couture peasant outfits and surrounding herself with chickens and sheaves of wheat (Figure 7).

Elite fantasies, however, were only that. Eighteenth-century French peasants may have possessed very traditional convictions with regard to king and church, but that did not mean they were quaint or backward-looking. In truth, they were pressing strenuously for change. By that time, all sectors of the economy had become commercialised, and even peasants were fulfilling a large proportion of their own needs from the market. This required them to have reliable cash reserves – and that, in turn, required innovation. Eighteenth-century peasants were attempting to transform their farms in response to market needs, and to supplement agriculture with associated commerce. Even common land – a relic of medieval times – was being used by groups of smallholders to expand the range of crops and animals they offered to urban customers.[4]

But every attempt by peasants to modernise their economic strategy was obstructed by France's feudal reality.[5] Besides the dues they owed to church and lord, they were constrained by seigneurial monopolies – which required peasants to pay a lord for the use of his mill, oven or wine press – and by much-resented hunting rights, which allowed lords to hunt on peasant fields, whatever damage they caused, and to have sole claim to certain game. Lords also controlled the civil and criminal courts and supplemented their income by levying arbitrary fines. They taxed peasant sales as well, which meant that the more peasants became commercialised the more money they lost.

Contrary to the backward-looking and inflexible stereotypes circulating in the cities, therefore, peasants had little allegiance to the status quo; in fact they were passionate advocates of modernisation. As in other times and places, their conception of a modern society was grounded in a moral framework all of their own. They did not merely criticise the injustice, venality and arbitrariness of seigneurial power; they also offered an alternative vision based on communal rights over ecological resources, collective political authority for the countryside, customary constraints on lordly power and subsistence guarantees in the event of hardship.[6]

But since there was no forum for direct inter-class bargaining, civil disobedience was their principal means of negotiation. And this was no longer directed solely towards local aristocrats. Peasants were aware that aristocratic power resided not in individuals, but in law and regulation: all feudal relations had been institutionalised by the absolutist state. Increasingly, therefore, the French peasantry found itself in opposition to the state. And though historians have found it difficult to countenance the idea that peasants might have instigated the foundational event of modern Europe – the French revolution – that is what happened. Not only did the bourgeois revolution emerge from the peasant revolt of the previous year, but the peasantry continued to manipulate events for three years until its specific ends had been achieved.

Resentment towards seigneurial dues had been flaring up since the early 1780s, and there were sporadic assaults on aristocratic estates. In 1788 it erupted into a full-blown Jacquerie which took over two-thirds of the country. In what has been described as Europe's largest peasant uprising before 1917, peasants raided castles, tax offices and courts, in order to dispute dues, renegotiate terms and compel lords and officers to put their signature thereto; they took over archives in order to burn the evidence of feudal rights and obligations; they seized grain stores and arms in order to defend themselves from state retribution. This was not simple mob mayhem. Peasant armies did little violence to private property, to merchants or to the clergy. Their target was the feudal order.[7]

The revolution is usually presented as an urban eruption which eventually spread to the villages. The opposite is also true: parliamentary elites were charting their course in reaction to news arriving from the countryside. Following the storming of the Bastille prison in July of that year, as deputies gathered to debate the ground rules of a democratic France, the upheavals sweeping through country estates and constituencies persuaded them that the state might actually collapse if they did not make radical concessions to the anti-feudal masses.[8] During the night of 4 August 1789, France's deputies voted to cancel all feudal dues, effectively dismantling centuries of aristocratic and ecclesiastical despotism (Figure 8).

The mood was momentous: 'the most memorable session in the history of any nation', declared one deputy. But the Marquis de Ferrières spoke not from simple political idealism. As far as he was concerned, the threat of rural discontent was so severe that, in the absence of extreme measures, his own aristocracy might not survive: 'open opposition by noble deputies would be dangerous, not merely for those deputies, but for the nobility in France as a whole.'[9]

And yet, despite the foundational role it had played, the peasantry was ultimately shut out of the revolution. Peasants discovered they still could not compete with urban speculators when it came to acquiring lands expropriated from aristocrats and the church; communal affairs were still managed by a coterie of the rich. By 1793, their tactics against the state were also ceasing to be effective. Not only had the Republic entered its most draconian phase – 'the Terror' – but all of Europe was declaring war on France's revolution, and peasants were needed for the army. Taxes were raised to unprecedented levels and in February 1793, the Republic issued a call for an additional 300,000 soldiers – who would be forcibly conscripted if there were not sufficient volunteers. A peasant uprising broke out in the Vendée, a western region at the mouth of the Loire River. The spirit reflected traditional peasant values: 'They have killed our king, chased away our priests, sold the goods of our church, eaten everything we have and now they want to take our bodies . . . no, they shall not have them.'[10] Rebels surrounded a group of soldiers sent to conscript them; in the ensuing skirmish they slaughtered 150 men. For urban radicals, this assault demonstrated that peasants threatened the entire revolutionary project, and all their prejudices rushed back. The Committee of Public Safety – France's de facto government – recommended the most violent response: 'exterminate this rebel race, destroy their homes, set fire to their forests, and cut down their harvests.'[11] As many as 170,000 were slaughtered; whether this amounted to a genocide is still debated.[12]

Only a few years before, peasants had been romanticised in revolutionary iconography: they were the benign – if dim-witted – masses whose liberation would be won by the heroic efforts of enlightened elites and intellectuals in the cities. Now, revolutionary leaders reverted to a more traditional conception: the peasant was brutish and retrogressive, opposed to civilisation and progress. Immediately, the peasant masses were shut out of politics. Though the Republic had, for the first elections of 1792, made a bold experiment with universal male suffrage, property requirements were then reintroduced which excluded peasants in their entirety. These requirements became ever more exacting thereafter: while 3.6 million voted in the election of 1792 (out of a total population of about 30 million), the electorate in 1815 was reduced to a mere 33,000.[13] Before peasants could be admitted to the body politic, they had to be rescued from savagery – for in France as in England the countryside was now seen through the lens of colonial encounter. In a landmark history of the French peasantry, we hear the voices of an officialdom filled with an almost racial hatred of their agrarian inferiors: 'Lazy, greedy, avaricious, and suspicious' (Landes, 1843) . . . 'Foulness, rags, miserable savagery' (Loire-Inférieure, 1850) . . . 'Vulgar, hardly civilised, their nature meek but wild' (Loire, 1862) . . . 'Animals with two feet, hardly resembling a man' (Limoges, 1865).[14]

A campaign of re-education and discipline began, of which roads, primary schools and military service were the principal components. This campaign intensified after 1870, and ended only with the First World War, when industrialisation and empire finally absorbed most of the peasantry.[15] In the end, the French revolution became a bourgeois revolution. This was not because the peasantry was not itself active or revolutionary; as we have seen, it was greatly responsible for the overthrow of feudalism. Nor was it because the bourgeoisie was necessarily 'modern'. The new ruling elite continued to draw most of its income from land rents, looked to the army and the bureaucracy for advancement, and, according to some historians, continued to resist the advent of capitalism for decades.* The point, however is this: 'only the bourgeoisie,

* This is the argument, for instance, of Alfred Cobban in *The Social Interpretation of the French Revolution*. He contends that the 'bourgeois revolution' was supposed not to

increasingly self-conscious as a class and endowed with sufficient economic, political, and cultural resources', was in a position to take over the apparatus of the state.[16] With state levers in its hands, this class could consolidate the rewards of the new system and alienate a peasantry of which it continued to harbour the greatest fear and suspicion.

If today our memory of the French revolution is mainly that of urban elites, it is also because they made the novels and paintings. As the memory waned of violent rural revolt, as France was swept up in the tumult of empire, war and capitalist development, artists became obsessed by the peasant, whom they now represented as poignant and dying – a beautiful symbol of everything that was disappearing into history. As a reaction to the priests and bureaucrats, who continued to decry the peasant's savagery, novelists and artists romanticised her helplessness in the face of ruthless modernity. In Millet's famous painting *The Angelus* (1857–9), the peasant couple repeat the timeless rituals of rural France: while the bell rings in the medieval church, they pause their labours to pray (Figure 9). As peasants began to join the throngs of imperial France's factory workers and emigrants, they seemed ever rarer and more exquisite to artists and aesthetes. Paul Gauguin arrived in Brittany in 1886 and began dressing as a Breton peasant: 'when my peasant clogs clatter on this granite ground,' he wrote, 'I hear the sound – deaf, matt and powerful – that I seek in my painting.'[17] French artists flocked to Brittany to capture the tragic power of a subspecies that had not long to live (Figure 10).

We ourselves are the heirs of that culture. We continue to use the word 'peasant' to mean 'incapable of evolution'. We too think of the peasant as some primitive relic, always about to die. Our memory, too, has waned of the European peasant as a dynamic

---

advance capitalism but to hinder its development, since it contravened the economic interests of the rentier class. Trade and industry, he suggests, were less advanced in 1815 than before the revolution, and land continued to absorb the bulk of investment.

agent of political evolution. Or rather: that memory has been covered up.

It was probably Marx who did most to convert the dying peasant of bourgeois fantasy into scientific 'fact'. Marx's prediction, of course, was that capitalism would eradicate all older economic systems, that the world would be divided between rich capitalists and exploited workers, and that the latter class would overthrow the former to create a universal proletarian republic. Eager to witness this final culmination of history, the German was enthusiastic about everything that swelled the ranks of the industrial proletariat. Factory workers had lost their connection to the land and could not return there to feed their hunger: there was nowhere for them to flee except the future. They were urban and densely concentrated; they were already used to working together in well-coordinated squadrons. In short, they were the modern force which could overthrow the glorious evil of capitalist exploitation.

Peasants were exploited too. But Marx did not think they were capable of Communist revolution. As far as he was concerned, they were too primitive, too attached to their own smallholdings and too ignorant of grand political forces. In his famously contemptuous simile, peasants constituted a political 'class' only in the unthinking way that 'potatoes in a sack form a sack of potatoes'.

> [They] form a vast mass [whose members] live in similar conditions but without entering into manifold relations with one another. Their mode of production isolates them from one another instead of bringing them into mutual intercourse . . . They are consequently incapable of enforcing their class interest in their own name, whether through a parliament or a convention. They cannot represent themselves, they must be represented.[18]

For Marx, as for French revolutionaries before him, peasants could not, therefore, be trusted, and he hoped for their swift departure from the historical stage. Peasants were too concerned with private property. Ultimately, they would abandon the revolution, and their attachment to their own land would stand in the way of large-scale agriculture. His antipathy to the peasant he formalised as prediction: in agriculture as in industry, large-scale production would eventually take over, and the peasantry would be converted into wage workers. 'There is no need to abolish [the property of . . . the small peasant],' reads the *Communist Manifesto*, which he wrote in 1848 with Friedrich Engels; 'The development of industry has to a great extent already destroyed it, and is still destroying it daily.'[19] This could not happen quickly enough: the peasants' 'relentless property fanaticism' made them a reactionary force within capitalism, and one that had already, in Marx's analysis, defeated several proletarian revolutions.

Russia, the country where these ideas would have the profoundest impact, had an even more mythological conception of the peasantry than did France. This great majority of the population had only become legal citizens in 1861, when serfdom was abolished. That moment produced emotional reactions as powerful as the almost simultaneous abolition of southern slavery in the United States: Dostoevsky thought it was akin to Russia's conversion to Christianity in the tenth century. Many of the artists and aristocrats who came of age at that time fell under the spell of the peasant, who represented everything they were not, who filled them with guilt at their own privilege and inauthenticity – and who seemed to represent, above all, the eternal spirit of Russia itself. Russian elites had traditionally contented themselves with a cartoonish conception of the peasant – childlike and simple – but attitudes had begun to change in the 1850s, especially after the publication of Turgenev's novel *Sketches from a Hunter's Album* (1852), which depicted real human beings with deep feelings and great practical intelligence.

Russia's closeted urban life began to turn outwards. In the early 1870s, bands of students set out from Moscow and St Petersburg to live with the peasants, even to dress and talk like them.[20] The hard life of the rural communes they set up gave them a refreshing feeling of penitence; 'we have come to realise', wrote Nikolay Mikhaylovsky, one of the leading theorists of the *narodniki* ('people's') movement, 'that our awareness of the universal truth could only have been reached at the cost of the age-old suffering of the people. We are the people's debtors and this debt weighs on our conscience.'[21] Tolstoy's *Anna Karenina* (1878) tells of an aristocrat who becomes disillusioned with city life, retreats to his country estate to live alongside the peasants and thereby learns the essence of his own land and culture (Figure 11). Dostoevsky hoped the peasant could provide an insight, not only into the Russian soul, but also into the Russian future: '[the peasant] will show us a new path . . . it is we who must bow down before the people's truth.'[22] It became a Russian truism, in fact, that the peasant represented the national destiny; each political camp therefore developed its own theory of that character (Figure 12). As one eminent historian writes, 'For the Populists, the peasant was a natural socialist . . . Democrats . . . saw the peasant as a champion of liberty. The Slavophiles regarded him as a Russian patriot, suffering and patient.'[23]

Such sentimentalism had little place in the Bolshevik regime which, led by Vladimir Lenin, began to administer the country in 1917. In the spirit of *narodniki* writers from the previous century, that regime embraced the sovereignty of 'the people'. True to its Marxist foundations, however, its conception of 'the people' allowed at best a transitional place to the peasant (Figure 13). Marx had written most of his theory in England, the only country on earth where the peasantry had all but disappeared, and where large-scale farming dominated all other forms – and yet that theory was assumed to apply everywhere. Despite the fact that – according to the 1897 census – 82 per cent of the Russian population lived in the countryside, Lenin was determined that the revolution should be uncorrupted by what he called the 'political backwardness of the peasants'.[24] This backwardness was reflected in peasants' constant appeals for land reform, which for Lenin were not only deluded but full of 'bourgeois prejudices'.[25] The peasants, in fact, were bourgeois in their hearts: 'Small-scale [peasant] production gives birth to capitalism and the bourgeoisie constantly, daily, hourly, with elemental force, and in vast proportions.' His irritation, when addressing them, was scarcely undisguised. 'Reforms', he wrote, 'will not rid you of poverty. That can only be achieved by one means: the victory of the entire proletariat – both industrial and agricultural – over the entire bourgeoisie and the formation of a socialist society.'[26]

'The people' had to be purified, in other words, of the peasantry – which meant terror. Joseph Stalin, who became leader in 1924, was even more suspicious of peasants than Lenin; he was also more preoccupied with the question of how to extract a sufficient surplus from agriculture to fund the Soviet Union's ultra-rapid industrialisation. Both problems, political and economic, had the same answer: the peasantry had to be destroyed. Between 1928 and 1940, peasants were stripped of their landholdings and brought to work on large-scale farms controlled by collectives (*kolkhoz*) or the state (*sovkhoz*).[27] These farms were required to make fixed contributions to the state; peasants caught withholding grain or gleaning in the harvested fields were sent to labour camps or executed. All traditional strategies for surviving bad years were therefore cancelled; some 7 million died of starvation during the failed harvest of 1932–3.[28]

Collectivisation was fantastically costly in human terms, but it was not necessarily viewed as a failure for all that.* The breaking of the peasant class and the imposition of large-scale farming were ends in themselves; and indeed the experiment continued until after the outbreak of the Second World War – for several years, in other words, after Soviet officials had understood its human consequences. So important was the establishment of large-scale farming, in fact, that it provided a rare point of convergence between the Soviet Union and the United States.[29] In Depression America in the 1930s, major banks and corporations were snatching up land

* Stalin is supposed to have informed Churchill at the Yalta conference in 1945, as if to display his own heroism, that collectivisation had been achieved at a cost of 10 million lives.

sold by destitute farmers, consolidating them into vast agricultural enterprises designed according to the rational principles of Henry Ford's factories, and deploying on them armies of tractors and combine harvesters. There, too, the motive was ideological: American technocrats shared with their Soviet counterparts a blind conviction that the peasant must be neutralised in order for society to become fully modern. As one enthusiastic journalist put it at the time:

> Collectivisation is posed by history and economics. Politically, the small farmer or peasant is a drag on progress. Technically, he is as antiquated as the small machinists who once put automobiles together by hand in little wooden sheds. The Russians have been the first to see this clearly, and to adapt themselves to historical necessity.[30]

Both the United States and the Soviet Union threw themselves passionately into the cause of big agriculture, often through direct collaboration over techniques and equipment.* Some kinds of farming were well adapted to the large scale, others were not. In aggregate, the American experiments – though far less catastrophic than Stalin's – were unimpressive. There was little evidence that the factory farm performed more efficiently than small farmers. In fact, they were so highly capitalised that they were extremely vulnerable to financial movements and price fluctuations – situations for which the peasant family was supremely well adapted. J. P. Morgan lost $1 million in the first three years of its 1920s large-scale farming experiment in Montana.[31]

---

* James C. Scott notes that there was intense exchange during the 1920s between Soviet and American agricultural experts and engineers. American agronomists saw the Soviet Union as a model of industrial farming, while the Soviet Union imported American machinery, expertise and technicians to advance its project of large-scale collectivised agriculture: 'Visitors traveling in either direction returned to their own country thinking that they had seen the future.' See James C. Scott, *Seeing Like a State: How Certain Schemes to Improve the Human Condition Have Failed* (New Haven, CT: Yale University Press, 1998), 199–200.

Britain, France, Russia, America: all the great experiments with modernity, in one way or another, eradicated the peasant – and that began to seem like a law of nature, as if modern air were too oxygenated for the peasant's primitive biology. In the self-declared 'modern' nations, she was starting to be a distant memory. Folklorists rushed around the countryside collecting peasant songs and tales before it was too late; photographers took images of frail peasants – whose great age suggested the imminent death not only of the individuals concerned, but of their entire archaic class.

The word itself ceased to have any currency in the industrialised centres of the world system. There were no peasants, any longer, in the West – at least not that anyone cared about. It was in their expeditions to other continents, now, that Westerners encountered them. Europe's colonial possessions in Asia and Africa, of course, were still constituted almost entirely of peasants. And yet these peasants too – precisely because of European rule – were in a less than optimal condition. Travellers and administrators who believed that the peasant was destined to die out in the modern era often found their ideas confirmed by the physical state of colonial farmers.

Rolling out in India the same ethos that had already destroyed the peasants of Ireland, for instance, British administrators found themselves superintending such stupendous catastrophes as the famine of 1876–8. Starving and emaciated peasants streamed into Madras and Bombay, where British ideology prohibited government 'charity' from impeding the free functioning of markets. Officials were therefore instructed not to feed the hungry unless they could purchase it with money or labour – and to flog them should they attempt to steal grain.[32] As enfeebled peasants succumbed also to malaria, and the death toll reached 10 million, news of the daily horrors was published back in the capitalist heartlands, where it confirmed the reigning ideology. All the world's nations, ran the thought, were arranged on a timeline: Europe was in front, with America slightly behind, and the rest of the world lagging by decades or even centuries. 'Backward' societies would catch up in time – that was the belief, at least, of 'progressives' – so Europe's past represented the future of Africa and Asia. The long-suffering Asian peasant, correspondingly, was like a fossil from Europe's medieval past and the fact that she was so skeletal was symbolic of the sad but inescapable truth: in order for Asia to become modern, she would have to die.

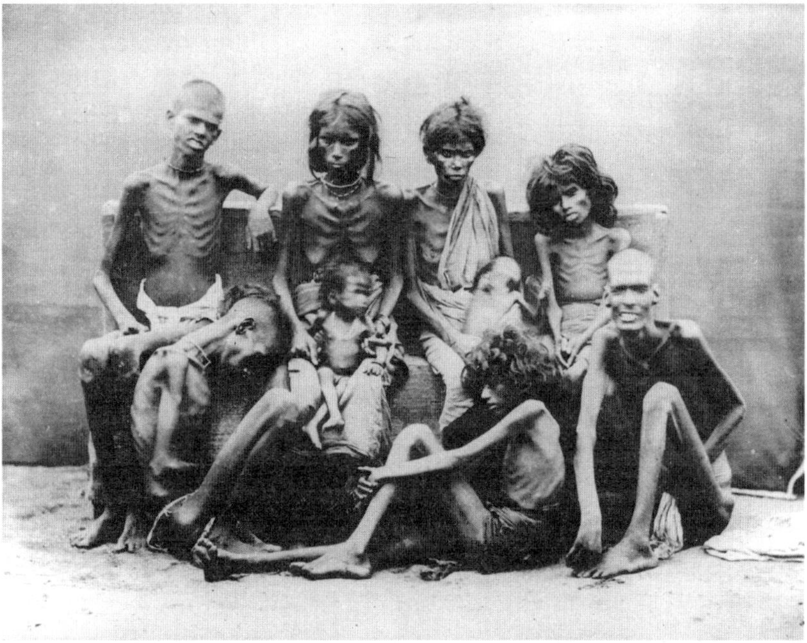

Inmates of a Madras famine relief camp. Photograph by Willoughby Wallace Hooper, 1877.

In reality, of course the parlous state of these masses was not an abstract statement about history; it was the real consequence of the policies of the imperial government. European propaganda spoke of the 'Oriental despotisms' under which Asian peasants had struggled and starved for so many centuries before the enlightened foreigners arrived. In fact, as we saw in China, rulers of agrarian empires had regarded the maintenance of the peasantry as their first priority. The same was the case in India;

it was the ignorance and venality of the colonial administration that were plunging the population into this condition. Such nuances escaped Western observers, however, who were subject to constant indoctrination with respect to race and history. The Asian peasantry was portrayed as a feeble subspecies, living its last days, about to disappear. Part of the reason Europeans felt so little remorse about bombing such people from the air is that they were, from the long-term perspective, expendable. They were simply an inconvenient residue, which would have to be cleared away for the modern age truly to begin.

That age seemed to begin in earnest with the end of the Second World War, which brought two technological superpowers – the USA and the Soviet Union – to the forefront of world history. What a shock it was, therefore, when the Third World peasant made such a dramatic comeback. Mao's revolution, as we have seen, was based on a very different idea of the peasant – eternal, powerful, world-changing. As decolonisation produced fifty and then one hundred new nations, Mao*ism* acquired immense importance: most of those nations had peasant populations who were suddenly forced into very modern political confrontations. Castro's successful revolution in Cuba showed once again the power of the peasant revolt. By the 1960s, the two superpowers were facing peasant armies all over the world – and soon the USA was bogged down in a mighty conflict with peasants in Vietnam. With the insurgents Che Guevara and Ho Chi Minh as its mascots, the cause of Third World peasant revolution found recruits everywhere, not only in Asia and Africa, but also on American university campuses. Maoist protesters in Paris and Berkeley believed that American imperialism would end with the uprising of the Third World peasantry.

And America was scared. Suddenly, the peasant became the number-one issue on the security agenda: nothing in American history could teach the superpower how peasants in Ghana or Indonesia might think. The CIA took over sizeable sections of American culture and academia in its attempt to generate knowledge about the Third World peasant: this was the era when so many 'area studies' departments were set up in US universities. Many PhD studies of the life of rural communities in Africa and Asia were funded by the CIA and the State Department (usually with the intermediary of the Ford Foundation, so the fiction of academic independence might be sustained). All the same, researchers were often subjected to a mandatory CIA debrief after completing their fieldwork. The CIA-sponsored coup in Indonesia in 1965, for instance, which ultimately resulted in the massacre of between 500,000 and 1 million 'Communist sympathisers', was precipitated by anthropology research in Javanese villages, which convinced the State Department that the Indonesian countryside represented a major vulnerability in the global ideological conflict.[33]

Elderly Vietnamese peasants suspected of being communists and detained by US forces. Unknown photographer, 1966.

Washington and Moscow were talking about peasants. Radicals were talking about peasants. Universities were talking about peasants. And then – suddenly, again – everyone stopped talking about peasants.

The Vietnam War demonstrated the impossibility of subduing Third World peasants by military means. It was followed almost immediately by a programme that would take hold of the peasantry by financial means – and this was much grander and more successful. By the 1980s, many developing states were seriously indebted and had enormous need of foreign capital; their financial dependency was used as a lever to subject agrarian economies to the discipline of markets. 'Peasants' were re-scripted along with everything else. Now they were just 'consumers' like everyone else: their collective identity was cast away. Locked into individual contracts with financiers and agrobusiness, these 'customers' of the global countryside would have no capacity for class consciousness or revolution. In the neo-liberal era, markets were the drivers of history, not classes or cultures. Finally, the long-awaited 'disappearance of the peasant' seemed complete, and modernity could take over the planet. The word itself became antique. People forgot that peasants – who had so recently threatened global apocalypse – even existed.

5

The Question of the Peasant

It is crucial we understand that our 'forgetting' has nothing to do with reality. Yes, the most industrialised countries destroyed most or all of their peasantry. But most of the world has become modern without doing so, and it is now unlikely that it will.

In order to explain further, we need a working definition of the peasantry. Who *is* a peasant? A smallholder farmer who lives off the land – either owned or rented – relies mainly on family labour, and farms both for subsistence and for the market. We can unpack this thus:

1. Peasant agriculture is characterised by the family farm. The land is tenanted or rented by a family, usually for generations. Family members do most or all of the work.
2. Peasant agriculture is embedded in larger systems of power. Peasant lives are shaped by their subordination to higher authorities – especially states, but also traders and corporations – which extract a surplus from them.[1]
3. Peasant agriculture is designed for survival and security. For this reason, it is structured to withstand external shocks, both natural and economic. As much as possible, peasants rely on nature and community reciprocity for resources, in order to insulate themselves from policy and market. When surpluses are meagre or commodity prices low, their

production may be directed solely to sustaining the family, the farm and the village.[2]

4. Peasant agriculture is supported by an understanding of nature and the cosmos which is markedly different from those of the city. The rituals which express that understanding are not just quaint ornamentation, but essential for sustaining a way of life.
5. As a result, partly, of the above, peasant agriculture is poorly represented in 'official' media and politics. Across history, peasants have had little access to the apparatus of power. This means they may easily be expropriated by other parties. It also means that marches and revolts are essential to peasant political expression.

Contrary to the lazy stories told by 'modern' newspapers and textbooks, the people matching this description never disappeared. Their form of life is, after all, far better evolved and more resilient, say, than factory wage-work. No other class has such a clear understanding of economic exploitation and political oppression; no class has had longer to develop strategies for dealing with them. No class has such an ability to adapt to ecological change or breakdown. Anyone who has actually spent time with peasants has been impressed by this ability to adapt and endure. Writing from a remote village in eastern France, John Berger observed in 1979 that 'For a century and a half now the tenacious ability of peasants to survive has confounded administrators and theorists. Today it can still be said that the majority in the world are peasants.'[3] A recent study suggests that things have not changed so much, even now: despite their 'manufactured invisibility' there are 'far more peasants than ever before'.[4] My own calculations suggest that, in today's world, about 2 billion people live in what might be described as peasant households.[5] Though there has been an undeniable urbanisation of our species over the last century, peasants remain, even in our twenty-first century, by far the largest constituency of all, overwhelmingly more numerous than modernity's more familiar characters: assembly-line workers, miners, office drones, taxi drivers. This quarter of humanity administers the vast majority of the world's 600 million farms and produces one-third of all food.[6]

In our desire to become modern, we wrote this largest and most essential of populations out of the world story. How was this even possible? Because the 'psychodrama' of modernity gave us an enormous need to divorce ourselves from the peasant, and so we developed a number of compelling – if unexamined – stories about her demise. Two of these stories are particularly widespread: many of the readers of this book will already have recited them in their heads. The first is that industry must take over agriculture; the second that cities must absorb everyone from the countryside.

We became used to thinking, first, that peasant agriculture must necessarily die off with the spread of large-scale plantations and heavy machinery. But this was based on an extrapolation from the highly specific experience of north-western Europe and, 250 years after the industrial revolution, it has still not happened.[7] Peasant agriculture has thrived in the industrial era, coexisting with and complementing newer forms. In many places – especially in Asia, but elsewhere too – large farms, industrial plantations and peasant operations are located side by side. Yes: wheat production can be carried out on a vast scale with little human labour and high inputs of fossil fuels and fertilisers; such techniques have become standardised from the US to Ukraine to India. Rice is grown predominantly by smallholder farmers, especially in Asia, where production is dominated by small family farms, which employ hundreds of millions of people – and provide the staple food for 3.5 billion.[8] Cotton production has been mechanised in the USA and Europe, but the quality suffers, which is why peasant production continues to dominate: small family farms in India contribute by far the greatest proportion of global supplies. Far from dying off in the face of industrial modernity, in other words, the peasantry is growing with it.

There are other reasons why peasant agriculture persists. It is often imagined that big plantations are more efficient and that corporations must therefore prefer them. But plantations require enormous capital – financial and political – and they are difficult to move when, as is almost inevitable with intensive farming, the land becomes less fertile. Many of the large industries feeding off agricultural produce, such as chocolate or textiles, choose to maximise their profits by dealing with suppliers who are small, dispersed and weak and passing on to them the problems of ecological degradation and commodity price variation. Some of the world's richest and most glamorous cartels and corporations therefore rest securely on peasant foundations. Because of the pressures from big capital, meanwhile, as well as the reality of ecological degradation, to which they are uniquely sensitive and exposed, peasants have made use of new industrial opportunities precisely to keep their farms running – combining agriculture with shifts in rural factories and seasonal jobs in the city, and so diversifying their risks and rewards. They are survivors, and the involvement of dedicated family members allows for considerable flexibility: the twenty-first-century peasant in the industrialising countryside of, say, India or China is sustained by a dizzyingly complex – we might even say hypermodern – mesh of economic relationships. Peasants, once again, are not 'prior to' or 'outside' the modern world: they are thoroughly integrated with contemporary economic systems, which could not function without them.

The second erroneous thought is that humanity is in the midst of an inexorable process of urbanisation to which there is effectively no limit – driven, in the main, by the peasant's desperate desire to leave the land. As we will see in Part Two, we certainly cannot assume that all peasants wish to leave the land – many are passionately attached to it and fight everything that attempts to drive them away. But it is also essential we understand that, in the absence of exceptional levels of industrialisation, nothing can sustain substantial populations so well as the land, and that peasants must think many times before forsaking its security. It is true that recent Asian industrialisation has been sufficiently spectacular that hundreds of millions of peasants have found new lives in industrial centres. China has seen the largest rural-to-urban migration in history: the urban population of this old agrarian empire now exceeds 900 million and continues to grow, approaching 70 per cent of the total.[9] But China is exceptional: it cannot become the general condition. Even in neighbouring India, whose industry has also received massive investment over the last few decades, the rural population remains at 65 per cent, which is 900 million people.[10] Indian industry is still too insignificant to absorb more of these rural millions. Since the world is already at a very high level of industrialisation relative to available fossil fuels and other natural resources, since advanced twenty-first-century factories require fewer and fewer workers, since overproduction is already a critical problem for the global industrial complex, there are many reasons to doubt the projection of historical graphs into the future. The UN predicts that, of the nearly 10 billion people alive in 2050, nearly 7 billion will live in cities. Is this truly feasible? Do cities truly have that capacity? Can cities of 50 million provide an acceptable standard of living? Many people are currently returning from the hypercompetition of Third World cities to a more dependable existence on the land – and there are good reasons to think that future population flows will be more multidirectional than we think. Even Europe is seeing traces of what some experts call 're-peasantisation', for alternatives to agriculture are threatened even there. When all else fails, land is the only thing; in this sense, peasant cultivation must have a significant role to play in securing humanity's future.

As we shall see, the world's peasants *are* in crisis – but not because they are weak or ill prepared for the modern world. It is because the world's managers have believed their own urban fairy tale: that the peasantry no longer exists – or that it should, in the interests of 'progress', cease to do so. They have therefore deliberately cut peasants off from the forms of support they have required from rulers since time immemorial. The current dispossession of peasants by mining companies, corporate plantations and other competitors for land is a result of this 'principled' withdrawal of political protection.

Peasants, we repeat, constitute the largest single class of humanity, guaranteeing the food supply, sustaining global supply chains and acting as stewards of the natural world. Protecting peasant communities and economies, therefore, is fundamental to our continued existence as a species. But we are doing precisely the opposite. In Part Two, we set out on a journey around the global countryside and speak to the people who are living the vast, composite crisis of smallholder agriculture. We will witness immense upheaval and misery; but we will also discover why it is that peasants have survived so many crises in the past. They will survive this crisis too.

PART TWO

Peasants in the Twenty-First Century

1

Sugarcane: Rebels from the Field

> Then the [Buddha] . . . set out on tour for Rajagaha [capital of India's ancient Mauryan empire]. And on the way, [one of his disciples] saw a sugar factory.
>
> – BUDDHIST SCRIPTURE, FOURTH CENTURY BCE[1]

In this saturated light, the earth glitters with detail. Every leaf is illuminated, every flower, every stone. Flies glint under the sun and are picked off by swooping birds. The manes of coconut trees blaze against the sky. Earth embankments run along the edges of the fields: their brilliant grid stretches to the horizon.

Colours are hyperreal. You could sink into the velvet brown of the soil; clumps of banana trees are more than green. The red of a dormant tractor hurts the eye.

Sugarcane begins as a spindly grass. Some distance away, I see newly planted fields: the seedlings are at knee level, their infant fronds spiky against the dark earth. A field of fully grown cane, like where I am standing, looks very different. Here is a vast and impenetrable vegetable mass, two or three times human height, great crests of foliage waving at the sky. The stems are dense with juice, thick and rigid. All space between them is packed with leaves longer than my arm and sharp as razors.

These giants were planted only a few months before the seedlings next door. Sun and irrigation have propelled them upwards at the rate of a centimetre a day. The canes are notched with characteristic green-and-yellow leaf scars – chronicle of this furious growth.

I am in the populous state of Maharashtra, in the heart of India. It is still morning, but work began hours ago and is far progressed. One-third of the field has been felled by an advancing line of brightly clad men and women. Their machetes flash twice: with the first arc, a towering stalk crumples; with the second, the length is cut in half. Leaves are deftly hacked away, the two sticks tossed down – and the cutter stoops to the next stem. Endlessly repeated, this coordinated action produces a zigzag weave across the field: leaves lie beneath, diagonal to the field, parallel stripes of cane on top.

The cutters are small and wiry, heads draped against the sun, feet and hands bare. Most are in their twenties, some not so old. Behind them follow young children – the cane scaffolding crunches as they walk across it – who gather the stems into bundles and tie them with leaves. There is a sense of urgency. Sugarcane must be processed within a few hours, otherwise the juice starts to ferment and the harvest is wasted.

The laughter of playing children tinkles in the air. At the side of the field, two young boys are staging a toy battle. One toy is a half-melted rubber superhero, the other the plastic body of a long-dead digital watch, whose buttons the boy nonetheless presses with murderous intent. Yesterday was a local new-year festival, and the girls are still wearing frilly dresses in pink and yellow. The children discover a mango tree; though the fruit is not yet ripe, they ask older siblings to reach up and pick it for them. Three girls draw together in a notebook.

As the morning advances, the temperature climbs to 43 degrees. Tripods sprout in the field, assembled quickly from full-length canes. Bundles of leaves are stashed on top to make shade. Water, food and babies find shelter beneath. I watch a young boy tying a checked cloth between two cane legs, laying his infant sister inside, rocking her and singing a lullaby. He smiles at me with tender pride.

On the embankment at the side of the field, dressed from cap to toe in clean white cotton, the farmer watches. He is in his mid-sixties, his posture is erect, his teeth are leonine. He has grown this sugarcane from seedlings, but his relationship with it is now finished. It is already sold to a contractor, who has brought the cutters and who is also here, surveying their progress.

The farmer is thinking about the next crop. To restore nitrogen to this exhausted field, he will plant onions, spinach, pulses. Though the cutting is far from over and the field still littered with cane, his son is already preparing to plough. He needs to find a way of getting the tractor over the raised embankment surrounding the field. With a hoe, he begins to cut an opening; from the released soil, he tries to shape a ramp. He climbs into the tractor, starts the engine and tries to reverse up the ramp, but the soil is too loose. The tractor sinks in, the engine roars, the wheels spin. He releases the power and lets the vehicle slide down the slope. He gets out and pulls down more earth, lengthening the ramp, packing it down. Other farmers have come to watch; then they bring their hoes and it becomes a community event. After four or five attempts, the tractor finally clears the embankment and lands heavily in the field. Tomorrow, all traces of sugarcane will be ploughed out of sight.

At the receding wall of cane, bodies continue to bend and rise, bend and rise. Though most sugar consumers will never witness their activity, it constitutes one of the defining scenes of our world. It is no exaggeration to say that the modern era was brought into being by the mass production of sugar – and, more than we understand, our reality is sustained even now by this endlessly repeated movement of arm and body. For the last five centuries, this same arrangement of human beings, tools and plants has been relentlessly reproduced in the tropical and subtropical regions where *Saccharum officinarum* grows. Cruelty is inherent to this arrangement, and it is no coincidence that sugarcane fields, for all their commercial importance, have always existed far from sight. During the terror years of European colonial production, iconically, the entire system was secreted offshore. Many of today's Caribbean tax havens were previously sugar havens, where civil laws did not apply and where imported slaves could be subjected to levels of violence which shocked the rare outside observers who did make it to those shores.* Such visitors witnessed scenes very like the ones before me now: there too, 'strong, youthful male and female adults' performed the gruelling cutting work, with 'younger, less mature or older slaves following behind . . . On all plantations there were . . . women with gaggles of children.'[2]

Where I am is not 'offshore'. Everyone around me is a citizen of the same democratic republic. No one stands behind these cutters with a whip. As we shall see, however, there are dark continuities between that crude coercion of old and the more abstract pressures applied to both farmers and cutters today. It is no coincidence that scenes from the most primitive stages of capitalism are so precisely reproduced here. Where I stand, from every point, the breeze carries the double chime of steel on cane: one-two, one-two. It is an eternal theme tune of our modern world.

The sound stops. It is time for lunch. Gathering under the sugar-cane tripods, workers take aluminium boxes from woven plastic bags printed with the logos of fertiliser manufacturers. They unpack home-made *roti* – the round flatbreads which provide the staple for so much of India. They pour water from the plastic drums they carried with them in the morning. At rest, they seem even younger. Some of the mothers reclaiming their babies for the half-hour break look hardly more than fifteen. Children gather around the food. The meal is strangely wordless.

The farmer has invited me to his house for lunch. He comes to usher me away. His son comes too, and we all leave together, walking along the raised embankment between two fields. On one side is a devastated melon crop. The vines lie in disarray. The farmer gestures with disgust at the rotting fruit.

'Unseasonal rain,' he says. 'So much fell in one day, the melons exploded. You can see they are all cracked open. That farmer lost

* Father Antoine Biet, for instance, who visited British plantations in Bermuda in 1654, later wrote at length of the horror he had felt when witnessing the beating, branding and mutilation of slaves. See for example Matthew Parker, *The Sugar Barons* (London: Windmill Books, 2012), ch. 12.

half a year's sustenance for his family. He has nothing left: he cannot even afford to clear the rubbish from the field.'

Climate change, and the enormous unpredictability it introduces to farming: we will encounter it again and again.

Across the flat land, we can see for several kilometres. The village is not far away; next to it runs the river, improbably broad and blue. In the distance, plumes of smoke rise from sugar factories. The heat is dry and enlivening. We pass a stony outcrop with a small shrine on top; the rock is covered with tomatoes drying in the sun. Their orange is like lava.

Everywhere, there is birdsong. Slow, rhythmic pulsing, excitable trills, passing shrieks – the chorus never ceases.

Right-angling between the fields, we finally reach the road. A tractor passes, pulling a sky-blue trailer piled high with bundles of sugarcane. It halts just ahead of us, and we soon catch it up. Several other trailers are parked too, ready for unloading. By the side of the road, under a high corrugated-iron shelter, is a little processing plant. This is a jaggery mill.

Jaggery is a massy brown-cane derivative which has been produced in Indian villages for at least 3,000 years. Long predating granulated sugar, jaggery is a less refined product which retains organic content from the cane and is therefore richer in nutrition and taste. This explains its perennial popularity. As late as the 1950s, more than half of all Indian cane was turned into jaggery, and it is still widely produced today. Traditional desserts such as *halwa* are not made with industrial sugar; their aromas demand jaggery, whose sticky rocks are therefore kept in households of every rank.

As we approach the mill, the farmer greets the supervisor, who gets up from his lunch to walk me around. His descriptions are shouted over a juddery din of diesel generators. Though a lone electric wire swoops over the fields to meet the corner of this corrugated shelter – and so to supply energy to the cane press – today there is a power cut.

At one end of the installation, a man feeds lengths of cane into a clattering grinder, which chews them greedily. Hindi songs are playing, and the man sings along joyfully, undisturbed by the noise. His machine spits out a mountain of discarded cane fibre, which another man removes with a fork and spreads on the ground to dry. This white pulp – known in the industry as bagasse – will dry in the sun and be used as fuel for the boilers.

The soupy green sap from the cane flows out of the press and through a wide plastic pipe into a large bubbling vat set into the ground. This is the first in a row of similar vats, each one hotter than the last to allow the juice to be clarified and then progressively concentrated, evaporating water in stages without burning the sugars. Two men are sprinkling white powder into the first vat.

'There are two additives,' says the supervisor. 'One is limestone. The other is okra powder – from the vegetable. These powders cause the impurities to coagulate, so we can remove them.'

Sure enough, the bubbling stew is disgorging a thick yellow scum, which the two men skim off with steel ladles on long poles.

'We keep this waste. It's sold for fertiliser. The farmers buy it.'

Ladled from one vat to the next, the boiling sap becomes each time purer and more viscous. I stand over the last vat, which bubbles violently, giving off a sweet and heady steam. From there, it is poured into a tub where it cools under the fans. Before it is entirely hard, it is shovelled into conical plastic moulds. Finally, the hard jaggery is taken out to be wrapped and dispatched.

The supervisor breaks a piece from one of the cooling cones and gives it to me. Still hot, the consistency is like paste; after a few seconds, it cools and turns crystal. I try it. It is heavenly.

'Where do you sell it?' I ask.

'Most we sell here in the market. Some is bought by a distiller. They use it to make rum.'

I wander around the installation. At the back, I find a group of women. They are forcing bagasse with their bare hands through a small hole into an underground furnace, whose heat hits me even through the tiny aperture. On its own, bagasse does not burn hot enough; to it they add shredded plastic bags and containers, which accounts for the acrid smell.

The women do the cooking, too. On a couple of gas stoves, they are making *daal* and *roti* which they serve to the men. They offer me food, which I decline in view of the meal to come. I complete my circumnavigation and rejoin the supervisor out front, who is chatting to my farmer and his son.

'Do you keep it running all day?' I ask.

'All day and all night,' says the supervisor. 'The furnace never dies. These ten workers will go home in the evening, and the night workers will come.'

'You have enough cane?'

He gestures to all the trailers parked outside. The quantity is stupendous.

'We process twenty tonnes every day,' he says.

We say goodbye and continue along the road. Another truck passes us, piled with cane, and another one, full of plastic waste. After fifteen minutes, we arrive at the farmer's house – a single-storey concrete structure painted cream.

At the entrance is a covered terrace, generous and breezy. The steps up to the terrace are decorated with geometric designs in coloured powder: another relic of yesterday's festival. Mythically connected to the creation of time and the universe, the Marathi new year, or Gudi Padwa, is celebrated as a new beginning. Many locals mark the occasion by eating a bitter neem leaf with a chunk of jaggery, symbolising their acceptance of everything the year will bring.

A line of coconut trees shades the building from the midday sun; washing is strung on lines between them. As we are taking off our shoes, the farmer's wife comes out, all smiles. She wears a cotton sari, whose end she has draped over her head to greet the stranger. She wears a great many bangles, and three gold earrings in each ear.

Inside, the ceiling is high and the room is cool, even though there is a power cut here too and the fans are off. A television is mounted on the wall; a frame of flowers has been painted around it, as if it were a shrine. The couple's granddaughter approaches: she is shy but eager to be part of the conversation. She asks if she can make me lemonade and disappears into the kitchen.

We sit down. The farmer is talking about his favourite television shows. He complains about the news, which leads him to complain about the government. The son, smiling at opinions he has heard before, offers me the plate of sweets his mother has put out ready. His face is outlined with black stubble; he wears jeans and a baseball cap.

I thank everyone for their hospitality.

'We are village people,' says the son. 'We farmers get excited: *Wow: I have a guest coming to my house, what can I do for him, what can I give him to eat?* It's not like this in the city. You don't find the same love there.'

'If a farmer has one piece of bread,' adds his father, 'he will give it to his guest. We give them the best we have. We don't tell them we don't have anything for ourselves. If we have nothing to give, we borrow it from our neighbour.'

The granddaughter emerges with lemonade. She is tall and pretty. Fifteen years old, she attends the village school. I thank her for the lemonade, and she flashes me a conspiratorial smile.

Her grandmother brings lunch. A basket of *roti*, a bowl of steaming *daal*, aubergine cooked with tomatoes and coriander. It smells fantastic. We begin to eat.

'Sugarcane is very difficult to grow,' wrote Kautilya in the third century BCE, 'being susceptible to diseases and requiring much . . . expenditure.'

Kautilya's great work, the *Arthashastra,* was perhaps the most comprehensive guide to statecraft until Niccolò Machiavelli in the sixteenth century, offering answers to every conceivable question of government. As adviser to the emperor Chandragupta, Kautilya directed his administrative expertise towards the building of the Mauryan empire, which became one of the largest of the age. Emerging from conquests in the north-west of the Indian subcontinent, the empire was intimately connected with Persia. Chandragupta's grandson, Ashoka, would extend the territory southwards and eastwards to the Bay of Bengal, so opening the sea routes to China. A giant between two giants, the Mauryan empire was blessed with immense trading opportunities. Ashoka enhanced them further by converting to Buddhism and promoting the new faith across his dominions – for Buddhists were not hampered by Brahminical concerns over purity and contact with foreigners and merchants, and preferred learning and trade to war. Buddhist temples became important nodes, in fact, in the Asian commercial network, and sugar was their essential ingredient. Buddhist monks were forbidden from consuming intoxicating drinks, but sugar-cane juice and sugar water were allowed; Buddhist scriptures even prescribed sugar as a medicine during sickness. Sugar was prominent, therefore, among the industries of the Buddhist monasteries, which were principally financed from this source (Figure 14).

The sugarcane plant itself originated in southern New Guinea, but it was eagerly transplanted by humans for the sweet sap that oozed out when it was chewed or crushed – and it arrived in India and China before 1000 BCE.[3] Since the sap spoiled quickly, however, it could not be stored or traded over long distances, so it remained – compared to what happened later – of limited use. It was in India that peasants learned how to turn the juice into jaggery, which could last for several months. They grew cane alongside rice and wheat, harvested it in the off-season and ground it in communal village mills, where it was crushed with a stone wheel powered by bullocks. Then it was boiled in kettles very much like how it is done today. Jaggery was a prominent feature of Indian life for much of the first millennium BCE, used not only to sweeten food but also to deliver a calorific jolt during labour – to animals as well as humans – and even as currency.[4]

At some point between 500 and 300 BCE, Indian artisans further elaborated this cottage industry, developing processes for extracting molasses, and so manufacturing a white, granulated sugar devoid of liquid and impurity. This product was light, it did not decompose, its taste was unrivalled, the method of its production was secret, and it could be transported over great distances without damage. It was, in other words, the ideal trading commodity – and it became as costly and coveted as such other luxury goods as silk, spices and sandalwood. This was the reason Kautilya devoted such attention to sugar in his treatise on statecraft: sugar created wealth and power. In the earliest Buddhist texts, sugar merchants appear as the epitome of worldly accumulation, their wealth so immense that it was an obstacle to spiritual achievement. In a text written about a century after Gautama Buddha's death, we read of a merchant who, leading 'five hundred wagons all filled with jars of sugar', encountered him on a highway and asked how he might demonstrate his devotion. The Buddha asked him to give sugar to his monks and to the poor. When the merchant had given away so much sugar that the crowd had filled their baskets and their robes, he still had much left and asked what he should do with it. 'Drop it into water,' instructed the Buddha, 'where there are no living creatures.' The merchant dumped his sugar into a barren pond, upon which the Buddha 'knew that [his] mind was ready' and sat down to offer him spiritual instruction.[5]

As if to remind us of India's primordial contribution to global eating habits, two Sanskrit words for cane derivatives – *sakkara* and *khanda*[6] – are still used, 2,500 years later, in English ('sugar' and 'candy') and many other languages. For centuries, sugar remained an Indian monopoly: traders had to source it from India, rather as they had to source silk from China. Like most Asian sugar production until the present, the crop was grown not on corporate plantations but by smallholder peasants. Manufacturers sent agents into the countryside to identify the best cane, which they bought from farmers in advance – a significant up-front investment which would have necessitated sophisticated financing. The cane was processed in regional refineries, where a caste of skilled sugar boilers produced different grades of sugar for different markets. Most of this production was destined for Indian consumers; the greatest profits, however, derived from caravan export to the courts of China, Persia and Egypt.

Knowledge of sugarcane cultivation and processing gradually spread. In Sasanian Persia, it became an important cash crop, especially in Khuzestan, where it was grown in centres such as Gundišāpur and Shushtar using extensive irrigation systems.[7] By the fifth century CE, Persia had an established sugar industry of its own, strategically located around the mouth of the Persian Gulf.[8] In the seventh century, Persia was conquered by the first caliphate, whose expansion transmitted Persia's abundant crop resources and advanced agro-industry to North Africa, Spain and the Levant. Egypt, whose sugar was particularly prized, would become the main supplier to medieval Europe and Arabia: by the eleventh century, and the first Crusades, caravans of hundreds of camels, transporting up to 150 tonnes at a time, could be seen departing Egyptian refineries for ports and markets all around the Mediterranean.

In the opposite direction, sugar science was transmitted to Tang China by Xuanzang (602–64 CE), a Buddhist monk whose sojourn at the court of King Harsha, ruler of much of eastern and northern India, resulted in a spectacular half-century of intra-Asian exchange. As a result of Xuanzang's transport of knowledge and seedlings, India's majestic sugarcane landscapes, whose descriptions fill his famous travelogue *Record of the Western Regions*, were reproduced in southern China. Six centuries later, Marco Polo would be astonished by their extent. 'I assure you that this province grows and produces more sugar than the rest of the world put together,' he wrote of the manufacture of Hangzhou, 'and this too is a prodigious source of revenue.'[9] Fifty years after Polo, the North African explorer Ibn Battuta arrived in China; he declared that 'there is abundant sugarcane, equal, nay superior, in quality to that of Egypt.'[10] Like sugar industries in other times and places, China's was internationalised: there were resident Egyptian technicians, as well as merchants from Persia and Arabia.* Cargoes left by ship for ports in the Indian Ocean and Persian Gulf.

By the medieval period, Asian and West Asian merchants had constructed a thriving transnational sugar system.† Europe, however, was for the most part excluded. Fifteen hundred years after the development of granulated sugar, few Europeans had ever seen it. Greeks travelling with Alexander the Great through modern-day Pakistan

---

* Modern scholars suppose Marco Polo's 'Babylonians' to have been Egyptians.

† Unlike the later European system, this made rather little use of slavery, depending instead on smallholder peasant cultivators for its supply – though a 'modern' shift was pioneered by the Abbasid caliphate which, in the eighth and ninth centuries, set up large-scale sugar plantations in southern Mesopotamia; these were worked by slaves from Europe, Central Asia and Africa.

were mystified to discover 'reeds [which] produce honey, although there are no bees'.[11] Some Indian sugar evidently reached Rome in the first century CE, where Pliny the Elder, the natural historian, encountered it as a crude curiosity: 'a kind of "honey" that collects in reeds . . . white like gum and brittle to the teeth . . . the largest pieces are the size of a hazelnut'.[12] But Persia's elaborate sherbets and sweetmeats, the dazzling sugar sculptures of China and Egypt, the medicinal sugar waters of Arabia and Central Asia – all these were unknown in Europe, and certainly, since sugar was paid for in gold, India's mass jaggery culture was unthinkable. As late as 1226, King Henry III of England asked the mayor of Winchester to obtain one and a half kilograms of Egyptian sugar from merchants arriving at the great Winchester Fair, 'if so much could be got'.[13]

Europe's slow integration began with the Crusades, which familiarised Europeans not only with the taste of sugar but also with its profits. After the conquest of Tyre in the Levant in 1124, the ever-commercial Venetian Republic laid claim to the rich sugarlands surrounding the city, from where it began to export to Europe. By 1291, the Mamluk sultans of Cairo had captured the last vestiges of the Kingdom of Jerusalem, and Venetian financiers began to look elsewhere. Centuries before, when the Abbasid caliphate had ruled much of the Mediterranean from its grand capital of Baghdad, sugar had been cultivated in Cyprus;[14] the Venetians took advantage of enduring knowledge and infrastructure to establish on the island their largest plantations yet.[15] Serviced by elaborate irrigation systems, state-of-the-art refineries and Balkan slaves, these plantations generated significant political power, as well as profits.[16] In 1361, Federico Cornaro, who had secured a fiefdom on Cyprus in return for a 60,000-ducat loan to its king, set up a plantation where as many as 400 workers, free and unfree, tended and harvested the cane. By 1379, his fortune was accounted the greatest in Venice.*

* A remarkable series of paintings was produced to celebrate the wedding, in 1468, of Caterina Cornari and James II of Cyprus – paintings in which, naturally, merchant vessels featured prominently. See Joaneath Spicer, 'The Abduction of Helen: A Monumental Series Celebrating the Wedding of Caterina Corner in 1468', *Journal of the Walters Art Museum*, Vol. 74 (2019).

Europe's principal sugar supplies continued to come, however, from plantations in Egypt and the Jordan valley, which were ruled by the Mamluks. Those supplies faltered in the fourteenth century, when plague swept through Mamluk lands, destroying agricultural labour. 'The people spat blood,' wrote the Mamluk historian al-Maqrizi of the five-year horrors which overwhelmed Cairo and Damascus in 1348.[17] Plague was compounded by droughts in the Nile delta and failed rains in the Jordan valley[18] – and sugar production collapsed in both centres. When, in 1400, Timur (also remembered as Tamerlane) led his armies from Central Asia into the Levant, depriving the Mamluks of their eastern plantations, the crisis was complete. Some sugar towns collapsed so completely that they were not inhabited again until the nineteenth century.[19]

This set European entrepreneurs on a sugar quest that would change the world. First, they attempted to make good their supplies from known lands in the Mediterranean. The Venetians grew cane on Crete, with little success; Sicilian aristocrats fared better on their estates, which drew in workers from all around the Adriatic. The Genoese funded new sugar ventures in the western Maghreb and in Granada – the Alhambra Palace is one vestige of the sugar wealth pouring into that kingdom in the late fourteenth century[20] – but the quality of the cane was low. The quantities remained small as well, compared to the lost production of Egypt. It is no surprise, therefore, that Genoa's attention – and that of its partners in Iberia and the Low Countries, who were united in their desire to end the supremacy of Venice – was drawn, ultimately, to the Atlantic.[21]

In 1425, Portugal's Prince Henry 'the Navigator' ordered Sicilian sugarcane to be transported to Madeira, an uninhabited island off the coast of modern-day Morocco, which his navy had occupied five years before. Technicians followed the plants,[22] their knowledge of crop and refinery inherited from the Levant, from Egypt and from Andalusia – all of which had learned from classical Persia. Large-scale production began in 1455 and, by the 1490s, Madeira had surpassed Cyprus as Europe's biggest sugar producer. With the new efficiencies of the Atlantic islands, indeed, Mediterranean producers now entered their terminal decline.

One of those efficiencies, no doubt, was slavery. While slaves had mostly been used in the Mediterranean to supplement conventional labour supplies, Atlantic sugar had no existence without them. Slaves were anyway one of Henry's principal motivations for seeking access to West Africa: plague had destroyed the Portuguese labour force too, and his Algarve estates had fallen into disuse. Shipping technologies introduced in the 1430s enabled Portugal to round the cape on today's Senegalese coast, and so to establish relations with traders who transported slaves down the Senegal and Gambia rivers. Henry's chronicler, Azurara, described the first arrival of 443 men, women and children in Lisbon:

> [W]ho among us was so hard at heart as not to be moved by compassion? They had heads downcast, and faces covered in tears. Some looked up towards heaven apparently praying to whatever God was theirs. I saw some slapping their faces with their hands, and then throwing themselves flat on the ground. There was a wailing chant, and although we could not understand their words, they spoke their grief to us clearly.
>
> Their anguish reached new heights when the moment of distribution came. For it to be fair, it proved necessary for children to be separated from their parents, wives from their husbands, and brothers from brothers . . . Fathers and sons, ranged on opposite sides, would break ranks and rush towards each other with all their might. Mothers clasped their infants in their arms, and threw themselves on the ground to cover them with their bodies.[23]

Several of the islands established by Portugal as distribution posts for this tragic trade – such as Cape Verde, São Tomé and Príncipe – also proved conducive to sugar cultivation. Since these islands were uninhabited, and since supply lines to the mainland were long, the Portuguese, from the very beginning, conceptualised slave-worked factories and plantations. The same model was then imported even where there were abundant native populations: the Guanche people of the Canary Isles were exterminated by the occupying Spanish, who re-engineered the landscape for sugar and brought West African slaves to work. The scale remained small compared to what would ensue in the Americas, but the intensity of violence was already full-blown: to maintain a slave population of about 10,000, the Portuguese had to import 140,000 individuals before the end of the fifteenth century.[24] As early as the 1450s, then, the system familiar to us from its sixteenth-century roll-out in Brazil and the Caribbean was fully operational off the African coast.

But the efficiency of the new sugar colonies derived also from the enormous resources, political and financial, invested in their success. Sugar was emerging, after all, as a crucial political concern. In 1453, the Ottoman capture of Constantinople completed Europe's commercial isolation from Asia, giving the western continent no choice but to acquire its own 'oriental' capabilities. As that scramble got under way, it was clear that sugar would make the difference between the dominant states and the rest. While grain, olive oil and wine were left to the merely affluent, kings and finance houses took control of the power crop. Atlantic sugar expansion was a joint venture of the Iberian kings, the leading bankers of Genoa, Florence and Augsburg and the most ambitious Spanish, Portuguese and Flemish merchants. The project depended, anyway, on influence such as theirs. Atlantic sugar would not be grown, as in India, China or Egypt, by smallholder peasants; it would be produced on large plantations adjacent to state-of-the-art refineries. Great powers were necessary to acquire and clear the necessary land, build the factories, create the hydraulic systems necessary for both irrigation and powering mills, and purchase, house and discipline the slave-labour force. As in the fifteenth century, so throughout the modern period: big sugar ruled.

At the end of the fifteenth century, this Atlantic system was transmitted to the Caribbean. Transmission was quite literal: on his second voyage to the Caribbean, the Genoese adventurer Christopher Columbus stopped first in the Canary Islands, where he collected sugarcane cuttings for transport to Hispaniola – the island that is home today to Haiti and the Dominican

Republic – and observed the modern slave complex up close. Columbus was well acquainted with sugar, married as he was into a family of Italian–Portuguese landowners who owned a sugar island off the coast of Madeira, where Columbus had lived with his wife in 1479–80. The Spanish monarchs had invested lavishly in his voyage, and Columbus was primed to commence operations: his seventeen ships also carried farmers, artisans, seeds and agricultural equipment. On his arrival in Hispaniola, he discovered that, half a world from its original home in the south Pacific, sugarcane grew exceptionally well. He wrote to King Ferdinand and Queen Isabella: 'Their Highnesses will give instructions to Don Juan de Fonseca' – a priest and counsellor who was already emerging as the controller of colonial affairs – 'he will have to see that sugar-canes of good quality be sent.'[25] And indeed the fragile

'Saccharum' ('sugar') from the late sixteenth-century engraving series *Nova Reperta,* or 'New Inventions of Modern Times' by Jan van der Straet. The advanced Dutch technologies shown here would later be adopted by other European producers.

botanical specimens sent from Spain were quickly turned into a world-changing enterprise, from which he and his family were spectacular beneficiaries. As Lords of 'the Indies' and of Jamaica, Christopher's son and grandson, Diego and Luiz, would administer substantial sugar plantations of their own.

For three centuries, the battle for European supremacy was prosecuted in New World sugarlands. Spanish, Portuguese, Dutch, French, British – all asserted monopolies over some piece of this industry. Britain was perhaps the most determined: Oliver Cromwell directed all the power of the Royal Navy – as did the kings who succeeded him – towards breaking into, and then dismantling, Spanish and Dutch dominance in the Caribbean.[26] Seized by British aristocrat-adventurers in the 1630s, Barbados became the laboratory where Britain's sugar formula was honed. Like the Portuguese system in Brazil, it was built on slave labour and state protection; the tiny island size forced British planters, however, into space-saving innovations. Brazilian mills were powered by cattle, whose pasture took up as much space as the plantations themselves; Brazilian refineries ran on wood, which required a large forest hinterland. Barbadian cane, by contrast, was crushed by Dutch-style wind power; the furnaces made substantial use of sun-dried bagasse; timber, coal and foodstuffs were imported from the American mainland. The island territory, in short, became entirely specialised and other tropical crops, such as tobacco and cotton, disappeared. Labour, too, was homogenised: forced white labour came to an end and the plantations were worked exclusively by African slaves. Sugar production absorbed at least half and possibly two-thirds of all the slaves abducted from Africa. Of all the territories where Europeans employed slave labour, lifespans were shortest in the Caribbean. Turnover was therefore very high: of the 12.5 million individuals transported to the Americas – 1.8 million having died on the way – around 40 per cent were unloaded in these small islands.[27]

The Barbados model was reproduced in all Britain's Caribbean possessions, most notably Jamaica, which was twenty times larger (Figures 15–18). Jamaican sugar was mainly responsible for propelling Britain to its position of nineteenth-century superpower. In 1673, Jamaica's fifty-seven estates produced 670 tonnes;[28] in the early nineteenth century, by which time the island housed a slave population of 320,000, there were 859 estates producing 80,000 tonnes[29] – and Jamaican planters had amassed private wealth equivalent to one-sixth of British GDP. By that time, Britain was responsible for more than half of all the sugar output from European colonies,[30] and there was a powerful impact at home. Caribbean sugar wealth, which sparkles in the pages of William Thackeray and Jane Austen, dazzled British society. But sugar produced much more than conspicuous consumption. In order to ensure that they could continue to obtain slaves, and that tariffs would continue to keep out sugar from other colonial blocs, sugar planters put together a formidable political coalition; families such as the Beckfords of Jamaica, the Codringtons of Antigua and the Lascelles of Barbados all 'had at least one family member as a Member of Parliament'.[31] 'If I am not misinformed,' wrote a contributor to the *Gentleman's Magazine* in 1766, 'there are now in Parliament upwards of forty members who are either West Indian planters themselves, descended from such, or have concerns there that entitle them to pre-eminence.'[32]

Along the way, European nutritional habits were transformed. Until the sixteenth century, sugar remained the preserve of the aristocracy, for whom it functioned as a status symbol. After 1600, however, new American supplies brought it within reach of the middle classes, which opened great culinary realms of cakes, pastries, puddings, ice creams and other desserts. European appetites were especially piqued, however, by the parallel spread of another exotic trio – coffee, tea and cocoa – whose bitter taste cried out for sweet. New rituals around tea and coffee were institutionalised in tea houses and cafés, where sugar contributed to the free flow of caffeinated conversation. By the early nineteenth century, sugar had transformed the diet of Europe's labouring classes, for whom bread with jam or treacle provided a welcome calorific bonus during the working shift. Tea breaks became integral to English factories, when workers were revived with two great products of the

British empire.* In an age when working-class alcohol consumption was decreasing, sugary tea became a major source of comfort and consolation – there were millions who, like the impoverished protagonist of Thackeray's *Vanity Fair* (1847–8), 'wheedled the grocer round the corner for sugar and tea'. Naturally, sugar consumption exploded. From their inception, European slave-worked plantations had inexorably increased supplies: in Britain, the price of sugar had already halved between 1630 and 1680.[33] During the ensuing century and a half, per capita consumption increased about twentyfold.[34]

In 1833, slavery was abolished in the British empire, and British sugar planters lobbied for the right to bring indentured workers to work their Caribbean estates. In 1837, John Gladstone, a prominent Jamaican planter and father of the future prime minister, wrote to the government warning that without 'a system of regular continuous labour . . . the cultivation of the sugarcane cannot . . . be carried on to a productive result' and proposing that such a system be based on 'a supply of Hill Coolies from Bengal'.[35] Similar systems would be established in French and Dutch plantations, producing a vast migration of people from India, China, Indonesia, Japan, the Philippines, Portugal's Atlantic islands and West Africa. Conditions could be very poor for these workers: plantation owners often saddled them with 'debts' which had to be repaid with work, so exposing them to levels of exploitation not dissimilar to those associated with slavery. Death rates were high, sanitary conditions terrible and – despite

* As one author notes, the highly organised West Indian sugar lobby and the East India Company used political pressure to create a cheap market for sweetened tea at the expense of coffee, with the result that 'the British Isles consumed more than 60 percent of all the tea shipped to Europe and sugar consumption was ten times higher than that of the rest of Europe.' Erika Diane Rappaport, *A Thirst for Empire: How Tea Shaped the Modern World* (Princeton, NJ: Princeton University Press, 2017), 49. By the mid-eighteenth century, tea drinking had spread far beyond elite circles, reaching even the poorest rural households and the most remote settlements, where it was commonly consumed with sugar, indicating how deeply sweetness had become embedded in the expanding tea market. See also Jon Stobart, *Sugar and Spice: Grocers and Groceries in Provincial England, 1650–1830* (Oxford: Oxford University Press, 2013); Markman Ellis, Richard Coulton and Matthew Mauger, *Empire of Tea: The Asian Leaf that Conquered the World* (London: Reaktion Books, 2015).

advertisements by recruiters to the contrary – there was rarely any provision for schooling, so children too slid into a life of plantation labour. Sexual exploitation of female workers was rife.

But without total control of land and labour Caribbean planters could never maintain their former dominance.[36] Slave-produced sugar was still cheaper, and for several decades slave plantations – now concentrated in Louisiana, Cuba and Brazil – remained the main source of industrial sugar. Those centres too declined with abolition; Louisiana's production did not regain 1861 levels until 1894, by which time it was no longer the dominant supplier to US consumers. And yet demand was exploding, along with the global population; in order to meet it, the problem of how to produce sugar 'legally' would have to be solved. It was time for peasant farmers – absent from European sugar cultivation, but never from Asian – to return to the centre.

The Dutch colony of Java was dominated by peasant cultivation, so there was no rural proletariat available for wage work, and plantation experiments collapsed for lack of labour.[37] Instead, the Dutch introduced a forced Cultivation System (*cultuurstelsel*), under which peasants would, in order to pay their taxes, give over a proportion of their land to the cultivation of sugarcane, which they could sell to colonial refineries.[38] This imposed extreme demands on Javanese peasants, who possessed no food reserves as a result; during the famines of the 1840s, they died in enormous numbers. Attempts to resist the hated system – strikes, marches, incineration of cane fields – were dealt with harshly, often by installed Javanese managers who were given a generous share of the profits when things went well but were subject to harsh fines in the event of unrest under their watch. Farmers who tried to run from their obligations were captured and punished under anti-migration laws.

The Cultivation System was spectacularly successful. Though it was underwritten by violence, its coercion was mainly abstracted into taxation and law. As such, it was much more efficient: while it delivered an agricultural exploitation as intensive as any other, it did not require the Dutch laboriously to acquire or occupy farmland, or to administer a mass incarceration regime. Johannes van

Harvesting cane for the Nieuw Tersana sugar company, Cheribon, Java. Photograph attributed to Ohannes Kurkdjian, around 1900.

den Bosch, governor general of the Dutch Indies and designer of the system, boasted that Javanese forced labour cost four times less than that of Caribbean slaves.[39] Java's sugar boomed, therefore: just when its rivals were beset by the crisis of slavery, the Netherlands rose to become the world's second-biggest exporter after Cuba.

The important point, as we move towards our own time, is that the Dutch system did not die. It proved an effective way to compel large numbers of independent peasants into intensive sugarcane farming – and many of its key elements were adopted by the independent nations of Indonesia and India. Both countries needed to supply sugar at very low prices to their own populations; both also possessed fiercely independent peasantries, which had resisted repeated attempts to force them to give up their smallholdings. It was difficult for them, therefore, to develop the kind of large plantation complexes still operating in Brazil and elsewhere.* Nor could

* Brazil's low production costs are still linked not only to scale and mechanisation but also to the persistently vulnerable status of plantation workers. See for instance Julien

they emulate the beet-sugar model expanding in the cool climates of the West. Beet sugar had been developed in nineteenth-century Prussia, which possessed no cane-growing colonies; the express purpose had been to reduce its dependence on tropical imports. By the twentieth century, many countries of Europe and North America had developed domestic beet-sugar industries, which they protected from Asian competition with significant subsidies and tariffs.[40] The future of sugarcane in Indonesia and India would rely on systems that preserved something of the coercive force of colonial times.*

When Sukarno declared Indonesian independence in 1949, he did so, like so many other post-colonial leaders, in the hope of returning to his people the rights and freedoms they had long been denied. The restoration of Javanese sugar, however, was essential to the building of the new state, which turned out to be incompatible with those privileges. By the time Sukarno was ousted in 1965, Javanese sugar production was still only one-quarter of the 1930 level. How could a modern sovereign state produce sugar on the same scale, and at the same low price, as coercive colonial powers? General Suharto, the strongman who replaced Sukarno, introduced a programme labelled 'Intensified Smallholder Cane' (*Tebu Rakyat Intensifikasi*) whose aim was to restore the power of factories over farmers and to lower the price at which they acquired cane. This represented 'a return to colonial times, if not the Cultivation System proper'.[41]

Bouissou and Kenza Soares El Sayed, 'Brazilian Plantations Accused of Forced Labour Supply Europe with Sugar', *Le Monde*, 31 December 2022. Similar abuses are documented in other countries working with such models – e.g. Ana Swanson, 'US Blocks Dominican Republic Sugar Imports, Citing Forced Labor', *New York Times*, 23 November 2022.

* Western countries developed beet sugar for the express purpose of reducing their dependence on imports from rival imperial systems. Prussian chemists were particularly important: Prussia possessed no sugar-growing colonies and could face shortages during times of conflict – for instance, during the 'Napoleonic blockade' of Britain and its colonies. Developing indigenous sugar production was therefore a strategic affair, receiving significant patronage from the state. See Ulbe Bosma, *The World of Sugar: How the Sweet Stuff Transformed Our Politics, Health, and Environment over 2,000 Years* (Cambridge, MA: Harvard University Press, 2023), 93–95.

For the Indian National Congress, too – effectively, the independence movement's government-in-waiting – a robust sugar industry was essential to the project of national development. Sugar cultivation needed to be restructured if it was to serve the mainstream economy and not just local needs. Most Indian peasants grew sugarcane as a mere component in a multi-crop cycle. Half of the total was still processed into jaggery, which remained the preferred form in most of the country; much of this processing was carried out by village collectives, which therefore retained the profits. Most of the rest became traditional *khandsari* sugar, a raw brown product unsuited to international tastes. Not much cane became white sugar for export. Peasants therefore needed to be induced into producing for industrial sugar producers. Indian officials knew the Cultivation System well: almost the first action of the Indian Sugar Committee after its establishment in 1919 was to visit Java and study the reasons for its success.[42]

The key lesson imported from Java was that of zoning: factories were given monopolies over the sugar produced in their immediate area. This relieved them from having to bid against other factories for cane supply. Measures were also taken to outlaw jaggery production except within the village, further reducing the competitive burden on granulated sugar manufacturers. These policies empowered factories against farmers; the hope was that farmers could right the imbalance by organising themselves into cooperatives. But factories always enjoyed fundamental advantages, especially since harvested cane perished within hours, and farmers with a crop to sell were always battling against time. The factories owned the scales on which the cane was weighed, for instance, and farmers always suspected tampering. The factories also assessed the cane's sucrose content and so its price – here too farmers had no way of contesting what they were told.*

* In his study of the Gorakhpur region of eastern Uttar Pradesh in the 1930s, Shahid Amin shows how the interests of sugar mills and peasants were structurally opposed. Mills promoted cane varieties with high sucrose content and sought to extend the crushing season and maximise sugar recovery; peasants prioritised early harvesting, high tonnage, fodder value and alignment with the agricultural calendar. Amin shows how peasants

After independence in August 1947, the government repurposed British-era legislation in order to centralise control of basic provisions. During the Second World War, the British had devised emergency provisions to compel Indian farmers to deliver essential supplies to the colonial state reliably and cheaply. Those laws persisted after independence, so the new government could use them to navigate the Republic's first precarious years. It turned out that the powers they gave – to regulate and even force the production of strategic commodities, and to control their price and distribution – were too valuable to surrender, and they were once again approved, in an expanded form, as the Essential Commodities Act of 1955. Ensuring that factories could procure sugarcane at low prices and in sufficient volume was a key aim of this Act, which is still in force today. Sugar, in fact, remains 'one of the most regulated sectors in the economy'[43] – a consequence of the continuing strategic significance of this crop to the Indian state.

This significance is reflected in the extraordinary mutations of the sugar industry in Maharashtra, where India's first sugar farmers' cooperative was set up in 1948. The purpose was to correct the power imbalance between factories and farmers. Individual cane farmers were given a share in the cooperative, which ran its own processing plant and returned the profits to members. Prime Minister Jawaharlal Nehru visited Maharashtra to study the model for himself, and declared that it should be emulated across the country.[44] From 1954, all new Indian sugar factories had to be cooperative-owned; most early cooperatives were founded and operated by leaders from ordinary village backgrounds.[45] The attraction for Nehru, a socialist hero of the freedom struggle, was clear. Zoning would ensure, on the one hand, that India's factories could acquire cane intensively and cheaply, so developing a robust industry capable of delivering effective supplies to a large and poor

were systematically cheated by sugar factories – through underweighing, arbitrary pricing, delays and coercive practices at mill gates. These were routine methods made possible by the mills' monopsonistic power. Shahid Amin, 'Unequal Antagonists: Peasants and Capitalists in Eastern UP in the 1930s', *Economic and Political Weekly*, Vol. 16, No. 42/43 (1981), 19–31.

population. On the other hand, thanks to the cooperatives, farmers would possess a bargaining voice and a commercial share, and the cruelty and injustice of colonial relations would be no more.

But it was not to be. Rich farmers were able to acquire controlling influence over these cooperatives which, like any strategic monopoly, could produce considerable rewards. Cooperative elections were furiously contested, since they provided a means for farmers to access the highest rungs of power: as in other times and places, the people who ran sugar ran the state. Leaders of sugar cooperatives controlled money and vote banks, which they could deliver to politicians; politicians, in turn, could suppress the prices paid to farmers (in the name of delivering sugar to consumers at a reasonable price), deliver crucial subsidies (especially in the form of irrigation and electricity) and control such competitors as jaggery and rum producers.[46]

Big farmers-turned-sugar-barons have always played a conspicuous role in Maharashtra politics: cane growers have been disproportionately represented in the state government, whose policies therefore protect their industry; the sugar cooperative movement has produced several chief ministers. The most influential of these, Sharad Pawar, came to resemble sugar barons in so many other times and places, from sixteenth-century Venice to eighteenth-century England and Cuba or Dutch Java in the twentieth century. A formidable political player at both state and federal levels, he also controlled immense financial resources.[47] Though Pawar exploited his position mercilessly – as agriculture minister, he was accused of profiting from wheat and sugar price fixing, even as the number of indebted farmers committing suicide began to skyrocket – he retained a widespread admiration in the Maharashtra sugar belt, whose abundant irrigation canals were chiefly his achievement.

In the long term, the colonial relations of the original model – the Cultivation System devised by the Dutch in Java – were reproduced in the heart of socialist India. The beneficiaries this time were not foreigners, however, but village elites. Sharad Pawar might have played exactly the same game as all the sugar barons of history; but unlike those marauding bankers, those colonial aristocrats, he too was a peasant.

'My father owned all the land you can see,' says the farmer, whose name is Hari. He sweeps the horizon with his outstretched arm. 'He was not a wealthy man, but there was nothing here but barren rock in those days. The land was plentiful and cheap.'

I am still in the farmhouse in Maharashtra, eating lunch with Hari the farmer, his son Deepak and Deepak's fifteen-year-old daughter Shivani. Hari's wife, Kavita, circles the meal; she is constantly monitoring the number of *roti* and, when necessary, disappearing into the kitchen to make more.

Supplying *roti* for a family meal is significantly more labour-intensive than, say, making a pot of rice. Each one is rolled and hand-shaped from an individual ball of dough, then cooked both sides on a smoking iron pan. Seeing women getting up at dawn to make another batch of dough, I always marvel at their relentless output. I wonder how many of these little bread circles are produced in India every day; the answer cannot be less than a billion.

Kavita serves them weightless, fresh and hot. In the mouth, they melt into the sharp taste of fried aubergine and mango pickle.

'In those days,' Deepak says, 'you could see big hills from here. Across the horizon.'

'We flattened the hills and took all the rocks away,' added his father. 'We had to bring machines to clear everything. We cut down the jungle. Only thorns grew on the land. We brought in soil and spread it, and made the land ready for farming. We cut irrigation channels from the river. That's how we started growing sugarcane. Now you can't see any hills – the land is flat to the horizon.'

'They cut down the hills,' repeats Deepak. 'Can you imagine?'

Deepak is in his late thirties. I doubt he has any memory of those hills; he is recounting what has become family mythology. The achievement is undoubtedly impressive. Looking out of the window, I see a meticulously managed agricultural landscape, flat and verdant, with soaring coconut trees for shade. For urban wanderers, hills and mountains provide a picturesque contrast to the plains, but hills and mountains have always presented a rude affront to the peasant's smooth activity. I am reminded of a Polish peasant's verdict on his journey to the United States in the 1960s:

> I like it where the plain is; when I was in America I saw a mountain, and this was an awful view. And when it's flat wherever you look, so that you could roll an apple, that is beautiful. Where you are perfectly flat, a lake, that's beautiful.[48]

'It was no joke,' Deepak reiterates. 'They had to build houses, roads, sewerage systems, cowsheds. Houses had to be elevated, so mud would not flow in. Until recently, it was all wilderness. My father was a teenager when they started. Now he is sixty-five.'

'Eventually, the land was divided between us brothers,' says Hari, 'and we built separate houses. There are five of us, each with five hectares. In my son's generation there are eight boys, so the farms are getting smaller.'

'When did you start farming?' I ask Hari.

'I gave up school when I was ten and went to work on other people's farms. Rich farmers would pay us to fill up their water tanks or remove garbage from their fields. In those days we had nothing.'

Deepak left school aged eighteen, having completed high school; no doubt his daughter Shivani will attend university. Such educational advancement over two generations is common in the Indian countryside. Many farming families take agricultural loans, not to buy seed or fertiliser, but to pay for education.[49] Despite this, rural people remain disadvantaged in the competition for urban jobs, and many return to the village after working in the urban informal economy. Often this return has become more desirable because of industrialisation: in the last two decades, factories have sprung up all over the countryside, providing alternative income sources. With urban experience, and new possibilities of subsidising agricultural incomes, the tenor of conversation has changed – the younger generations are more strategic in their planning, more impatient and more aware of farming practices in other countries.[50]

I ask about water. Sugarcane is a thirsty crop.

'We have no shortage of water,' says Deepak.

'We have water all year round,' confirms his father. 'Otherwise the sugarcane burns out and dies.'

'We have good irrigation around here. You saw the river as we were walking – that brings clean water from the lake.'

One of the reasons India produces so much cane is that the politicians who profit from it have invested significant public funds in waterworks. All local water bodies, in fact, have been pressed into this service, which leads to significant depletion elsewhere. The river I saw earlier is seasonal; in the summer it dries to a trickle. Farms are not the only culprits – sugar factories too use vast quantities of water, which is mostly returned to the land and rivers as polluted sludge. From beginning to end, sugar production hijacks water systems, which is particularly serious in a state whose giant conurbations – over 20 million people live in Mumbai's metropolitan sprawl – have already pushed those systems to the limit.

Indeed, ecological strain is the dominant reality in this region. The present decade is decisive: Maharashtra is being subjected to some of the most graphic consequences of climate change anywhere in the world.[51] Its cotton farmers are thrown into crisis by the altered seasons, which bring rain too late, and then produce catastrophic floods.[52] Amid such uncertainty, sugarcane is a good bet. A hardy plant, which is rarely attacked by pests, it does not fear storms or off-season rain. Most of all, however, sugarcane enjoys such political backing in Maharashtra that it has first claim on the state's fresh water, which insulates it significantly from the chaos afflicting other crops.

Sugarcane is, as it has always been, a *political* crop. Indian sugarcane farmers continue to be dependent on services which can only be organised at the political level. Irrigation is just the most obvious of these. Equally crucial is the infrastructure required to process the mature cane. The armies of sugarcane cutters who move through Maharashtra, and the complex of factories whose chimneys striate the rural horizon – these are also controlled by politicians. This is especially true of the factories, which in Maharashtra have almost completely abandoned their original cooperative promise. The remaining cooperatives are run by political families who manipulate the books – this is Deepak's contention – to show endless losses: there are no profits, therefore, to share with farmers. Precisely because their performance has apparently been so poor, however, many have declared bankruptcy and been reacquired as private businesses by the same political families – for a fraction of their value. All the attempts to democratise the Cultivation System have therefore been ineffectual: the profits from sugarcane are overwhelmingly monopolised by a small group of sugar barons.

Those profits are protected by policy and law. Sugar, as we saw, is designated one of India's 'essential commodities', and considerable political resources are devoted to ensuring that its price remains low. In theory, all sugarcane buyers are required to pay the same 'fair and remunerative price' (FRP) which, according to the officials who each year unveil it with great ceremony, provides 50 per cent more to farmers than they spent on production.[53] For many of the farmers I meet, the production cost is in reality much higher than the official figure, so farmer profits are slim from the outset. The FRP does, however, secure a dependable profit margin for sugar processors: one tonne of cane, purchased for the FRP (in 2024) of roughly $40, delivers nearly $80 in sugar, molasses and bagasse. And yet many processors try to find ways to avoid paying farmers the FRP. That is possible because of the now familiar properties of sugarcane itself: after harvest, it must be crushed within a few hours or it becomes useless. Sugarcane is quite different, in this respect, from rice or cotton, which farmers often store for months, waiting for the best moment to sell.

'We are very vulnerable during harvest,' says Deepak. 'The factories know we cannot allow anything to go wrong, or our cane will spoil in the sun and we lose everything. So they say, "We will give you the official price, but we cannot give you all the money now. We'll pay you in instalments, over several months." They know we can't accept, because our loans are due for repayment at that time.

Most farmers cover the cost of growing cane with loans from banks and moneylenders. So we have to accept the other deal, which is offered by middlemen. They provide all the cash up front, but they pay thirty per cent less.'

'Yes, the middleman gives us less,' says Hari, 'but the money is guaranteed. And he can take our entire production, which the jaggery mills cannot. We don't worry about the losses. The farmer has a very big heart.'

His son Deepak is not amused.

'No – we feel very bad about it. We hardly cover the cost of production. And we don't even take into account the cost of our own labour, so we essentially work for free. Of course we feel bad! The middleman takes our income without doing a day's work. He doesn't set foot in the field. He doesn't wear bad clothes. He just turns up with his mobile phone, makes a call – "Move this from here to there! Deliver this at this time!" – and for that he takes our money. For a year or more, we raise the cane like we raise our children. And he earns the same as we do with just five minutes' work.'

'So what can you do?' I ask.

'We have to digest it as it is. We have no option. If the regulations were lifted, and all these agents and businessmen left us alone, we could make some profit from our crop. But it's impossible. This is how the system is designed: they take all the fruit of our hard work.'

Deepak is becoming fiery with our discussion.

'We call it the *negative subsidy*,' he says. 'Western farmers also have to deal with low prices, but their losses are made up by governments, who pay subsidies. In India, we receive *negative subsidies*. That means farmers subsidise everyone else. We subsidise the sugar factories, and in turn the consumers, with our own money. We subsidise them with money we earn in factories or in trade, or with money we borrow. That's why the processors earn such good profits. And remember, we don't include our own labour when we calculate our cost. We only include the price of fertiliser, pesticide, electricity, fuel. We work for free.'

I have heard this analysis from other farmers too. For those who imagine peasants to have automatically socialist instincts, it turns out to be a surprisingly free-market stance.

'People think India rejected socialism,' continues Deepak. 'After all, Indian businesses are completely free – they sell to anyone they like, at the price they wish. But Indian peasants still operate in a socialist system. They must sell to certain people at the price set by the government.'

The implication is that, when Deepak sells his cane, it moves from the socialist system into the capitalist system. The frontier between the two is preserved by the Essential Commodities Act, whose purpose is to keep incomes low on this side and high on the other side.

'We want these restrictions removed,' Deepak concludes.

In 2020, the international media broke their habitual silence over rural affairs to report on the farmer protests which brought much of Delhi to a standstill. Blocking Delhi roads with their tractors, the farmers were attempting – successfully, as it turned out – to stall new legislation which would have deregulated agricultural markets. Urban journalists concluded what they already believed: peasants were not equipped for capitalist exchange, from which they needed to be insulated and protected. But these were not just any farmers. Mostly they were from Punjab and Haryana's wheat–paddy belt, where many farmers produced for the public grain-distribution system and were consequently dependent on fixed prices and state procurement. Forced to sell their crop for less than the market rate, many Indian farmers – Deepak included – would love a bit more capitalism in their lives.

That is all the more the case because of another set of laws, whose effect is to make it much more difficult to exit farming – forcing many farmers to continue delivering their subsidy to industry and consumers. These are the agricultural lands acts, which prohibit agricultural land from being sold to non-farmers. Enacted after independence to protect the agricultural base, today these laws serve to keep the price of agricultural land artificially low, since it may only be bought by other poor smallholders.[54] Selling land does not therefore deliver a significant enough windfall for farmers to expose themselves to the vagaries of casual employment – often in the informal economy. As a result there is remarkably little dynamism in the distribution of land. Even when they are producing at a loss, most farmers feel their land provides the surest form of security and end up staying put. This is additionally the case because they feel that land passed on to them by previous generations is sacred and must remain fertile and productive so it may safely be delivered to the next generation.

'They tell us these laws are for our own protection. I say, we do not wish to be protected. We wish to be free.'

Hari does not contribute to his son's political contentions but looks steadfastly at the floor. While his face is expressionless, I sense he enjoys hearing Deepak speak in this way.

'The government is constantly launching programmes to relieve farmer poverty,' Deepak concludes. 'They give us grants and handouts. Occasionally, they forgive our debts. It's all pointless while those laws remain in place. One year after the debts are forgiven, everyone is in debt again.'

Our lunch is finished. Shivani, Hari's granddaughter, has left the room and returned to her homework.

Hari breaks his silence to add an opinion of his own.

'The truth is, farmers do not have good prospects if they leave the land,' he says. 'Some become factory workers, which is a good job. Some drive autorickshaws. Some become construction workers or security guards. But these jobs come today and go tomorrow. The best thing for farmers is farming.'

The electricity has returned, and the fans are roaring overhead: the afternoon heat is at full blast. Kavita has put out tea. I take a sip of mine – it is almost ostentatiously sugary.

Hari says, 'If farmers are to survive, they have to diversify. They can't survive on sugarcane alone. They are all trying to diversify into crops whose price is not controlled, like fruit or poultry or silkworms. These experiments are difficult on small plots – they need capital and they carry risk. But diversification is essential. We have only survived because we also have a small business. We run fruit and vegetable transport to the wholesale market. We have a truck, people bring us their crops early in the morning, and we deliver to nearby cities. There's a long queue of people contacting us on the mobile. Everything is worked out on the phone, it takes just a few hours each day, and it gives us steady income.

'We've run this business for nearly forty years. Back then we had a lot of land, and we could sell some parcels to set it up. My brothers did the same. One has a timber business. Another raises poultry. A big poultry firm gives him the newly hatched chicks, and he raises them and returns them to the company when they're fully grown. With this extra income, we've managed to expand our households over the years.'

'So why do you farm at all?' I ask. 'If your income comes from business?'

'It depends on prices,' says Hari. 'Some years farming covers its costs, some years it does not. But the important thing is that we have inherited this land and its promise, which we must pass on to future generations. If we leave the land barren, it will soon be overgrown with thorns. It is so much work to clear land when it becomes overgrown. It is shameful to treat land like that. Land is security and heritage. When everything else fails, it is still there.'

There is a widespread assumption, particularly in the West, that peasants play no significant role in today's global economy. And yet the 350 million tonnes of sugarcane produced each year in India – the most substantial output of any country – are all produced on family farms like Hari's, most of them significantly smaller, in fact, than his. This peasant production is anything but static: cane output has increased ten times in the last century; it has tripled since 1980.[55] Nor is it quaint or old-fashioned – once it leaves the field, Indian cane is securely in the realm of large-scale twenty-first-century business. Some of India's own sugar producers, such as EID Parry or Balrampur Sugar, are billion-dollar corporations in their own right. Others are subsidiaries of international giants – Shree Renuka Sugars, for instance, which is owned by Wilmar Sugar Holdings, a Singapore-based conglomerate with revenues, in

2024, of US$67 billion. Far from being held back by their dependence on peasant producers, modern corporations have turned it into a world-beating relationship.

My discussion with Hari and Deepak helps us understand why Indian peasants fit so well with today's corporate economy. As we have seen, the perennial fear of big sugar producers – like their counterparts in the cotton industry – was always that they would not be able to produce at a profit without slavery or some equivalent form of coercion. Contemporary India shows that coercion can take many forms. Though there are no whips or chains in sight, Indian farmers are compelled, by a complex array of legal and cultural instruments, to continue producing at a loss – or, in other words, to subsidise big businesses, not only with their cash, but also with their own free labour and that of their family members. No corporation could resist such a gift, handed down from the socialist past – especially because these small farmers have a commitment to their land which is far more than economic, and they will do whatever is necessary to ensure that it continues to be productive. The costs of climate-change adaptation, which corporations themselves would have to bear were they to administer large plantations, are mainly absorbed by the farmers themselves.

The majority of Indian farmers, however, lack Hari's commercial safety net. Though they are, like all peasants across time and space, an endlessly resourceful group, and though they have found many ways, in booming India, to combine their agricultural work with other kinds of income, they cannot escape forever the basic negative formula of their lives. Over the last thirty years, corporations have expanded their control over the supply of seeds, fertilisers and pesticides. Assailed by low commodity prices and climate change, farmers have seized gratefully on these powerful new products, but this has added enormously to their cash requirements. Peasants cover this outlay by taking out loans which they hope they can pay back when they sell their crop. Too often, this is not the case. Since many of these loans are obtained from local moneylenders, who charge between 5 and 15 per cent interest a month, many farmers find themselves sucked into a vortex of debt.[56] Of course the system continues – peasants are eternal optimists, with something of the gambler about them. They are always looking forward to that jackpot harvest, when all the debts of the past will be redeemed. But debt remains the fundamental condition of the Indian farmer.

Deepak is pressed for time. The sugarcane cutting will soon be complete, and he needs to plough the entire field in readiness for tomorrow's sowing. There is much to do before sunset. But he does not want to leave this conversation – which ends up, inevitably, with farmer suicides.

'We have had no suicides in this village,' says Hari. 'But every year one or two kill themselves in the villages nearby.'

Official statistics show that around 12,000 Indian farmers kill themselves every year – some 300,000 this century. But this number is based on very narrow definitions, of both 'farmer' and 'suicide'. A farmer is defined as someone with farming land registered in their name, which excludes nearly all women, as well as younger farmers working on their fathers' land. It excludes the young daughters of farmers who kill themselves to spare their parents the expense of their wedding. It excludes members of those tribal communities who hold land in common, where suicides related to agricultural debt have also increased in recent year. Any death preceded by alcohol consumption, meanwhile, is not considered suicide, even though the alcohol is what may be needed for farmers to gain the courage to kill themselves – which they often do by drinking pesticide. Everyone close to this phenomenon knows the actual number of farmer suicides this century must exceed 400,000. The greatest number of them are in this state of Maharashtra. The greatest of those are among cotton farmers.[57] Cotton goes through many more industrial processes than sugar, and there are much bigger negative subsidies. Cotton farmers are also far more exposed to climate change and regularly experience crop infestation or failure.

'With sugarcane, the expenses are not so great,' says Deepak. 'The factories or the middlemen pay to cut the cane. But cotton farmers, their price is already very low, and they must pay workers to pick the cotton. They are only spending, never earning.'

'But sugarcane needs water,' says Hari. 'Until now, we have always had enough. But look how the river is changing. If that disappears, we are finished.'

'When we hear about suicides, we feel very bad,' says Deepak. 'We wonder what will happen to us.'

'One day, we are all going to die,' says Hari. 'But no one should die before that day. Farmers are in charge of fertility. Why should the ones who give life be forced to die early?'

Our discussion comes to an end. Deepak rushes back to the farm. Hari is tired: he turns on the television and sits in front of a Marathi-language drama. Kavita offers me more tea, which I decline. Her granddaughter Shivani asks me if she can show me the village.

We leave the house and walk down the lane. We pass a pink temple, newly put up by Hari and his neighbours. Shivani shows me the shrine, a white box with a sliding grille, fastened with a lock pad. It is filled with grain.

'There will be a statue of Lord Krishna here,' she says. 'But he hasn't come yet. For the time being, we've stored wheat inside.'

In Hindu mythology, Lord Krishna is associated with the birth of sugarcane. After a series of terrible battles with demons who threatened the earth and its fertility, Krishna restored sweetness and prosperity by planting sugarcane on the barren land. Thereafter, he became a peace-loving, pastoral figure, a lover of field and forest and the most feminine and sensitive of male gods. He is much loved by farmers.

The tarmac road, too, is newly made, and the houses are attractive. We come to a village square, at the centre of which is a giant neem tree. Under a little tiled roof, some farmers just returned from the field are playing cards.

We leave the square by another lane, and enter a more dilapidated part of the village. This is the low-caste – *dalit* or, formerly, 'untouchable' – area, which is evidently poorer and more cramped. India's villages are still segregated by caste, with *dalit* families relegated to the periphery. Members of this group are mainly landless and work as day labourers. The street is unpaved, and some of the houses are just corrugated iron and tarpaulin. Kneeling in the street, women spread barley on big plastic trays, separating the chaff.

Shivani tells me about her school. She has spent the afternoon studying for an exam tomorrow morning, about the geography of Brazil. She is a bright student, and her parents want her to do well. Next year she will leave the village school behind and go to boarding school in Nashik, a major city 400 kilometres from here.

The street turns into a country path bathed, once again, in a symphony of birdsong. On one side, there is a recently harvested cabbage field, where goats have been set loose to eat the stems. Poultry batteries line the other side of the field.

I ask Shivani what she would like to do after school.

'I want to join the army,' she says. 'Then I can travel all over India. I can serve my country, and people will give me respect.'

We reach the river. We sit under a tree and watch the water. This beautiful spot has been chosen for the village's last rites: an elegant marble shelter has been built for cremations. All is tranquil – except for the noise of the electric motor, pumping water up to the fields.

I ask Shivani about her friends and family. But she does not want to talk about herself. She wants to hear stories of distant lands. I tell her about Iran, where I grew up, and England, where I now live. I show her photographs of my home, my family, my university. She is delighted. She takes my phone number and asks me to send her more pictures of places far away.

Fifteen minutes away from the village, adjoining the main road, are two rows of tents. This is where the sugarcane cutters stay. The constructions are untidy and basic: sheets of blue and yellow tarpaulin are slung over bamboo frames and held together with a mesh of ropes tied down to rocks and bricks. The floor of each tent is another tarpaulin sheet. I see no bedding anywhere, though jeans and saris are hanging from every available protrusion.

The two rows face each other across a patch of earth flattened by foot traffic. All around the settlement are piles of firewood and fertiliser sacks stuffed with belongings.

When I arrive, the place is still deserted, save for two old women. One prods smoking embers with a bamboo pole, the other sits in the opening of a tent watching an old television screen propped up at the other end: brightly clad Bollywood lovers are singing ecstatically on a mountain top. There is electricity here. The residents have connected a slim wire to the pylon overhead, which snakes down to the settlement, where it is looped over the tents on a circle of bamboo poles. In addition to the television, this tent has a naked lightbulb hanging from the roof.

Stray dogs wander listlessly around. Nearby, a brown cow chews on some discarded sugarcane leaves. An uncomfortable mouthful, I think.

As the sun begins to dip, the cutters make their way home. Before I see them, I hear the steel clink of their machetes and cooking pots. Ahead of the ragtag procession, a barefoot boy runs behind a rolling tyre, which he propels along the road with a stick. Dressed in bright pink, his elder sister chases him, laughing.

The cutters deposit water canisters and dirty pots at the entrances to their tents and sit down to rest. The fires are soon flaming again and pots of milk set to heat. I see a young woman rushing into her tent to breastfeed her infant. The air smells bitter: the fires burn not only wood but also plastic bags, old shoes, bits of rubber tyre.

I have arranged to meet a young sugarcane cutter named Anil, who was introduced to me earlier by the labour contractor, or *mukadam.* The *mukadam* comes to find me, Anil following timidly behind. We all sit down on some tractor tyres.

The *mukadam* is employed by the middleman to organise the cutting of the cane and its delivery from the field to the plant. He has brought Anil here, and he is responsible for all aspects of his employment. I sense that Anil cannot speak freely, but there seems to be no choice: the *mukadam* is visibly reluctant for Anil to talk to me without supervision. I ask Anil anodyne questions in the hope the *mukadam* will lose interest and depart. He tells me he is from

Beed, a district in the centre of the state, 300 kilometres from here. He speaks quietly and hesitantly.

'Answer properly,' says the *mukadam* brusquely. 'What are you afraid of?'

'All of us are from the same place,' continues Anil. 'Our land is there, our families are there. Two of my children are there. Eight months of the year, we are away cutting cane. We cut all the cane in one area, then after a few weeks we travel to another area. Finally, we go home and rest. We look for work there too, but it is a barren place.'

'Two or three months is their resting period,' says the *mukadam.* His numbers never quite correspond to Anil's. Anil seems to understate his efforts and overstate his rewards.

'You are alone?' I ask Anil.

'No. My wife is with me, and our youngest child.'

'At least you are not alone.'

'We are happy that at least we are together in this work.'

'What time do you start in the morning?'

'We go to the field at six or seven. We finish at four.'

'What do you do in the evening?'

'I play with my son. Eat some chicken.'

'With rice,' says the *mukadam.*

'Then we go to sleep.'

'They have a full meal,' says the *mukadam.* 'Their nutrition is excellent.'

'Do you have a day off?' I ask.

'Of course they do,' says the *mukadam.* 'Twice a month.'

'What do you do on those days?' I ask, looking pointedly at Anil.

'Two Fridays a month, we go to the market with other cutters and buy little things for the children.'

'How long have you been doing this work?'

'Since I was a child of five or six. My parents were cutters, and I used to travel with them. Then my father said, "Go cut sugarcane." So I said, "OK, I will go and cut sugarcane." '

'How old are you now?'

'I cannot say.'

'Approximately?'

'I don't know anything about that.'

'When is your birthday?'

'I don't know.'

'Your parents must know?'

'I think my parents know.'

Small and boyish, Anil wears a pair of jeans and a bright orange shirt; his hair is thick with dust and sweat. I do not think he can be much above twenty-five, but he seems entirely absent to himself. Perhaps this has something to do with the fact that he is employed not as a person but as a 'knife'.

'We are two knives,' he says, 'my wife and I.' The Marathi word is *koyta*, which is the word for the local variety of machete. 'In this group, we are nine and a half *koyta.* Each *koyta* receives eighty or ninety thousand rupees for the season.'

The halves are young boys. Girls also work alongside their parents, but they are not counted.

'They try to get their children married quickly,' comments the *mukadam*, 'so each half-*koyta* can become two.'

In addition to the cash payment – around $1,000 per *koyta* for eight months of work – the cutters are also allowed to keep the sugarcane leaves, which are used to make cattle feed. A bundle of these leaves sells for about three rupees (five cents); each week, the team sells about sixty dollars' worth, which is enough to pay for their food and other expenses.

The *mukadam* organises all this. He comes from the same region as the cutters, so he is able to negotiate with a community far removed, culturally speaking, from the factory owners. He pays them a cash advance at the beginning of the season: about $700 per adult and $350 per working boy. The *mukadam* then takes care of all the necessary arrangements. He organises the cutters' transport to the cane-growing region and gives them bamboo, tarpaulin and cardboard to build their tents. He keeps hold of jewellery and other valuables – since most of the cutters have no formal residence where it may be stored back home.

'Sir is from our village,' says Anil, referring to the *mukadam*. 'He collects all the workers from our village and another four or five villages around. He provides gas cylinders for cooking. He gives us money for grain and meat. He keeps us safe: if something happens, he takes us to the hospital. He handles the police, if there's a problem.'

Anil's portrait, once again, is designed for the *mukadam*'s ears. Most cutters complain they can never visit a doctor.

'Do you have any problems with money?'

'No.'

As is obvious from Anil's discomfort, the *mukadam* exerts enormous control. This is very close, in fact, to bonded labour. Cutters may not break the contract halfway through, and the penalty for missing a day of work is double the pay. Some cutters find themselves in debt to the *mukadam* at the end of the season, and their labour obligations roll over to the next year. Hence their desperation never to avoid work. They work even when they get injuries or snake bites, and they avoid taking sick children to the doctor. It is hardly surprising if Anil's responses seem bland and uncritical: neither his body nor his mind is free.

'Sometimes we feel dizzy in the sun. But it's OK. We can manage. We cut twenty tonnes of cane in one day. With nine and a half *koyta*. Each one cuts two tonnes a day.'

The fear of missing workdays is one reason for the most notorious aspect of this system – early hysterectomies. Government surveys show that one in five female sugarcane cutters from Anil's home district have had their wombs removed.[58] Women as young as twenty undergo such operations; most do so in their thirties. The conventional rationale is that sugarcane cutters have no effective way of washing menstrual rags. This leads to frequent infections, and so to doctor visits, medical bills and penalties for missed work. But the details are murky, and Anil will certainly not talk about them. Some say that women are forced into these operations by the *mukadam*. Others believe it is a medical scam: women are told that persistent abdominal pain is an early sign of cancer, for which a $500 procedure is the only sure solution. Still others suggest that hysterectomies are a defence against unwanted pregnancy. There are constant rumours of rape, sometimes at the hands of the *mukadam* himself.

'Are women safe here?' I ask Anil. 'Do they face any problems?'

'No,' he says flatly.

'Nothing at all?'

'What problem could there be?'

'There is nothing like that,' confirms the *mukadam.*

For hundreds of years, as we have seen, the sugar industry has relied on racially stigmatised groups to perform its most gruelling jobs, and things are no different here. These cutters mainly come from an aboriginal community whose name – *bhil*, derived from an ancient word for bow and arrow – gives a sense of their traditional livelihood. The *bhil* were exposed to arbitrary violence during colonial times and probably long before. Designated a 'criminal tribe' under British law, they were forbidden from moving outside a specified territory on pain of detention, maiming or death. Today, they are among the poorest and most neglected peoples in the world. The majority of *bhil* families spend less than $40 per month; most – like Anil himself – cannot read.

Anil's family belongs to the minority of *bhil* who own farmland. Previously, they used to grow cotton. Today, however, the land is dry.

'There is no water in our village,' he says. 'So there is no work there.'

'Nothing at all? Construction work, nothing?'

'Without water, nothing can happen.'

'Can you grow anything at all?'

'If we could, we would never leave. That would be better. But our land gives nothing. If you spend ten thousand rupees, you will earn five thousand. There is only sugarcane to fill our stomachs.'

Far from the well-irrigated sugarlands of Western Maharashtra, Beed district's years of drought have made cultivation costly and difficult. Its rural communities are increasingly turned into climate refugees and must accept whatever agricultural labour they can find.

Large numbers of such refugees work as sugarcane cutters – not only in Maharashtra, but also across the neighbouring states of Gujarat and Karnataka. We saw how the sugar industry gratefully collected the 'negative subsidy' provided by sugarcane farmers; it is equally happy to profit from the ruin of cotton communities such as this one. Anil's plight helps us to understand why farmers like Hari will do anything – including farming at a loss – to hold on to their land.

A woman brings Anil an aluminium beaker of steaming milk. Her name is Dagubai. She sits down on the ground to listen to our conversation. She is probably in her thirties. I soon learn she is Anil's elder sister.

She and Anil grew up like the children running around these lines of tents – constantly on the move, and far from school. As soon as they were old enough to handle a machete, they began to cut cane. With his own children, Anil is determined to break that cycle. He and his wife have left their two older children, a boy and girl of six and seven, to attend school in the village. The youngest is not yet of school age; he is in one of these tents with his mother.

'We are not educated,' Anil says. 'At least we should educate our children.'

'Who looks after your other two?'

'My mother and father are there. They are tired now, so we are taking responsibility, they are resting at home. My children stay with them. Other people have no one in the village. Or their parents are weak and cannot offer protection. No one can leave their children without security, especially girls. So they bring them along. But here we are constantly moving, and the children cannot attend school. They grow up in the fields.'

The situation of the children I have watched today is anathema to Indian law, which prescribes compulsory education until the age of fourteen. But tribal communities have always existed somewhat below the threshold of state life, and it is anyway beyond the capacity of these migrant labourers to conform to such laws. In Hari's family we saw a rapid increase, from generation to generation, in educational achievement. No such benefits have flowed to these sugarcane cutters.

'How often do you see your children?' I ask Anil.

He does not know what to say. I ask another question.

'How long does it take to go there?'

'Seventeen hours.'

'They all have mobile phones,' says the *mukadam*. 'So they don't feel the distance.'

At this point, there is a money problem, and someone calls on the *mukadam* to advise. To my relief, he departs.

'I am glad your children are going to school,' I say to Anil.

'That's why we are working hard,' he says. 'I have no dreams for myself. We are just working hard and filling our stomach. That's it. My dreams died when I was born. But I dream for my children. They will not be cutters like me. They will go further.'

To my surprise, I realise Anil is crying. As he stares into the distance, a tear runs down his cheek. Dagubai stares at him for a second and says, 'Your children will do the same thing as you. You feel bad. But you have to eat. One day you will be too tired to do this work, and your children will have to support you. Old age will come soon – there is no option.'

'Perhaps they can do other work?' I venture.

'Back in our village, there is nothing,' says Dagubai. 'The cotton is finished. Nothing can grow except onions. But you cannot survive on onions.'

I ask Dagubai if she is here on her own.

'No. My husband is here, and my children. But my husband injured his leg with his machete, so he cannot cut cane. He has to do other jobs. Right now, he is filling the tractor with diesel.'

'Do single women come?'

'Widows come. But it is not good. They have no house. They live under a piece of cloth. Animals can come in and bite them. Men can also come. We are tribal people, so anything can happen to us, no? No one can predict when someone will make advances. Her safety is in God's hands.'

I ask her when she got married.

'I cannot say exactly. I actually cannot remember. We are all so busy with this work. Days and seasons are the same in the field. So it does not stay in my mind.'

'Where are your children?'

'My daughter is right here!' She points out a girl in her early teens who is chewing happily on a length of sugarcane. Standing by the fire outside her tent are her two sons, who are old enough to be full members of the cutting team. They are watching the food boiling in the pot for dinner.

'They all work with me,' says Dagubai. 'They have not been to school. But they are very strong. They have been moving behind us in the fields since they were three or four years old. In the hot sun, in the heavy rain and wind.'

I ask her what her day is like.

'The women get up at four. We go to fetch water from the village, bring it here. Heat water for everyone to wash.'

The endless labour of fetching water – this too is women's work. Dawn processions of women carrying water on their heads are a common sight all over rural India.

'Then we start the cooking. Feed the men and the children, and make *roti* for lunch. We join the men in the fields about nine. Come home at four or five. Then again we do the cooking and cleaning. Then we go to sleep.'

'Do you feel tired?'

'After working so much, of course I feel tired. But it's OK.'

Anil takes out some chewing tobacco, which he kneads in his palm before putting it in his mouth.

'Your brother said he has no dreams,' I say to Dagubai. 'Do you feel the same?'

'I can't say anything about that.'

'What do you do with the money you earn?'

'Nothing remains from this money. When we go home, we spend it all on wheat and millet. Then we eat for three months, and the money is exhausted. Nothing remains. In the village we stay with my husband's parents, who live between four sheets of corrugated iron. We have never saved money to build a house.'

I ask what they think of this sugar system. Why do they not earn more? Who is benefiting?

'We really don't know how to talk about that,' says Dagubai.

'But the *mukadam* earns much more than you do.'

'I don't know what he earns,' says Anil.

'We used to get rations from the government,' says Dagubai vaguely. 'We don't get that any more.'

There is something hermetic about this conversation. There is no sense of what *should* be; only what *is.* Breaking the silence, Dagubai expresses something similar in her own words.

'My complete life is in sugarcane,' she says. 'This plant is like my god. If there is no sugarcane, I do not exist. I am bonded with sugarcane forever.'

The sun is setting when I leave the cutters. Adjacent to the road is another field of proud sugarcane, waiting to be cut. I wander across the verge and grasp one of the thick stems in my hand. I look up at the lush leaves, far above my head, waving serenely in the evening breeze.

For thousands of years, we humans have been bonded to this plant. What turbulence it has unleashed upon us.

I think of a film scene. In *I am Cuba*, the 1964 masterpiece by Soviet director Mikhail Kalatozov, a peasant speaks to his soaring field of cane:

> I hoped and prayed that it would rain for you, cane. I have helped you. Now you help me. Grow tall. Taller than me!
>
> I used to think, the worst in life was death. Now I know better. The worst is life. I am so frightened for my children. All my life I have worked, and all that time I have lived in debt.
>
> Grow tall, sugarcane. Not for me; for them. You hear me? Grow tall. Very tall!

But the crop does not answer. The plant itself has nothing to say to his suffering. For that he must take another route: revolution. The film is of course a love letter to the Cuban revolution of 1957, which was brewed in the sugar fields. Fidel Castro's father was himself a sugarcane farmer.

With sugar, however, there is no final deliverance. Despite the abolition of slavery, despite revolutions and independence struggles, this 'political crop' has always managed to domesticate everyone who touched it. Today, in the world's largest democracy, it continues to extract a terrible price from those who grow it and, above all, from those who cut it.

Certain areas of the world became modern by eradicating their peasants. But that is not the only way. Many places became modern by preserving peasant systems and serving them to the global economy. India is one such place. Thanks to the regulatory controls which still constrain Indian peasants, sugar companies can exert great power over them – and they are booming. There is no reason to think the system is in decline.

2

Rice: Struggling Ecosystem

> The entrance to the great lake of Cambodia is grand and beautiful. The river becomes wider and wider, until at last it is four or five miles in breadth; and then you enter the immense sheet of water called Tonle Sap, as large and full of motion as a sea . . . The waves glitter in the broad sunshine with a brilliancy which the eye can scarcely support, and, in many parts of the lake, nothing is visible all around but water.
>
> – HENRI MOUHOT, FRENCH NATURALIST AND EXPLORER, 1863[1]

I am looking at the immense expanse of the Tonle Sap.

Near to shore, rows of brightly painted houses rise above the waves on wooden stilts, each one a self-contained water world, with fishing boats moored below and a twisted TV aerial on the roof. Steps lead from the lake up to ornate balconies hung with drying laundry and decorated with potted flowers, household shrines and – above the main doors – framed photographs of past generations. A boat is doing the rounds of this aquatic village, peddling snacks and cooking oil. The boatwoman places purchased items in baskets lowered on ropes from balconies, which are then hauled briskly up.

Rain is approaching. Far away, a billowing downpour dulls the horizon; a chill wind blows off the water. October clouds churn, pregnant with monsoon. Distant fishing boats speed towards shore. The lake darkens.

I am standing on a broad earthen dyke, raised several metres above the lake's surface. Running along the dyke is a strip of road planted on either side with fast-growing acacia trees, whose roots reinforce the packed earth. Scattered shacks sell snacks and cigarettes. As the boiling clouds draw close, their owners rush to take down hanging displays, shutting hatches and piling plastic chairs lest they blow away. The humidity crests and the afternoon sky turns black. The first drops fall, and I huddle with others under a tarpaulin shelter strung between the trees.

At the water's edge is a row of tied-up fishing boats, already glistening in the downpour. A little girl emerges barefoot from a cabin, lifts her arms to the sky and – ignoring the protests of her mother inside – jumps gleefully up and down on the deck.

Over the lake, a watery curtain joins land to sky. There is no horizon, just a great miasma flickering with inner electricity. The rain drums deafeningly on the tarpaulin above our heads; we are soaked by spray. Torrents of red earth run over our feet. On the boat, the girl is drenched through: her heart-covered T-shirt clings to her skin, and rivulets pour from her pigtails.

Each time the roar increases I think, *This is the peak* – and then it becomes more furious again.

Finally, after about twenty minutes, it lessens. The deluge begins to abate, the lightning disperses. Nature releases its hostages. We venture from our shelter, and boat engines start up again. Surprisingly quickly, the heat returns, and steam takes off from every surface. The water cycle resumes.

I turn away from the lake and wander to the other side of the dyke. Looking towards land.

But the land is water too. As far as I can see are flooded rice fields. The landscape is like one giant mirror, bright with the reflection of the post-storm sky above. A few coconut trees ornament the view, and, in the far distance, the green outcrop of Phnom Krom – 'a small hill with two peaks', in the words of a French surveyor working during the time of his country's nineteenth-century colonial expansion in the region, 'which dominates the entire surrounding plain and which, at the time of the great waters, is bathed on all sides by the waters of the lake'.[2]

As I gaze over the endless rectangles of water, held in place by a filigree of smaller dams, the clouds part behind me and sun breaks through. A rainbow shimmers over the silvery rice fields – its arc doubled, in reflection, to a vast ellipse.

Water above, water below, water on every side: it is easy to understand why Cambodians long believed their country to have come from water. Creation myths recounted by the Khmer society which dominated Cambodia in medieval times tell of a prince expelled from India – some call him Kaundinya – who, when Cambodia still lay submerged, arrived by ship in the middle of the ocean. There, he met a princess from the underworld, a water-snake goddess in human guise. After accompanying her into the submarine realm, he married her. But Kaundinya was earth-bound and could not survive in water. His father-in-law, the snake king, drank up the ocean to expose the submerged continent, where he built a city designed by the architect of heaven. From this cosmic capital, Kaundinya and his wife ruled over the new kingdom of Kambuja, installing there a Sanskritic culture brought from Kaundinya's native land.[3]

Given that the Khmer emperors claimed descent from Kaundinya, it is striking how underwhelming is his portrait in the myths. A fourth son, who is sent away from his birthplace for disobedience, for his oppression of the people or simply for his foul smell – depending on which version you read – Kaundinya is tossed helplessly by natural forces. It is significant that he is dependent, even for the air he breathes and the earth beneath his feet, on the much greater powers of his serpentine in-laws. Formidable serpent spirits have continued to play a central role in Cambodian culture. In 1296, several centuries after the myths were written, a Chinese visitor found that the political power of Khmer kings was still insufficient; true power was ecological, which made the male ruler perennially subservient to a snake-goddess consort:

> Inside the palace there is a golden tower, at the summit of which the king sleeps at night. The local people all say that in the tower

> lives a nine-headed snake spirit which is lord of the death for the entire country. Every night it appears in the form of a woman, and the king first shares his bed with her and has sex with her . . . If for a single night this spirit does not appear, the time has come for this foreign king to die. If for a single night he stays away, he is bound to suffer a disaster.[4]

Even today, the nine-headed serpent is everywhere. Whether ancient or modern, sculptures of this all-powerful figure are part of the Cambodian furniture, protecting human beings wherever they transition from one realm to another: at the entrance to towns and museums and temples and, especially, on bridges, whose snake balustrades keep land creatures from watery danger.

Cambodia has an objective reason to believe in the magic of water spirits. That reason is the Tonle Sap itself. The miracle of this 'natural wonder of the world'[5] is most dramatically observed in the Tonle Sap River, which drains the lake into the Mekong and thence into the South China Sea. For eight months of the year, this river behaves like any other, flowing downhill and seawards. But in June the waters reverse their course and, for the other four months, the river flows upstream, back into the lake. This seemingly supernatural behaviour explains the Tonle Sap's unusual mythological aura. It also creates a uniquely varied and fecund ecosystem, which in premodern times supported one of the biggest urban populations in the world, and which remains the foundation of the Cambodian economy even today.

How does this implausible reversal happen? For most of the year, the Tonle Sap is fed by the dense system of rivers flowing off the Cardamom Mountains to the west and Thailand's Dangrek Mountains to the north. But in the summer the swelling of the Mekong overtakes this local order. Torrents of meltwater pour from Tibetan peaks into the upper reaches of the region's mightiest river. These are further enlarged by monsoon rains captured by the Annamite mountains, whose slopes run 1,100 kilometres down the eastern edge of Laos and Vietnam. As the river's volume increases by fifteen times, its level rises higher than the Tonle Sap, and it

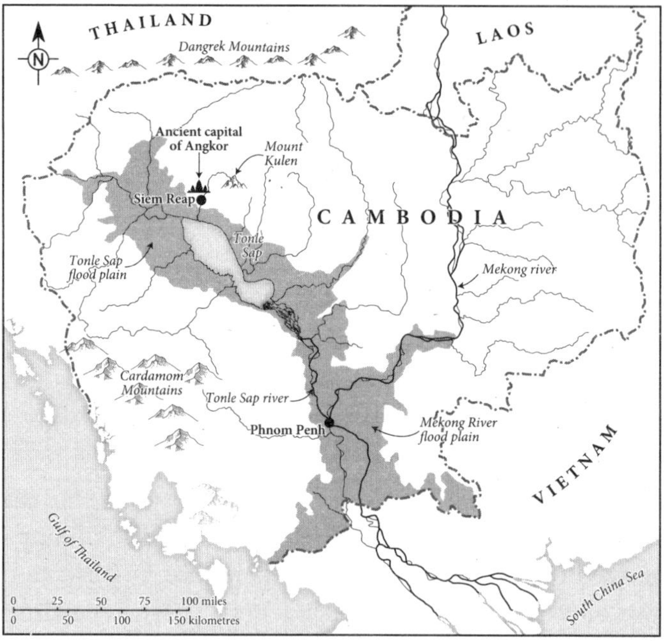

Tonle Sap and the Lower Mekong Basin.

begins to discharge water upstream. The surplus floods into the lake, whose volume, in turn, is multiplied by forty or more. The surface of the Tonle Sap can rise by as much as ten metres – hence the extraordinary elevation of the stilt houses – and expands from 2,500 to 15,000 square kilometres.[6] Louis de Carné, a nineteenth-century French diplomat, described an 'inland sea' which, 'when the inundation begins, spreads over the country till it triples its surface'. He travelled up the Mekong as part of the Mekong Exploration Commission (1866–8), sponsored by the French government to discover whether the river could provide trade access to China and thus rival the British port in Shanghai. His most awestruck descriptions were reserved, however, for the side-trip to the shapeshifting Tonle Sap:

> During the months of August and September the roads are covered in the lowland parts of the country; boats sail through

> the fields, trees show their heads above the water, and the wild beasts withdraw, en masse, to the heights, nothing could give a more vivid idea of the deluge. The people of the plains themselves take refuge on the mountains, or send their domestic animals there.[7]

In late October or early November, as the Mekong dwindles, the Tonle Sap River turns around again to resume its normal flow, and the lake begins to subside. This restoration of the hydrological order is marked by a grand water festival known as Bon Om Touk. The best-known manifestation takes place on the stretch of the Mekong in front of the royal palace in Phnom Penh, where teams of rowers race dragon boats painted with crocodiles, elephants and, especially, serpent gods. This is said to commemorate the Khmer's naval victory over the rival kingdom to the east – Champa – in 1181. But the boat race is a comparatively recent addition to a festival whose oldest elements, dating from at least a thousand years ago, are more explicitly ecological. Scheduled to coincide with the full moon, the festival centres on two Hindu deities credited with authority over the waters: Ganga and Indra. Ganga is the goddess of the Ganges River – part of an Indian sacred geography which is transposed, in the Cambodian context, on to the Tonle Sap. The Sanskrit texts tell how the Ganges was once stopped by a demon so fearsome he 'swallow[ed] the whole sky with his mouth . . . and lick[ed] up all the stars in the sky with his tongue'.[8] This demon was defeated by the lord of the gods, Indra. With this act, Indra 'broke (a way) for the torrents of the mountain' and order was restored: 'the flowing waters quickly hastened to the ocean, like cows (hastening) to their calves.'[9] During the festival, fireworks evoking Indra's celestial lightning, and lamps floating on 'Ganga' waters, create the parallel between this myth and the Tonle Sap River's annual turnaround.

It should be clear that the Tonle Sap sits at the centre of a uniquely dynamic and promiscuous water system. The lake unites waters and soils from six nations, producing a diverse mineral environment, which gives rise to a corresponding abundance of algae. This in turn

Detail from a bas-relief illustrating a mighty naval battle fought between Khmer and Cham navies (Bayon Temple, Angkor Thom, early thirteenth century). The depiction of the Tonle Sap includes anatomically precise depictions of many local fish and other sea creatures.

creates an incomparably rich ecosystem for the fish which are concentrated through the same riverine network. The Tonle Sap acts in fact as a fish incubator: the back-and-forth motion of the river creates a regional pump which draws in fish larvae from far afield, nourishes them to adulthood and then expels them in their billions – along with their eggs – into the Mekong. At the end of the calendar year, the Tonle Sap River becomes one of the densest animal migration corridors in the world. The most numerous migrants are the tiny *trey riel* (in Khmer; L. *Henicorhynchus siamensis*), which give their name to the Cambodian currency, and which are used to produce *prahok*, the fermented fish paste at the heart of local cuisine. Either side of the first full moon of the calendar year, around 15,000 tonnes of these fish are caught by commercial fisheries as they swim towards the Vietnam border. But many of the Tonle Sap's nearly 300 fish species – such as the 1.3-metre iridescent shark catfish (L. *Pangasianodon hypophthalmus*), which migrates up the Mekong River to Laos – end up very far away. This great dispersal means that 'the most densely populated natural fishbowl in the world' is a protein source for the wider region: in addition to the 500,000 tonnes extracted from the lake itself, 2.6 million tonnes of fish originating in the Tonle Sap are harvested each year in Vietnam, Thailand and Laos.[10]

Though Cambodia is only the eighty-eighth-largest country, it is the fourth-largest freshwater fish producer in the world – exceeded only by much vaster China, India and Bangladesh. Fishing provides the basis for numerous specialised populations – including the famous villages floating on the Tonle Sap, which are inhabited not only by ethnic Khmers but also by Muslims from Cambodia's Cham community and by fisherpeople from China and Vietnam. Cambodians are greatly defined by their relationship to fish, which generates 80 per cent of dietary protein. But the same water system that supports this extraordinary density of fish – as well as frogs, shrimps, crabs, molluscs, snails, water snakes, turtles, crocodiles, otters, water rats and 150 species of waterbird – also supports a crop that has shaped Cambodian history and society in even more fundamental ways: rice.

Much of Cambodia's natural soil is poor. The flooding of the Tonle Sap, however, disperses alluvial sediments brought from mountains and plateaus far away. It also generates mineral-rich irrigation across great swathes of the country's land surface. This is the basis of Cambodia's rice production, which is even more extraordinary than its fish. Cambodians have been growing rice in the Tonle Sap floodplain for over 2,000 years; more than 2,000 varieties are grown today.

'He's a very naughty boy!'

The boy is about five, running barefoot on the smooth floor, screaming with laughter. He comes to a halt, holding aloft the potato chips he has just snatched from the table. His slim calves emerge comically from baggy denim shorts.

I am talking to his grandmother, Dem, whose lithe frame sits easily in a red plastic chair. She must be in her fifties – her hair is silver at the edges – but she exudes physical power. Even her trackpants and sweatshirt seem ready for action.

We are sitting in that emblematic Cambodian space: the shaded area beneath a raised house. The family has built a broad corrugated-iron skirt around the house, so the covered area is large. It is designed to channel breezes, and the concrete floor is polished and cool – so it is pleasant to sit here, though the day is hot and humid. The whole family is here: in one corner, Dem's husband is fixing a new mirror on his motorbike; in another, her granddaughter kneels at a table, bent over schoolwork. There is also a strutting chicken and a sleeping dog. A hammock is slung between two pillars.

'We have two hectares of farmland,' Dem tells me, 'and we do three harvests a year. We use OM [Oryza Mekong] seeds. Each crop takes three months. Three days after harvest we plough again and broadcast seeds. Then we spray with herbicide. We rent a machine and workers at harvest time. We keep nine hundred kilos of rice for our own needs. The rest we sell to middlemen who send it to Vietnam.'

It is a simple formula, but it rests on cutting-edge technology, particularly when it comes to seeds. The seeds Dem plants originate in Vietnam, whose government institutes take the lead in breeding high-yield varieties for the Mekong delta. Known by their serial numbers – Dem grows OM 5451, which is a hi-tech derivative of jasmine – these Oryza Mekong seeds are commercialised by large Vietnamese agricultural conglomerates, and they are not cheap. But they are resistant to disease and pests and therefore do not require intensive supervision.

'My youngest two children work in Phnom Penh,' Dem says. 'My eldest son and daughter work in factories in Korea. My son has gone there with his wife, who also works in the factory. These are their children.'

Two people – Dem and her husband – look after this farm, even as they bring up their grandchildren. It is the same everywhere: most farms are missing their middle generation. Men and women in their prime go away to work in factories and construction, leaving their children in the care of their parents. Cambodian rice farming is totally integrated, in fact, with the Asian industrial boom, without whose subsidies it would hardly function. Rice did not generate the cash for this concrete floor, this sturdy iron roof, the wedding-cake pillars now adorning this once modest wooden house. Those were bought with remittances from South Korea, where wages are about fifteen times higher. That is the paradox of a country so dominated by rice farming: fewer and fewer rice farmers actually earn their money from rice. This farm covers its own costs, but not much more. Cash needs are met overwhelmingly from three Korean salaries of $300 a month.

A farm with cash but no labour: that is the opposite of the norm, and it overturns traditional rice practices. Dem spoke of 'broadcasting' the rice seed: this is a technique developed for the new era of empty villages. Here in Siem Reap province – we are in the floodplain of the Tonle Sap, though the waters have subsided from their peak – the traditional technique, perhaps for 2,000 years, was 'transplanting'. In May, when monsoon rains had softened the ground for ploughing, rice seeds were sown in flooded seedbeds; after a few weeks, the seedlings were transplanted to carefully prepared fields. This was fantastically time-consuming, and it could only happen when villages were well populated. Farms pooled their labour. The whole village worked together on one farm and then the next, digging up seedlings and planting them in rows in the fields. Festivals were designed to celebrate and reinforce this spirit of mutual assistance.

Broadcasting works differently. Seeds are spread directly in the ploughed field, which soon becomes choked with rice and weeds. Forty-five days after sowing, the field is ploughed again, dislodging the weeds and killing enough of the rice plants for the remainder to mature. This is much more labour-efficient. The ploughing can be done by one person using a rented wheelbarrow plough – a diesel-engined machine on paddled wheels, which is driven by hand across the flooded field. It is also far less precise than traditional techniques. It weakens the roots of the rice plants and leaves them in a random distribution, so they are more difficult to maintain.

In addition to the enormous seed wastage, therefore, broadcasting relies on much greater inputs of fertiliser and herbicide. Even so, broadcasting produces only half the yield of transplanting. But this too is mitigated, in part, by technology: new seeds like OM 5451 mature very quickly, and they are resistant to drought, which – in the exceptional conditions close to the Tonle Sap – enables three harvests per year, in place of the traditional one or two.

Dem wants me to inspect her fields, which are right behind us. Even from our shelter beneath the house, the blinding green of the rice field overwhelms the view. Cambodian villages are more dispersed than the one we visited in India – farmers live not in a cluster, but on their separate parcels of land. We have only to step around the house's hydraulic infrastructure – a concrete well, a row of large clay rainwater tanks – and we are in the rice fields.

The fields themselves are sunken, so we navigate the raised paths between. Dem's grandson goes ahead, eager to show me the way. He runs sure-footed on the narrow track; I follow more cautiously behind. The intersections of these paths are marked with little flags fluttering on poles. They are for navigation, I realise, when everything is flooded.

We walk between two thick fields of knee-high crop, the white rice stems still in flower. The roots are submerged in water. When I crouch down and part the leaves, I can see the mirror surface. It's uplifting to walk here. The sky is deep blue, and all colours are vivid: the pale green of one crop, the emerald of the other, the grassy strip of the path, the cluster of deep green trees beyond the fields.

'These are two different varieties,' says Dem. 'This is OM 5451' – she points to the deeper green – 'which we sell for export. We don't like to eat it. The other field is our rice. Cambodian rice, part of our cooking.'

In a country so rich in rice varieties, the new standardised strains do not arouse much love. OM 5451 is an agribusiness triumph, but even the companies whose job it is to promote the crop waste little time on romance. 'Very easy to cook,' says one brochure. 'OM 5451 rice is also the optimal choice for the cafeteria of companies with large staff, industrial catering suppliers, etc.'

We stand for a moment under the sun. Dem calls after her grandson, who is far ahead. Paying no heed, he runs giggling in the distance.

'He's a very naughty boy,' she says again.

I detect the slightest hint of fatigue. She has a lot on her hands. Shading my eyes, I look over the expanses of green on either side. How much labour for two people.

'When will you harvest?' I ask.

'In three weeks,' she says.

'You harvest by hand?'

'No, no!' She laughs. 'We rent a team with machines. They come and everything is done in three days.'

We begin to walk back towards the house. She has given up on the boy. She walks briskly ahead of me in her rubber sandals. Then she turns back.

'Can you hear?'

I listen to the birdsong. The breeze.

'The fields are quiet,' she says.

I don't know what she means.

'When I was a girl, rice fields were full of noise. They were full of frogs and crickets. They were full of birds catching fish. Used to make so much noise!'

She laughs.

'Now just chemicals,' she says.

She hurries inside the house. I wander on my own. Along the side of the house is a pretty garden. A three-rowed lantern of bananas hangs from a banana tree, the purple lobe of the flower still fleshy beneath. Orange butterflies graze a pink hibiscus; a spiny cactus erupts into improbably lush red flowers.

A huge millipede crosses my path, brown and glistening in the sun. It is nearly as long as my forearm.

I come around to the front of the house. The 'spirit house' is here: an ornate shrine standing on a post in the ground, painted in red and gold. Someone has decorated it with fresh flowers this morning.

Cambodia's is the neatest society I know. Everything is pristine, everything in its place. The streets are immaculate, houses sparkling, gardens beautifully arranged. Even the bin where this family collects discarded plastic bottles is somehow exquisite – a world away from the sugarcane villages of India, which are disfigured by ubiquitous plastic waste. Intuitively, this neatness feels like an extension of rice culture, which depends on continual, almost obsessive, upkeep of the landscape. Most agrarian landscapes are flat and horizontal, with borders traced lazily on their surface. The rice landscape is engineered vertically: roads and houses stand above the water, seedbeds and fields below. In addition to sunken fields and raised paths there are even higher islands where machinery and tools are stored under shelters. All these layers are separated by dykes and dams, which must endlessly be maintained to prevent leakage from one zone to another. This defines the culture: I have never been to a place where zonal divisions are so energetically preserved. Even in Phnom Penh, the capital city, where enormous trees line the French colonial boulevards, fallen leaves are swept up immediately lest they impede the traffic. City houses are separated from the street by dense bamboo barricades, which filter sound and dust.

I rejoin the family in the shaded area under the house. Dem is setting lunch. Her husband is already sitting at the round table. Next to him is an old woman he introduces as his mother. The grandson has come in from the fields; he and his sister also take their places. Rice is steaming in a bowl – it has a light pink colour. There's a bowl of broth, too, and some cubes of fried pork seasoned with fish paste.

We begin to eat. The rice is light, with a beautiful nutty taste. The children eat with gusto.

'What would happen if you did not grow rice?' I ask Dem's husband, whose name is Soun.

'What do you mean?'

'Farming is hard work. Your children earn good money. You could sell your farm and have an easier life.'

He looks at his wife. They laugh.

'We are Khmer people,' Dem says.

Soun says, 'Khmer are rice farmers. We're not like the Cham or the Chinese, who live in the market and sell. They don't need land. We are different. The moment I get married, my parents give me land to grow rice. Otherwise, my family cannot perform the rituals.'

'We don't sell our land,' says Dem. 'It is our identity.'

'In our language,' Soun explains, 'we don't say, "to eat". We say, "to eat rice". If you ask someone if he has eaten today, and he has not had rice, he will say "no" – whatever else he has eaten. The kitchen is "the room where rice is cooked".

'Rice is our companion. We say human beings have nineteen souls, and rice has the same number. If you plant rice at the wrong time, we say it will not have enough souls. All our rituals involve rice. Every year, we give thanks for the harvest at the festival of Og Ambok, which happens under the full moon. We make cakes of pounded rice with coconut juice and banana, and everyone feeds each other.

'Rice is with us from the moment of birth to the moment of death. Newborn babies are placed on a basket of rice. We throw rice at weddings. When dead people are brought to the pagoda, we throw rice backwards over our shoulder.'

This extraordinary symbiosis between Cambodian society and the botanical family known as *Oryza sativa* has been apparent to visitors since time immemorial. Coming from a rice society himself, the thirteenth-century Chinese traveller we met earlier was still astonished by the range of uses Cambodians had found for their crop:

> As soon as they give birth, the local women prepare some hot rice, mix it with salt, and put it into the entrance of the vagina . . . Because of this, women do not fall sick when they are giving birth, and usually contract so as to be like young girls again.[11]

Even today, Cambodians seem to use rice in every conceivable context. They make alcohol from it, and glue. There is an endless range of rice-based medicines, shampoos and cosmetics. Rice stems are used for thatching and matting, rice husks are used for industrial fuel and to reinforce cement. Paper and fertiliser are made from rice, pillows and mattresses are stuffed with it.

'This is who we are,' Soun says. 'We are the people who grow rice.'

'That's why we get angry', his wife adds, 'when the government doesn't take care of rice growers. They sell the land to businessmen from Vietnam and China, who cut down the forest and silt up the canals. They don't provide irrigation.'

'And the king says nothing,' says Soun's mother.

'Yes,' agrees Dem. 'Money is changing hands, the country is sold, and the king stays silent.'

I ask what they think of the government. The country has effectively been a one-party state since 1979, when a rival left-wing faction, the Cambodian People's Party, replaced the disastrous and genocidal Khmer Rouge.

Soun laughs again. I have observed a particular kind of Cambodian laughter which has nothing to do with humour. On the contrary, it is a kind of sweetening applied to bitter subjects.

'They were better before,' says Soun. His voice is close, suddenly, to a whisper. 'Now they're not so good.'

The children have already finished eating. They go outside to play.

'Fifteen years ago,' Soun says, 'they created the "one million tonnes export target". They wanted to make the country famous for rice exports. They cleared a lot of forest. In 1990 we had under two million hectares of rice fields, now we have three and a half million. They put pressure on farmers to grow short-term rice varieties and use a lot of chemicals. In many places, it was compulsory. If you did not grow the new varieties, you could not sell your crop. Many farmers complained.

'On our farm, we started three harvests a year. In parts of Cambodia, there is one harvest a year. Around Tonle Sap, where the water lasts longer, there are two harvests. But now we do three harvests. Two hundred and ninety-four days a year we grow rice, each time praying the government irrigation will last that long. It is good for us, and bad. Short-term rice matures in just ninety-five days, but it has only twenty or thirty ears per stem. Six-month jasmine rice has seventy or eighty, and it doesn't need pesticide.'

His old mother is nodding as he speaks. Her gaze is deep and thoughtful. She is in her seventies, but her skin has barely a wrinkle.

'The fields have changed,' Soun continues. 'In the old days, everything was fertilised with animal waste. There were thousands of fish in the rice fields, whose faeces fertilised the crop. We used to eat the fish too. But chemicals killed the fish and the frogs. So then the birds disappeared – there used to be thousands of storks and ibises hunting in the fields. And those birds also ate rats. When the birds disappeared, we were overrun with rats, which we never had before. And we had to poison them. For years, I refused to put poison in my fields, but the other farmers used poison, so all the rats came to me. Eventually, I had to use poison too.

'It all costs money. Many farmers run out of money, because they need so many chemicals. We all have to pay for water now, even where there is plentiful rain, because we are cultivating long after the season has ended. So farmers have cash problems. The people who sell fertilisers make a lot of cash and they start giving farmers credit at eight or ten per cent interest per month. Debt is everywhere.'

'What about cooperatives?' I ask. 'Isn't the government pushing farmers to join cooperatives? So you can get cheap credit, buy fertilisers in bulk?'

'There are cooperatives,' Soun says. 'Many foreigners come to lecture us about them. Personally, I don't like them. I don't like to share with strangers. Family is the best investment – that's what our religion says. My mother can tell you what happens when they take that away. They collectivised the country when she was young, and everyone died.'

Soun is referring to the depredations of the Khmer Rouge, a revolutionary movement which seized power in 1975 after a protracted guerrilla war. The Khmer Rouge was led by a former schoolteacher calling himself Pol Pot, who had studied Communist ideas as a student in Paris. The 1970s saw the peak of an idea we examined in Part One, which was much cherished on left-wing Western campuses: that the Third World peasant was the last defence against superpower imperialism. In Pol Pot's puritanical vision, the nation would be stripped back to its peasant essence. He sought to eradicate from Cambodia what he regarded as its colonial decadence, not only the vestiges of the French empire itself, but all trace of modern education, culture and commerce. Anyone who was not a rice farmer had to be either executed or returned to that condition.

Pol Pot's regime abolished 'money, markets, formal schooling, Buddhist practices and private property'.[12] In three short years, it also wiped out 1.5 to 2 million out of about 7 million Cambodians – a level of national fatality perhaps unequalled in modern history. Hundreds of thousands died by execution. Even more deaths stemmed, however, from the regime's reorganisation of Cambodian society. Businesspeople and intellectuals were wiped out, as were medical doctors, whose absence alone probably caused 200,000 deaths. City dwellers were sent to the countryside, which was turned into a giant forced-labour camp. Though the regime constantly invoked peasant virtues, it was determined to destroy every system on which peasant life depended, especially small landholding and, tragically, the family. Land was collectivised and families split up. The government set astronomical targets for rice production; these required large-scale irrigation works which

Cambodian two-riel banknote, late 1970s. Since the country functioned largely without money during the Khmer Rouge years, such banknotes never circulated widely.

had to be carried out by hand. Regime propaganda showed happy peasants celebrating bumper harvests, but the reality was catastrophic. Vast numbers died of starvation and exhaustion.

Soun's mother worked in a Khmer Rouge rice collective.

'In 1975, when they came to power, I was married, and Soun was already born,' she says. 'The Khmer Rouge moved me from my village. My husband was taken to a different place. I never saw him again. I lost my parents then, most of my family.

'I was forced to marry a Khmer Rouge soldier, and I had another child with him. In 1979, the Khmer Rouge was overthrown by the invading Vietnamese army, and my husband fled. I returned to my village with my children. It was like a ghost town – there was almost no one left. But our house was still standing.

'Years later, I was allocated this land by the government. I farmed it alone, bringing up my son and daughter. Now it is farmed by my son and his wife.'

It is a heavy story. But in this country nearly everyone has a similar tale.

'What do you feel about rice?' I ask. 'After all that?'

'Rice is the only constant in my life,' she replies. 'Rice has kept me attached to the earth.'

Soun smiles at me.

'We did not have machines for harvest,' his mother continues. 'All the households helped each other then. We were all together – we harvested one farm, and then moved to another.' After a moment's reflection, she adds, 'We used sickles. Sickles came in different shapes. I always used one with a half-moon shape.'

Dem has begun to clear plates away. She does not seem to be one for old stories. Soun is more talkative. He is knowledgeable about many subjects – he has a remarkable memory for dates and figures – and he is energised by discussion. He wants to take me to visit Dem's father in the next village.

'He's a fortune teller,' he tells me. 'A very interesting man. You have to meet him.'

He leads me outside, wheeling his motorbike. We walk on to the street, which is empty except for a couple of floppy-eared white cows grazing at the verge. I jump on the back of the bike and we speed away.

'My mother has had many experiences,' Soun calls over his shoulder. 'Now she spends her days in the Buddhist pagoda. She likes to pray and be quiet.'

We drive along a red earthen track, muddy at the edges with the recent rain. We pass several stilted houses and turn on to the main road. It is lined by shopfronts, restaurants, automobile workshops, the occasional temple. There are giant beer advertisements and endless posters showing the humourless faces of the Cambodian People's Party leader and his son. All along the road, rice is sun-drying on sheets of tarpaulin. Then the buildings give way and there is only the expanse of rice fields.

We turn off the road on to another track. We travel a kilometre through the countryside, trees shimmering overhead, humming-birds darting between village flowers. We pass a Buddhist monastery, impressively large, the tiled green roof twisting at the corners into golden serpents.

'This is my father-in-law's village,' says Soun. 'He moved here after the Khmer Rouge. My wife grew up in this house.'

He parks his bike outside a raised wooden house with blue shutters. He calls up as we climb the stairs, and a voice responds merrily from inside.

We leave our shoes on the landing at the top of the stairs and enter the house, which floats four metres above the ground. As in all traditional houses, there are no partitions inside: the entire house is one room. Adapted for very particular conditions – climatic, hydrological and familial – such houses can be found throughout Cambodia, as well as in the riverine regions of Laos, Vietnam and Thailand.

The father-in-law greets us, all smiles. He is shrunken and toothless, dressed in a cotton shirt and pants. We sit together on mats of woven rush.

'My name is Chheav,' he says. 'I am sorry – I have just come in from the fields and my clothes are dirty.'

He laughs engagingly.

'I am eighty-four years old. I have six children. I am a rice farmer, like my father before.'

Over our heads, a pigeon watches from a hanging cage.

'I have seen many changes,' he says. 'The most important is the weather. The rain is early or late. We have floods some years, most years we have drought. This is because we have cut down the forests. Forests preserve the weather. Without them, it is destroyed.'

Soun is nodding. 'In 1990,' he says, 'three-quarters of Cambodia was forested. Today, it is under a half. Most of that change has happened in the last fifteen years. They have cut down two and a half million hectares of forest in that time.'

Everything in this house is made of woven rattan. The walls are lined with rattan matting, which also covers the floor. Innumerable rattan baskets hang from the ceiling; clothes, rice, medicine, fruit – everything is stored in this way.

'I was born in this village,' says Chheav. 'During the Khmer Rouge time, I was sent away for three years. I moved with my wife and young children. It was very difficult – we had to grow rice with no tools. Everything was done by hand. We had to build dams with our hands, all the earth was dug with our hands. There was nothing to eat. My wife died of hunger.'

How naturally such truths are delivered.

'My wife remembers,' says Soun. 'When she was three years old, she was lying in her mother's arms. Her mother died while she was holding her.'

He laughs nervously. That same Cambodian laugh. A mask for suffering.

'Since the age of sixteen,' says Chheav, 'I have been a fortune teller. I learned the art from my father. People come to me to ask about their marriage problems, advice about farming. Many things.'

'They come from far away,' says Soun admiringly. 'He is very famous.'

Parakeets are shrieking merrily in the trees outside.

'Cambodians wish to please the spirits,' Chheav says. 'You see in front of every Cambodian house a little shrine, where the domestic spirit lives. The spirit walks out at night, spreading protection. We feed it with tea and incense.

'Other spirits take care of the land, the water, the trees. We are in touch with all these spirits. Outside my house, there's a two-metre termite hill. It's a place where the earth is alive. We place offerings there, to the spirits of the earth. When we have to cut down trees – let's say we are making a road – we ask for forgiveness. We make offerings to the trees. We ask them for peace and safety along the new road.'

'That's why deforestation hurts us,' says Soun. 'We take such care of five trees, ten trees. But millions of trees are cut down without a thought.'

'For rice farmers,' Chheav continues, 'the most important spirits are water spirits. After the harvest, we have the water festival of Bon Om Touk. We thank the spirits. We pray there will be enough water next year. We give offerings to Indra, as the ancient Khmer kings did.'

Soun becomes excited at the mention of the Khmer kings.

'They had a deep understanding of water,' he says. 'In the twelfth century, King Jayavarman VII built a huge reservoir: three thousand five hundred metres by nine hundred metres. The water was stored behind raised embankments: it was higher than the surrounding land and could be directed anywhere he wished.

'At the same time, he built a temple devoted to Indra, the god who controls water. So there was both a physical and a spiritual infrastructure for water, and the irrigation was so good they could grow rice all year. He was the most popular king. He was deeply concerned for his people – he built universities, guesthouses, more than one hundred hospitals. The country was very developed under him.'

Such spectacular functionality leaves a long memory. Many Cambodians still draw their image of the ideal state from those far-off times.

'About ten years ago, there was a drought,' Soun says. 'Everything was dry. A statue of a nine-headed serpent was put up outside the king's palace. To bring water. In our system, good water provision is still associated with the king and the spirits.'

It is possible to think farmers are foolishly superstitious, that they waste too much time with rituals and offerings. But that would be a simplistic response. Spiritual 'work' has always been essential to the peasant mode of production – just as essential as tilling or reaping. It is not that farmers believe that weather systems are controlled by prayer. Their method, after all, is scientific: each cultivation is like a fresh experiment, whose results are closely monitored, in the pursuit of constant improvement. A man like Soun is deeply aware of scientific realities; as we have seen, he uses advanced inputs on his own farm. But farmers must constantly reassert, also, the cosmological order on which their activity depends. The idea that forests and rivers are sacred is not just a quaint premodern relic. It is essential to the sustainability of the agrarian enterprise, whose pursuit of productivity must never be allowed to erode the ecological foundation. Over prolonged periods, the sacred offers a much stronger form of environmental protection than the law. In that sense, this idea is never archaic. It is always modern.

Farmers are deeply concerned with environmental degradation, even when – especially when – they are the ones doing it. Of course they use chemicals on their land, but they hope to keep that land for ever, and they are troubled by the long-term effects. The wider destruction of ecological systems, meanwhile – whether because of deforestation, dam building, industrial pollution – fills them with an almost religious foreboding. One reason we should be concerned not to undermine peasants is that they keep alive an environmental cosmology that is beyond the capacity of city people. They function as a kind of buffer, holding in check an industrial system which has none of their reverence for nature. Our fragile world is only as intact as it is because of them. Were they to disappear, or were their ideas of the sacred to succumb to the same opportunism which characterises the rest of humanity, our last protection against environmental collapse might be lost.

I ask Chheav how his system works.

'I work with astrological calculations, which are based on an individual's birthday. When it is not an individual issue, they go to Buddhist monks. Monks take care of all the festivals and rituals. You saw the monastery when you came into the village. Many villages have monasteries like that.'

'The monks are entirely fed by the village,' says Soun. 'Even when a village is poor, the monks always have enough, because that is how farmers invest in their next life. Monks feed the hunger of the ancestors, resulting in blessings for the living. So farmers are happy to give their rice away. The monks do the spiritual work of rice farmers – they conduct the main festivals and keep the community together.'

'My work is different,' says his father-in-law. 'A farmer comes to me and asks me when he should plant his crop. I look for the connections between the time of his birth and the time he has come to see me. I advise him not only which date he should plant, but also which side of his field he should start from.'

'Only people who have studied for more than twenty years can do this,' says Soun. 'My father-in-law can close his eyes and see the spirits. He doesn't even need to visit the field.'

Chheav smiles at Soun, whose passion for his father-in-law's skills is indeed endearing.

'Often, they ask me about building a house. Is the land good? Which season should they start to build? Where should they place the first column? Nowadays people ask less about farming. They ask about jobs and business. Their mentality is changing. They are not so passionate about farming any more.'

Chheav has to end our conversation. He is expecting some clients. A couple: they want to talk about having children.

'I must change my clothes!' he says.

While he changes, Soun and I go out on to the landing. Down below, a rooster is crowing loudly. I see a mongoose burrowing in the undergrowth.

'Is it a business?' I ask Soun. 'Does he charge money for his services?'

'Some people give him money. Others bring rice or bananas or cigarettes. He doesn't tell them what they should give. Some people give fifty cents, others five dollars – it's all the same.'

A strange twanging noise starts up in the house. We go back in.

Chheav has donned the garb of a fortune teller, exchanging his black cottons for white. He is sitting on the floor playing an *angkuoch*, or jaw harp. He holds the steel instrument in his mouth with his left hand and plucks the struts with his right. For a small and slight figure, his hands are large and powerful.

He changes the tone by opening and closing his mouth. It is hypnotic more than musical, the beats speeding and slowing in waves.

'He played better when he had teeth' is Soun's harsh opinion. 'Now he has no teeth.'

I see a couple come up the stairs. They are young and hesitant. They wait at the entrance. Chheav lays off his playing. He welcomes them and beckons them to sit. They smile and bow many times.

Soun and I go down to where his motorbike is glinting in the afternoon sun.

'They have no children,' he explains. 'They want my father-in-law's help. So there will be someone to take over their farm.'

The history of Cambodia flows from a basic ecological mismatch: though temperatures are warm throughout the year, there is rain only from May to November. One hundred and fifty centimetres fall in that season, which is characterised by violent storms and floods. The waters then retreat, giving way to six months of drought.

Human beings began to domesticate wild rice plants in China's Yangtze River basin some 10,000 years ago. By 2000 BCE, Chinese seeds and farming techniques had spread through Vietnam into Cambodia. After 1500 BCE, trade contact with India brought new rice varieties; from the resulting interbreeding emerged the exceptionally rich botanical resource which characterises the region even today.[13] What limited Cambodian rice production was the irregular availability of water. From earliest times, therefore, Cambodian agriculture depended on engineering projects designed to extend the growing season by 'stabilising, storing and dispersing water'.[14]

These works were concentrated between the Tonle Sap and Mount Kulen, forty kilometres to the north-east. The steep edges of that plateau rise 500 metres above the Siem Reap plain, creating a microclimate with distinctly higher rainfall than surrounding areas. Several streams and rivers flow down the plateau; they are fed beyond the monsoon by waters retained in the Kulen sandstone. ('The kingdom of Cambodia . . . is very big,' observed the Spanish monk Gabriel Quiroga de San Antonio, who visited in the 1590s. 'It has only one mountain, from which emerge many rivers.')[15] Cambodian engineers began at least 1,500 years ago to trap these streams before they drained into the Tonle Sap and from there into the Mekong. The core technology was the *baray*, or reservoir. The Khmer name comes from a Sanskrit word whose meaning – 'to traverse' or 'to cross' – suggests the technological evolution: first, dykes were built across the plain, blocking the waters' flow; later these dykes were used to channel the water into storage tanks.[16] Water accumulated in these tanks to a level higher than the surrounding land, allowing for its redistribution through a network of downward-sloping canals.

From earliest times, the water supply was understood to depend on the propitiation of ancestors. But from the fifth and sixth centuries CE Cambodia's indigenous animism was transformed by waves of ideas and migrants arriving from India, whose language – Sanskrit – was established as the medium of courtly and intellectual life. Sanskritic elites took credit for the engineering innovations at the heart of Cambodian society.[17] A Chinese chronicler reported how, according to them, that technical know-how had arrived with Kaundinya, the mythical Indian prince we encountered earlier: 'Then a Brahman named Kaundinya ruled the kingdom . . . He changed the institutions to follow Indian models. He wanted his subjects to stop digging wells, and to dig reservoirs in the future; several dozen families could then unite and use one of these in common.'[18]

Indian culture also supplied the spiritual vocabulary with which Cambodian kings began to describe their relationship to these works – and to the heavens, from where water originated.

They were particularly influenced by Hindu ascetics arriving from southern India, who spread an ethos of personal and passionate devotion to Shiva, which they considered more authentic than the mere observance of Brahmanical dogma and ritual.[19] Animating force of the cosmos, Shiva was represented in stone either as an all-powerful male figure, with multiple arms and a third eye in the forehead, or as a sacred phallus or linga. By identifying with this god, Cambodian rulers set themselves up as prime movers of the water system, and as sources, therefore, of all fertile energy. According to myth, after all, it was Shiva who dispensed celestial waters. When the river goddess Ganga descended from heaven to purify the earth, the gods were afraid that the impact would bring universal destruction. Mighty Shiva therefore stood below and caught her, and channelled her waters gently to the land through his long matted hair. In the Cambodian setting, a similar fecundity was attributed to the Shiva-king, who dispensed sky water into reservoirs and fields.[20]

Until the ninth century, Cambodia was made up of several small kingdoms, bound by shared conceptions of rice, water and kingship. These kingdoms probably competed not only for land but also for slaves and subjects. Human resources were the most urgent requirement of the rice economy, which required large labour forces both for cultivation and for constructing and maintaining the irrigation system.[21] Unification began under the first Khmer emperor, Jayavarman II (r. 802–50), who developed a sacred geography for his newly expanded realm. In particular, he projected on to Mount Kulen the attributes of Mount Meru, sacred mountain of Hindu mythology, which was surrounded by a great ocean, just as Mount Kulen rose from the floods of the Tonle Sap. The scriptures described Mount Meru as a cosmic axis connecting the celestial and terrestrial realms. Cambodian emperors ascended their own Meru, therefore, to receive the power to mediate between the two and so control the waters. Jayavarman constructed a temple on the summit of Mount Kulen where he was crowned *devaraja* or god-king; this would be the coronation site for all his successors. During the ensuing centuries, the rocky beds of the rivers rising on Mount Kulen were carved with Shiva lingas. Passing over those carvings, the water flowing down into Tonle Sap – and so into the rice system – was charged with divine fertility.[22]

The Cambodian plains were gradually engineered into an artificial landscape consisting of four main elements: rice fields, human settlements, temple complexes and, linking these three, a dense network of ponds and canals. This landscape was intensively worked by the Khmer peasantry, whose enormous productivity was not achieved without relentless coercion. Along with irrigation technology, in fact, the capacity to mobilise large labour forces according to the seasonal demands of rice farming formed the foundation of Khmer power. Farmers had heavy corvée (forced labour) obligations to the king, to other overlords and to temples, while unfree workers (including prisoners of war and hereditary slaves) performed the most arduous work of digging canals and building temples and monuments.[23]

It is clear that from earliest times Khmer rice cultivation was sufficiently prolific to release much of the population from the fields. As we have seen, rice was an exceptionally efficient way of deriving calories from land, especially given Cambodia's botanical variety: long-stemmed floating rice, for instance, could be cultivated even when metres of water covered the earth. But the empire also saw constant technical improvements: Emperor Suryavarman II (r. 1113–50) generalised new techniques to allow three rice harvests per year, further increasing the nutritional surplus. Visiting in 1296 from China – another rice empire – the traveller Zhou Daguan was impressed to note that Cambodia had no winter, that the whole year is 'like our fifth and six months with days that know no frost or snow' and that 'crops could be harvested three or four times a year'.[24]

The astonishing 'profit' of this rice-based economy is impressive even today: archaeologists have documented over 1,000 temples on the Khmer plains; some of the earthworks, meanwhile, were also massive, rising twelve metres high, containing close to a million cubic metres of packed earth and reinforced on the water side with slabs of laterite.[25] The city of Angkor, imperial capital for 600 years, was 'possibly the largest complex of low-density urban development in the pre-industrial world',[26] spreading over 1,000 square kilometres, ten times bigger than the next-largest such development we know (the Mayan centre of Tikal, which reached its maximum extent between 200 and 900 CE). The population was 'low-density' because of the dominance of temples and water bodies, but it was considerable nonetheless: at some points, Angkor may have had as many as 1 million inhabitants. By the twelfth century, this urban population featured a formal bureaucracy, as well as a substantial merchant class, which was chiefly constituted, as throughout Cambodian history, by ethnic outsiders – Chams, Chinese and Vietnamese – who imported commodities and manufactured goods from neighbouring countries. The maintenance of the empire and its population also required sizeable armies and navies to prosecute continual military campaigns. Each of the large temples was also serviced by tens of thousands of people, as we know from an inscription at Ta Prohm, built by Jayavarman VII in 1186 CE:

> There are here 400 men, 18 high priests, 2,740 other priests, 2,232 assistants, including 615 female dancers. In addition, there are 66,625 men and women who perform services for the gods.[27]

The greatest of these temples was Angkor Wat, built by Suryavarman II. Suryavarman waged military campaigns against the eastern kingdoms of Vietnam and Champa, considerably expanding Khmer territory; he also sent tributary embassies to China and so declared Cambodia's place in the 'global' economy. His temple was conceived on a scale appropriate to this new imperial sweep: more than eighty hectares were enclosed by the temple walls, themselves surrounded by a vast moat covering a further ninety hectares. The temple's corridors and colonnades were carved with nearly a kilometre of continuous bas-reliefs, including 1,800 *apsaras* or celestial dancing girls, whose flowing robes and gestures appear even today to make the building sway.[28]

Devoted not to Shiva but to Vishnu, Angkor Wat was designed as a five-peaked Mount Meru. According to one archaeologist, 'the

View of Angkor Wat by the French explorer and artist Louis Delaporte, who travelled on the government-sponsored Mekong exploration of 1866–68. His book, *The Monuments of Cambodia*, was published in 1873.

great enclosure wall around the temple represents the mountains at the edge of the world, the surrounding moat the Sea of Milk around Meru where gods and demons churned ambrosia.'[29] But Angkor Wat was not merely a celestial diagram. Recent aerial scans have demonstrated that the area within the temple walls was marked by a grid of ponds and dwellings similar to the urban expanse outside.[30] The temple itself probably sustained about 4,500 people; the ponds supplied water for household needs and for cultivating vegetables and medicinal plants. Aligned with the planets, Angkor Wat's walls and moats and ponds were a ceremonial extension of the hydraulic network, and a monument to the rice economy from which it sprang (Figure 19).

The empire reached its greatest extent under Jayavarman VII (r. 1181–1218), largely thanks to his victory over Cambodia's rival sibling to the east, Champa. Cambodia emerged, in fact, as the regional superpower, drawing tribute from Champa and other surrounding kingdoms and taking over Cham ports on the South China Sea – so

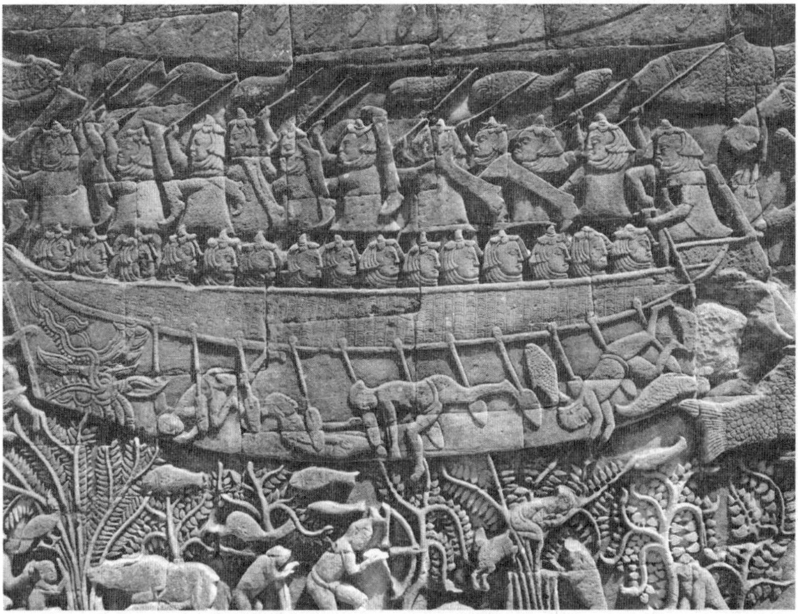

Detail from frieze depicting the Khmer-Cham naval battles of 1177–78, Bayon Temple, late-twelfth century CE.

opening new trade connections with China. The empire's increased scale and stature were reflected, once again, in stupendous building works – most famously, the geometric walled city of Angkor Thom, whose enclosure was nearly five times that of Angkor Wat. Like other emperors, however, Jayavarman considered hydraulic works to be the most important fruit of a meritorious reign and oversaw the construction of a great reservoir, which he called Jayatataka. Collecting as yet untapped run-off from Mount Kulen, this was the last major component of the Khmer water system. Unlike his predecessors, Jayavarman was Buddhist; for his reservoir, he drew on his personal religion to create a new poetry of the water he stored from the sky and fed into the rice system. In the precise centre was a cruciform island containing four small ponds connected to a large central pond by stone conduits, each one in the shape of an animal head: elephant, horse, lion, human. In the middle of the central pond was a small temple dedicated to the bodhisattva Lokeshvara, healer of the sick and lame. The temple was built on a platform carved with lotus petals and seemed to rise therefore from a sacred lotus floating on the water. Around the base were wrapped two intertwined nagas, or serpent gods. All this had cosmic resonance: the central pond was a replica of the Anavatapta, the lake which, according to Buddhist cosmology, lay below Mount Meru at the centre of the continent of Jambudvipa; from its cardinal points flowed the four great rivers which ran throughout the world.[31]

It is likely that the Khmer system was reaching its ecological limits by the time of Jayavarman's death in 1218. The plains were mainly deforested and much of the Kulen plateau too, which meant that silt flowed unimpeded into the canals and reservoirs. As the network choked, the expense of maintaining it became unsustainable. It became more and more difficult to support Angkor's substantial population, which was increasingly exposed also to military invasion. During the thirteenth century, many of Cambodia's vassal states turned their allegiance to the trading behemoth that was Mongol China, depriving the Khmer of both tribute and defensive buffer lands. A Thai raid reported to Zhou Daguan during his Cambodian sojourn of 1296–7 placed such strain on local defences that 'all the ordinary people were ordered out to do battle, often with no good strategy or preparation.'[32] In 1431, a more formidable Thai invasion resulted in the capture of the walled city of Angkor Thom, from where great quantities of treasure and documents, as well as thousands of dancers, artisans and administrators, were carried off to the court of Ayutthaya. In the aftermath, the old capital was abandoned. A replacement court was set up in modern-day Phnom Penh. From its new position on the Mekong, the state became more focused on trade, which gave an enhanced role to immigrant merchant communities such as the Chinese and Malays.

In the absence of a centralised hydraulic bureaucracy, the old irrigation system fell into ruin, and rice farming was confined to the rainy season – which meant one harvest per year. Farmers built local dykes and reservoirs, and life shrank to the scale of the village. So did religion: no longer the vast temples, Hindu and Buddhist, of imperial times, but village monasteries embedded in rural life. By this time, the Cambodian peasantry had largely converted to Theravada Buddhism, a tradition imported by wandering missionaries from present-day Thailand, Myanmar and Sri Lanka.[33] Buddhism became integrated with older Khmer ideas of spirits, ancestors, forests, water and rice, and peasants shifted their tributary obligations to local monks, many of whom were themselves sons of peasants. In return, the monasteries offered teachings which imbued natural systems and agricultural work with moral meaning and so gave dignity to peasant life.[34]

As a regional power, however, Cambodia was considerably diminished. Rulers no longer had the moral authority to organise labour on the previous scale, and rice production fell off. The population thinned accordingly, and cities declined in step with the rural hinterland. By the 1690s, a visiting Chinese merchant could give this dismal report: 'Cambodia is a poor country with a poorly organised government and armed forces. There are virtually no rich people . . . Rice is much cheaper there.'[35] Feeble as it was, Cambodia struggled to resist takeover by rising Vietnam and Thailand, which occupied it from both sides and assumed significant de facto control. By the nineteenth century, the countryside was so devastated by invasions and rebellions that the king was forced to beg from these hostile neighbours:

> In the year 1827 . . . a dispatch from the King of Cambodia [said that] the harvests in that country had failed in those years, and the troops and people were suffering greatly from hunger. [Vietnamese Emperor] Minh Mạng ordered the grain storehouses to be opened to provide emergency relief and timely aid. Therefore, the King of Cambodia submitted a memorial expressing his gratitude.[36]

It was against this backdrop, in 1863, that King Norodom (r. 1860–1904) submitted to a French protectorate – the only way, he judged, of securing his dynasty and avoiding total absorption by regional powers.

The French empire ultimately swallowed all of Cambodia, Vietnam and Laos. The colonial government used Cambodia as a source of cheap agricultural exports; its rice would supply the mills in the regional headquarters in Saigon, where it would be processed for global distribution.* This reorganisation did little for Cambodian peasants. The core of the French system was the large-scale plantations in Battambang Province, which were connected by railway to Phnom Penh. During the creation of these plantations, many Battambang peasants lost their land to foreign entrepreneurs and were re-employed as wage labourers. In other provinces, rice farmers continued to farm as they had before, but with a greatly increased tax burden. Often this tax had to be paid in cash, which required peasants either to sell rice or to work as day labourers; those who could not pay could be required to perform up to ninety days of corvée labour.[37] Moneylenders benefited from peasants' new cash requirements, often building up sizeable landholdings and contributing to the growing class of landless peasants. French administrators used Cambodian taxes to build ports and railways and to build up their colonial centre in Vietnam; they did not involve themselves in the ancient activity of storing water in order to extend the growing season. Rice farmers were fully exposed, therefore, to rainfall fluctuations – 'there were frequent famines, and epidemics of malaria and cholera.'[38]

So it is no surprise that, after Cambodian independence in 1953, successive political regimes proclaimed their legitimacy by invoking the still-present memory of the Khmer emperors – and particularly their investments in irrigation. Even in the twentieth century, they supplied the formula for genuine Cambodian sovereignty, and under King Norodom Sihanouk, who abdicated in 1955 in order

* Alongside this agrarian extraction, the colonial state relied heavily on monopolies over opium, alcohol and salt. Opium provided a particularly important source of revenue. John Collins, 'Imperial Drug Economies, Development, and the Search for Alternatives in Asia, from Colonialism to Decolonisation', *International Development Policy | Revue internationale de politique de développement*, Vol. 12 (2020), 44–63; Christian C. Lentz, 'Cultivating Subjects: Opium and Rule in Post-Colonial Vietnam', *Modern Asian Studies*, Vol. 51, No. 4 (2017), 879–918.

to serve as prime minister, there was considerable investment in barrages, canals and reservoirs. The US Agency for International Development (USAID) provided most of the funds: with the creation of a Communist agrarian state in neighbouring North Vietnam, the State Department was extremely concerned to keep Cambodian peasants from radicalisation. In 1961, a French scholar was struck by the way these modernisation attempts proceeded by way of the classical past: 'Great works are being undertaken today in the region of Siem Reap to restore to working order the reservoirs and irrigation systems built during the era of the monarchs of Angkor.'[39] USAID also set up seed research centres across the country and, with new strains developed from traditional stock, each year's rice production began to set new records. That came to an end in 1970 when the countryside was overwhelmed by a three-way conflict between the US-backed government, invading armies from Communist Vietnam and Khmer Rouge insurgents. With the abolition of the monarchy in October of that year and the proclamation of the Khmer Republic, the last symbolic ties were broken between the state and the peasantry, which now entered a decade of overwhelming catastrophe.[40] As part of its wider campaign against Vietnam, the United States dropped over 2.7 million tonnes of bombs on Cambodia's eastern and central regions, where rice fields and irrigation systems were totally destroyed. Many peasants joined the Khmer Rouge – not usually out of conviction but rather because the collapse of rural communities and economies created conditions in which it was possible for rebel armies to intimidate and recruit.[41] Tens of thousands of peasants flooded into the cities, meanwhile, where they accumulated as an urban underclass. By 1974, an estimated 80 per cent of rice fields were abandoned, and rice production had fallen to 16 per cent of the 1970 level.[42]

In 1975, the Khmer Rouge defeated its rivals in what its leaders presented as a peasant revolution. Hoping to re-establish the hyperproductive rice economy of the mythical past, the new regime immediately emptied the cities, forcing over 2 million urban residents to leave and become rice farmers. Maximising rice production was an all-encompassing obsession, in pursuit of which other crops such as tobacco and maize were eradicated and forests were cleared to expand the growing area. The regime committed farmers to two harvests a year where for centuries there had been only one, and set targets for rice production that had no relation to the underlying reality: the hastily compiled Four-Year Plan demanded average yields of three tonnes per hectare, which was more than triple the pre-war average.[43] To focus the population on this task, private property was abolished and all land, draft animals and tools were collectivised. The regime sought to abolish all structures that might compromise the productivity objective, especially the family – family members were often separated and sent to join agricultural brigades in different parts of the country – and the village community. Buddhist temples were destroyed or turned into granaries; some 50,000 monks were murdered.[44] Labour was planned and directed by the regime, which decided agricultural schedules, daily rations for farmers and quotas of earth moved and rice delivered.

Farmers were expected to meet their targets without fertiliser or machines; revolutionary fervour and large-scale irrigation works were to suffice. Pol Pot was particularly aroused by the hydraulic feats of ancient Angkor, which symbolised for him the national spirit. 'If we can build Angkor,' he declared in 1977, 'we can build anything.'[45] The Cambodian countryside was reimagined as a grid of one-hectare squares outlined by canals; everything needed to be dug with spades or, more frequently, with bare hands (Figure 20). As the Party exhortations rang out – 'dig canals, raise earthworks' – as many as 1.2 million died of their labour. The Khmer Rouge viewed the peasantry, in fact, as the expendable fuel for revolution. Peasants were less important than the rice they produced, on whose calories alone Pol Pot imagined he could power the nation's development. Among the modern systems he rejected was money itself; he hoped to use rice to buy industrial machinery from China, North Korea and Yugoslavia.[46] The speed at which he could modernise the country was therefore dependent on the amount of manual labour he could deploy – hence the stupefying coercion and fatality of his so-called Super Great Leap Forward.[47]

There was brutal persecution of those segments of the population not involved with rice growing.[48] This included not only urban professionals but also such 'enemy insiders' as the Vietnamese, Chinese and the Cham, all associated with trade. Many Cham had converted to Islam during the great dispersal which followed the fall of Champa to Vietnamese expansion in 1471; the Khmer Rouge destroyed mosques, executed Muslim clerics, massacred Cham villages and forced survivors to change their names, eat pork and join rice-growing collectives. Also targeted were Cambodia's indigenous peoples – the Kuy, for instance, who, because they collected plants and resins from the forest, were regarded as both backward and possessing an unhealthy attachment to private property. The Kuy and other indigenous communities were resettled in villages, their language and ethnic markers were prohibited, and they too were forced into collectives.[49]

Despite everything, Cambodian rice production stagnated under the Khmer Rouge; according to some analyses, it actually fell. Pol Pot and his fellow leaders came typically from privileged backgrounds, and they were mainly ignorant of rural affairs. Production quotas, for instance, were standardised across regions, without regard for the stark differences in ecology and soil quality; failed harvests were attributed to treachery and punished – often with execution. The quality of the infrastructure built during those years was extremely low, and floods and collapses were common. By 1977, famine was beginning to spread across the country. There were almost no long-term benefits from the inhuman expenditure of energy, in fact, and much of the irrigation system had to be rebuilt by the Kampuchean People's Revolutionary Party, which took over after the fall of the Khmer Rouge in 1979 and which, in various guises, has been in power ever since.

As in a cathedral, as in New York City, so in a primeval rainforest: it is impossible not to look up. Everything is vertical: there is not a kink in the thousands of tree trunks, which soar like parallel pillars towards the sky. They are built hard, for height. Even young trees, their trunk still narrower than my wrist, are inflexible as marble. Their mature ancestors, which are old enough to remember when the first Europeans set foot in these lands, have anchored themselves with wooden walls radiating out from the base of the trunk, their diameter large enough to enfold a small village. Far above, the canopy is intricate and dense, like some impossible needlework. From that height, beige leaves fall in a light and constant rain, carpeting the fragrant ground. I watch a seed helicoptering: it takes many minutes to reach the ground, gliding this way, then that. Almost all the sun is absorbed by the trees' elevated panel of green; only rare golden rays penetrate below.

I am in Prey Lang, the last significant expanse of a forest which once covered most of the Indochinese peninsula. Deforestation, which is the precondition of the rice landscape, has been a persistent theme of this chapter, but the process has been even more comprehensive in neighbouring Thailand, Vietnam and Laos. If this 500,000-hectare remnant survives here, it is due in part to the protective efforts of the Kuy people, who have been gathering produce from it since long before the foundation of the Khmer empire.

'We are the custodians of the forest,' says Chup Lin. In her sixties, she wears jeans and flip-flops. 'We collect rattan vines for weaving. We collect resin to sell in the market – resin for sealing houses and boats, sweet-smelling resin for religious ceremonies. But we don't cut the trees.'

'The small trees we can cut,' says Luun, her husband. 'We cut young trees for building houses. Then we give offerings of food and drink to the spirits, otherwise they get angry and we fall sick. But when the trees grow big, they do not belong to us any more. They belong to the spirits, and we may not cut them at all.'

The couple live on the fringes of the forest, in a part of Kampong Thom province that is assailed by plantation and timber interests.

'We had one and a half hectares of land,' says Chup Lin. 'We grew rain-fed rice. We mixed it with sesame and cassava.'

'All for our own consumption,' adds her husband. 'For cash, we sold products from the forest.'

'But they took our land, without giving us any money,' says Chup Lin. She chuckles that tragic laugh that has become so familiar on my travels in Cambodia. 'An officer came to take our land for a rubber plantation. The men came with guns – it was very scary. Everyone in the village lost their land. They left us our houses but took our fields.'

'Before that, we could feed ourselves,' says Luun. 'Our land was good. Years ago, someone offered us ten thousand dollars for our land but we said no. You can spend that money very soon, and then you are hungry. But now we have no land and no money either. We can only work on the rubber plantation. All we have is a daily wage. Six dollars a day.'

'We tried to get the land back,' explains Chup Lin. 'For three years we made petitions in Phnom Penh, without result. Now the plantation is there – it's pointless complaining. The government cannot do this. But they do it.'

'We have three children,' says Luun. 'They have moved to Kampong Cham province. They are all rice farmers. But they don't have enough for themselves. They are missing two or three months of rice each year. So they can't give any to us. We have to buy rice in the market.'

'They had guns,' repeats his wife. 'What could we do?'

As a Marxist-Leninist party taking over a traumatised and devastated country, the Kampuchean People's Revolutionary Party placed peasant concerns at the forefront. As a corrective to the Khmer Rouge's total assault on families and private property, land was distributed once again to peasant families for private cultivation, even though tools and labour were still shared. The rice output, which rebounded considerably during the 1980s, was directed to peasant food security, while significant investments were made in village life – not only irrigation systems, but also hospitals, schools and roads. Given the lack of capital, there were limitations to all these initiatives. Nevertheless, between 1979 and 1991, calorie intake regained normal levels and infant mortality was cut nearly in half. An energetic adult literacy drive, meanwhile, raised the number of reading adults from under a quarter to about 60 per cent.

With the end of the Cold War, international sponsorship disappeared for Cambodia's socialist system, and the state entered a liquidity crisis. Rebranding itself the Cambodian People's Party, the administration solicited loans and aid from the World Bank, the International Monetary Fund, Japan, France and the USA. In return, it had to promise various reforms, of which the introduction of 'multi-party democracy' was the least noticeable. Far more consequential was 'market liberalisation', which would eventually give foreign corporations unfettered access to Cambodia's extraordinarily rich land resources. In a country where most rural households depended on small-scale rice cultivation, this shift was transformative. Between 2001 and 2010, an expanding array of 'land concession' laws demonstrated what rural dwellers could already see: selling land to international bidders was becoming the state's primary business. Technically speaking, the land was leased, not bought – usually for ninety-nine years – and concessionaires were obliged to submit to certain environmental guidelines and to comply with legal procedures regarding resettlement of displaced populations.[50] But land concessions also provided opportunities for large-scale corruption within the Cambodian power system – opportunities which were so lucrative precisely because land concessions were bound by a long list of environmental and social responsibilities, so offering officials the possibility of charging corporations that wished to evade the regulations.[51] Land concessions became the means, in other words, by which some of the world's richest land was removed from the orbit of the rice-growing peasantry and privatised instead by bureaucratic entrepreneurs. By 2012, around 2.1 million hectares of Cambodian land – about one-ninth of national territory – had been allocated to concessionaires, some of which, through multiple companies or spousal arrangements, were able to accumulate as many as thirty times the legal limit of 10,000 hectares.[52]

Some of these parties were senior Cambodian military figures or politically connected tycoons, but most were from Vietnam, China, Thailand and Korea.[53] Their usual purpose was to set up plantations for rubber, sugarcane, cassava and oil palm. Since they were paying significant bribes to officials, they could be confident that the necessary evictions would be taken care of by police and army personnel. Nor did they usually pay compensation to those who lost their land – not only because they paid further bribes to avoid that expense, but also because destitution made former rice farmers more susceptible to being hired back as labourers.[54]

Concessionaires were lured by the promise of a nine-year tax holiday, so many of these developments never delivered any local revenues except for the negligible lease fees. According to my interviews, many concessionaires came and went without even building the infrastructure which was the one purported benefit of these otherwise profitless contracts. For their real interest was often nothing more than looting timber.[55] Though they arrived with promises of plantations and jobs, in fact they simply paid as little as $2 per hectare – according to my interviews again – to extract ancient woods probably worth $5,000 per hectare or more and then exited, leaving only wilderness behind them.

That is why the period of land concessions has been a period also of catastrophic forest loss: between 2000 and 2024, approximately one-third of Cambodia's tree cover was removed.[56] Even though fresh concessions were suspended in 2012 – a response to widespread protests against the eviction of tens of thousands of families, as well as conspicuous environmental depletion – control over the Cambodian countryside had retreated into backrooms by then and the damage did not abate. Nearly 60 per cent of the twenty-five-year loss has occurred in the last decade.[57] Prey Lang is not exempt, even though this uniquely surviving lowland rainforest was declared a protected area in 2016.

'City people do not have the education to understand what a forest is,' says Luun. 'If no one stops them, they will cut everything down.'

That is why he and Chup Lin have resorted to protecting Prey Lang themselves. They are part of a network of local people – which includes ethnic Khmer, as well as other indigenous communities – who patrol the forest, collate information about tree loss and confront chainsaw gangs.

'The law prohibits commercial logging in protected areas,' says Luun. 'But many land concessions were signed before 2016, so they go on logging here. If we find them, we take photos. We tell them they are illegal. Sometimes we set their timber on fire.'

All this is highly risky, since the government has declared such community patrols illegal.[58] Luun and Chup Lin have often faced armed guards and threats. Everyone knows the story of Chut Wutty, an environmental activist who in 2012 was shot dead, probably by military police, while investigating illegal logging in Koh Kong province.[59] But, for this couple, there can be no abandonment of the cause.

'We have no life without the forest,' says Chup Lin. 'Our livelihood comes from here. All our medicine comes from here. Will the rubber company pay to give us medicine? No. The forest must take care of us.'

We walk in deeper. The giant spirals of ancient creepers float through the space above our heads. Armies of butterflies, black and lemon-yellow, suck at the forest floor. Far away, we hear the mournful cries of treetop gibbons.

'These provide medicine for menstrual problems,' says Chup Lin, showing me a patch of bushes she has transplanted herself. She indicates roots that cure stomach infections, leaves that help complexion, bark that is used to treat wounds. She carries knowledge gained through centuries of experimentation. She prunes as she walks, breaking overgrown shoots, tearing off dead leaves.

Luun places his hand on a towering *chheuteal* tree – one of the rainforest hardwoods known as dipterocarps – whose broad mast erupts into pale green leaves forty metres above our heads.

'This is a resin tree,' he says. He shows me where he has cut a blackened hollow in the trunk, about chest height. 'I heat the hole with fire,' he explains. 'That releases the resin, which begins to drip after a few minutes.'

We walk on. The forest opens up and we see the sky. They point out simple mounds where ancestors are buried. There are small shrines at the base of trees where offerings are neatly arranged: leaves, fruit and – it seems completely incongruous – cans of beer.

Because of their forest identities, these people are managing a much denser web of botanical and spiritual connections than most peasants. Their forest is not just a place or an object. It is a giant system of interdependencies. That system can only operate at scale, which is why the endless erosion of the forest, as well as its transection by powerlines and logging roads, fills this couple with such alarm.

We see glorious metallic lizards. A fashion parade of forest birds. Lacquered ants speeding in their thousands along overhead root bridges.

Everywhere we go, there is water. The forest floor is criss-crossed by microchannels of water, flowing invisibly under the blanket of leaves. These streams rise from the ground; they are also fed from the canopy above, which catches rainfall and then drips it to the floor from specially designed leaf tips. The air inside the forest, meanwhile, is close to 100 per cent humid – we human beings are dripping too. Every night, this humidity condenses on the underside of the canopy: another cycle of drips. All these micromovements eventually coalesce into massive water flows. Four rivers rise in the Prey Lang; three flow eastward into the Mekong, while the other – the Steung Saen – is the largest tributary of the Tonle Sap.

'The forest makes rain,' says Luun. 'It also holds water and feeds it to the land. Without the forest, we have drought and flash floods. And we have no rice.' He blames the rapid disappearance of Cambodian forests for the disrupted climate of recent years. 'The climate is getting worse,' he says. 'People round here grow rain-fed rice. There is no irrigation. If there's no rain, it's a big problem. Before they sow, they pray for good weather. But some years the crop is lost.'

'We used to pray that our fields not be destroyed by wild animals,' adds his wife. 'We offered branches of leaves and made our prayers. But those ceremonies are not necessary any more because there are no wild animals! Nature is so polluted, they cannot survive.'

She laughs bitterly.

Her bitterness has a long history. Indigenous communities like the Kuy were not part of the rice-growing mainstream. Though rice cultivation was essential to their subsistence and ritual life, it was embedded in a diverse forest economy. For centuries, they were regarded as culturally inferior. Mostly, they were left to themselves, though there was always a market for their resin, rattan, beeswax and ironwork; in times of war or agricultural stress, they were forcibly relocated and even enslaved. Later French administrators added their own contempt, using insights from European 'race theory' to determine how far different communities could participate in their modern state. While the Khmer had shown themselves in the past to be capable of sophisticated government and were therefore mere 'barbarians', Cambodia's 'aborigines' were 'savages' in need of colonial 'pacification'.[60] Sihanouk's government attempted, without much success, to assimilate indigenous peoples. Pol Pot, as noted above, viewed their way of life as backward and treacherous and attempted to purge them.

The post-1979 regime supposedly abolished ethnic and religious distinctions, recognising the equality of all citizens. But it has not worked out like that. There is a reason the burden of corporate land grabs falls so disproportionately on the Kuy. Old attitudes die hard: even today, these people's claim to citizenship – and everything that goes with it – is weaker than that of the Khmer majority. In an age of hyper-exploitation, their frugality is even seen as subversive. As far back as 2010, a United Nations special rapporteur on human rights noted with concern that Cambodian lawyers representing indigenous peoples whose lands had been expropriated were themselves charged with 'incitement'.[61] Such are the cultural and legal avenues which lead to Luun and Chup Lin's situation: where questionable deals struck between a foreign businessman and a Phnom Penh bureaucrat may result, the next day, in the arrival of officers with eviction notices, of men with guns, of mechanical earth movers, of fences and barbed wire. The situation is critical. As the chainsaws roar on every side, it is not clear that these people – who survived French 'pacification' and the Khmer Rouge's ethnic cleansing – can survive today. The regime of transnational capital might turn out to be conclusive.

In fact, the fate of Cambodia's unique ecology, and that of the peasants who depend on it, is even more precarious than my Kuy companions make out, because the land concessions and forest depletion are taking place in the context of a large-scale reorganisation of regional water systems, which has the potential to alter even the mythic rhythms of the Mekong and Tonle Sap. At the heart of these changes is China, which has built several dams upstream on the Mekong in order to generate hydroelectricity. These dams obstruct the rich sediment which has nourished the Cambodian soil since the beginning of agricultural time, as well as the movement of fish and their eggs; fish levels have dropped alarmingly in the last decade.[62] The Tonle Sap floods are less plentiful than in the past, while the reversal of the Tonle Sap River is weaker and more short-lived – all of which has drastic implications for the ancient rice economy of this region. Commentators fear that these changes may 'impact the food security of urban people throughout Southeast Asia'.[63] Such concerns are particularly relevant in Cambodia, which China is increasingly reconfiguring to service its own food-security needs:[64] new Chinese-built highways, ports and airports serve to ensure that Cambodian produce can be transported as efficiently as possible to Chinese plates. New Chinese-built agro-industrial Special Economic Zones add value and efficiency to this transfer.

National states have become a vehicle for extracting natural resources as quickly as possible, not in order to benefit their citizens, but simply to enhance balance sheets of various kinds – their own GDP account, the accounts of major corporations or even the accounts of more powerful states. With the loss of ideological diversity that has occurred over the last forty years, there is less and less language for urban people to critique this situation. This is one reason we are so in need of peasant societies. They are on the front lines, they understand how monumental are the current stakes and they possess the alternative. They are already living that alternative. Most urban people will not risk their lives to protect trees, because they do not know enough about trees to do so. People like Luun and Chup Lin will take that risk – because they can see what urban people cannot. As Chup Lin put it to me, 'If the rivers weaken and the forests fall, there will be no rice. And without rice, the spirits will withdraw.'

3

Coca: The Illicit Peasant

> Coca (Erythroxylon coca) . . . is cultivated in the moist valley floors and on the lower slopes of the mountains . . . It is consumed almost entirely in Bolivia and Peru . . . [and] serves the indigenous people as both food and stimulant.
>
> – PAOLO MANTEGAZZA, 1859[1]

There are few road journeys as spectacular as the one that takes you over the Peruvian Andes and down into the verdant valleys of the Apurímac and Ene rivers.

I am already far from Lima. The capital, set slightly inland from the Pacific, once governed the vast wealth of Spain's South American empire, while nearby Callao – its great port on the ocean – connected the viceroyal city to the wider world. The palaces and cathedrals of Lima still bear the imprint of that age of empire and seafaring. But the flight from Lima to Ayacucho, high in the Andes, has extinguished all maritime thoughts and sensations. There is a reason most Peruvians, if you ask them where they are from, respond not with a town or a nation but with an ecosystem. Stupendous physical barriers divide this large country, and the *costa* (coast) can seem unimaginably remote to inhabitants of the *sierra* (mountains) or *selva* (jungle). Even today, physical connectivity is patchy and, just as in ancient times, considerable energy is devoted to the challenge of *moving stuff around*. What is banally abundant in the *selva* – a ripe papaya, say – may arouse joy and amazement when transported up into the *sierra*. Here, in Ayacucho's little airport, passengers embarking for Lima are purchasing suitcase-sized sacks of the delicious mountain bread known as *chapla.*

Outside, I am met by a man who calls himself Chacal. He has spent his whole life in the region we are going to – a region so notorious that, one after another, Lima folk have discouraged me from this trip. He has rented a car for the journey, a massive Toyota Hilux pickup, whose most important quality is well captured in Chacal's translated Spanish description: 'double traction'.

We set off through bustling sixteenth-century streets, which are soaking wet. It is early morning. The rain has only just stopped, and the women selling fruit and snacks on the pavements still wear protective plastic bags over their flat-brimmed felt hats. Now the skies are clear, and their layered skirts and floral blouses shine in the mountain sunlight. Chacal stops to buy a large sheet of plastic to cover the back of the truck, where our bags are exposed to the weather.

As we pass through the town outskirts, buildings become basic – brick and concrete, many unfinished. Numerous gas stations and tyre workshops compete for the attention of drivers embarking on the arduous drive ahead. For a while, the urban influence persists – most obviously in the deep scars in the mountainside, where construction rock has been unceremoniously excised. But before long we are alone with the Andes, whose giant teeth soar on every side, gnawing at the clouds. Pablo Neruda called them the 'spine' of South America, a 'torrential stairway' whose 'ultimate geometry' runs through the continent, ancient, austere, the 'destination of time'.[2]

The road meanders around the near-vertical slopes. My mind has to expand to accommodate this vastness. We zigzag up rock faces and over crests that seem stratospheric, only to discover a forest of higher peaks. Below, the receding valleys become miniature. Beyond the edge of the road is a terrifying drop into the abyss. Piles of tyres, painted yellow, highlight the hairpin bends. Wild dogs sit at each of these corners; they get up to bark at passing cars as if to warn them of the danger. It is remarkably systematic, as if some canine council has expressed concern about the inadequacy of human safety measures.

At first, the slopes are forested. With altitude, the trees disappear, and there is only bare rock and grass. Flocks of sheep and llamas freckle the mountainsides. Sometimes we pass a cluster of small houses with donkeys tied outside and gardens abundant with red hibiscus.

In his late fifties, Chacal is introverted and thoughtful. For some of his life, he was a farmer; as we drive, he tells me about different plants and trees. He points out how the vegetation differs on north- and south-facing slopes. He identifies the crops in the neat farms on the valley floor. He tells me about potatoes of which, famously, Peru possesses about 3,000 varieties.

We ascend into the desolate heights. Sometimes we pass a family carrying wood, leading a couple of sheep and cows, but there are no houses here. Finally, at 4,200 metres, we reach the highest point. I had had some fantasy that, from this vantage, I would see the continent laid out before me: the winding Amazon, the forests of Bolivia and Brazil. In fact, we are blanketed in heaving cloud and cannot see beyond the edge of the road. The top of the world is veiled and dim. Sometimes the mist parts enough to reveal giant beds of fleshy cacti, the sodden tufts of ichu grasses double my height.

We pass over to the eastern side of this great range. The downward journey is more fraught. Our destination is in the foothills. To get there, we must make a vertical descent of three and a half kilometres through water, mud and fallen rocks. I realise why the Toyota Hilux is such an iconic piece of engineering in these parts – to the extent that smaller cars and motorbikes display heart-shaped stickers saying 'Toyota Hilux Peru'. The 'double traction' is reassuring in this dynamic landscape, where nothing is stable – least of all the hopeful strip of man-made tarmac under our wheels.

It is as if nature is in a hurry – there is so much work to do, and the work is *moving water*. Waterfalls pour down the mountain slopes, streams cascade over the road, leaving crunchy deltas of pebbles and rocks. Everywhere you look, water is moving at enormous speed. All this water must flow east, away from the Andes. There is no outlet for it until it reaches the opposite side of the continent. The creature that will gather all these streams and rivers on its back, and transport them 3,000 kilometres to the Atlantic coast – that creature is the Amazon, whose mighty volume arouses terror, even at this distance.

Amid this endless flow, nothing is solid. Mud and rocks follow water down the mountainsides; sections of the road collapse. Driving here, you live your own death several times over. Not hours before our passage, massive boulders have dislodged from the slopes and fallen onto the road. Previous drivers have used their vehicles to push them aside just enough, but there has not yet been time for cranes and trucks to arrive. I am reminded of *Death in the Andes* by the Nobel Prize-winning Peruvian novelist Mario Vargas Llosa, in which huaycos or landslides become symptoms of the demonic powers governing these mountain heights: 'These hills are full of enemies . . . That's why there are so many accidents . . . Trucks that lose their brakes or drive off the road . . . They send down huaycos, too . . . Who else could loosen all that rock?'[3]

The slopes are steeper on this side. We descend so rapidly, I can feel the pressure mounting in my head. We pass below the treeline, and highland brush and grass gradually become woodland. Streams become rivers – churning, frothing, muddy rivers, tearing rocks and trees from the banks. The slopes acquire a covering of lush forest, which extends unbroken to the valley below. There are almost no people here. The rare houses are built only of what can easily be transported by truck: board and corrugated iron.

After another couple of hours, human systems resume. We hit a small town called Machente, where we are stopped at an army checkpoint. Passports are checked and we are waved on.

'They don't check much when you come in,' says Chacal. 'They're more interested in what you take out.'

This is the administrative gateway to the VRAEM – an acronym for Valle de los Ríos Apurímac, Ene y Mantaro (Valley of the Apurímac, Ene and Mantaro Rivers), a region which can only be accessed by long journeys over the Andes. The remoteness and rugged terrain of the VRAEM make law enforcement difficult, and crime and armed insurgency have flourished. Until the 1990s, there was an airport here, which became a major cocaine-distribution hub; it was shut down as part of the government's attempt to take back the region. Road is now the only way in. But because of the enormous natural barriers, the state's reach remains limited. The VRAEM remains a congenial refuge for illicit activities of all kinds.

Machente marks an ecological, as well as a political, frontier. The town sits about 1,200 metres above sea level, which marks the transition from airy montane forest to the lush lowland rainforest of the Andean foothills. As we drive out of the town, the mountains are behind us. We descend into the Apurímac valley, which is verdant beyond anything I have seen. This is the super-fertile band which locals call the *ceja de selva*: not the eye of the jungle, but the 'eyebrow'. Massive Andean cedars are ragged with vines and creepers. Graceful tara trees spread broad umbrellas of yellow blossom hung with woven nests of oropendola birds. Farms and gardens are bursting with cocoa pods, coconuts, papayas and countless varieties of banana. The road is strewn with fallen flowers and berries.

Another transition after Machente – the roads are suddenly terrible. An unbroken tarmac ribbon has brought us over the Andes, the edges scrupulously planted with eucalyptus to hold the soil in place. Down here, the tarmac disappears for long sections – another kind of state absence, perhaps. Rain carves the muddy tracks into valleys and hills; our Toyota lurches from one side to the other to avoid potholes. These are not roads for regular through-traffic. There are few cars and no freight trucks. Nearly everyone weaves through on a motorbike.

An hour after Machente, we finally encounter the broad and raging Apurímac. The other side of the valley is impossibly distant, and yet this great river is only a sub-sub-subtributary of the eventual Amazon. We drive along the river for some time, the road cut in places by white streams pouring into the valley. Our Toyota plunges in up to the wheel arches, while groups of halted motorbike and tuktuk riders impotently survey the torrent.

At some point, we turn on to a little track, and Chacal announces he is taking a detour to pick up a friend. We enter a village of banana trees and corrugated-iron houses. A man with a backpack is waiting for us. He slips his backpack under the plastic covering the back of the truck and jumps in. The coordination seems almost supernatural. The man is introduced as Chuzo. He is a similar age to Chacal, with a pockmarked face and a timid smile.

'Chuzo will help you a lot,' says Chacal vaguely.

We U-turn and rejoin the valley road. The sky is heavy with rain clouds, which appear yellow in the evening light; the hills are glowing.

'There,' says Chacal, pointing upwards. I lean forward to look up through the windscreen. There at last is the plant we have come to see. The slopes are carpeted with emerald-green coca bushes, which have shaped the culture of this valley for centuries and form the basis of its economy even today.

'See the brown patches too,' says Chacal. 'Those big brown scars on the hillside. There was coca there once. They put so many chemicals that the earth became completely polluted. Nothing grows there now. Coca destroys everything.'

I detect a powerful dislike for the plant.

Chacal talks about the forest that has been cut down for coca and the consequences for animal life. He talks about bears, monkeys, jaguars.

'Snakes are the most dangerous,' he says. 'Jaguars can kill, but they keep away from human beings.'

Chuzo wants to tell a story.

'Once I was transporting cocaine – this was ten years ago. I was one of the *mochileros*, the so-called backpackers, who transported coca paste into Brazil. We did all our walking at night.

'One of the men in our group fell behind. We didn't notice until we reached one of our rest points and realised he was not with us. It was too dark to look for him, so we decided to wait there until daylight. In the morning, we hid our backpacks in the woods and returned along the path to look for that man, thinking he must be lost. All we found was his bones. We thought he must have been eaten by a jaguar. His backpack was sitting there untouched, next to a tree.

'We shared the carrying of his backpack. But we could not abandon his remains. So we took his bones with us until we reached a town and could put them on a bus back home. We sent a note explaining to his family that he had been doing agricultural work in Bolivia, picking nuts, and he had been attacked and killed by a jaguar.'

'Was the dead man your friend?' I ask.

'You never know the other people in your group until you embark on the journey. But while you are travelling you are friends.'

'Did the traffickers provide any compensation?'

'They told us to tell his family he was harvesting nuts, and they would pay for his funeral. The family believed the story and didn't ask any questions. If they had known the truth, they would have asked for much more money.'

It begins to rain, and within seconds the downpour is full force. Water pours off trees and mountain slopes, turning the middle of the road into a gushing river. Daylight is disappearing and we struggle painfully along, a deafening drumming on the roof. Finally, after ten hours on the road, we arrive in the town where both Chacal and Chuzo live.

'Keep your phone in your pocket while you're here,' says Chacal, who has watched me photographing every detail of our journey. 'Don't take photographs in this town.'

I am reminded of the transit towns of the American West, as seen in old movies. Everything is makeshift; the well-clad façades disguise a jumble of poor-quality brick constructions. Houses and shops have steel front doors, which in turn are set into impregnable steel plates covering the ground floor. Even here, there is no tarmac on the road – a broad lake divides one row of shopfronts from the other. Street lighting is scarce and, in great contrast to other Peruvian towns I have seen, there is no street life. Illegal trade, and mutual suspicion, hang everywhere in the air.

We turn on to a main avenue. Next door to a ramshackle church – which has the words '*Jesús murió por ti*' ('Jesus died for you') scrawled in paint on the façade – is our hotel. Its blinding lights distinguish it from the shadowy surroundings. The lobby is plush, and there is a hint of the illicit: the marble, the chandeliers. I take the lift up to my room, which is cavernous. There are mirrors on the ceiling. The bathroom has a jacuzzi fit for ten people.

'I am an immigrant.'

I am sitting in the house of Carlos, a farmer in a nearby village.

Carlos is seventy years old. In his baseball cap and jeans, in the easy power of his physique, he looks twenty years younger. Because of his age, however, Carlos has adult memories of the tumult which took over this region in the 1980s.

'I came here with my family in 1970, when I was fifteen years old. We came from the *sierra*. From Andahuaylas.'

Most of the farmers in the VRAEM are 'immigrants' like Carlos. Until the 1960s, this area was inhabited almost exclusively by semi-nomadic Asháninka, Kakinte and Matsigenka peoples. In addition to hunting and gathering, they cultivated manioc and bananas for their own subsistence and tobacco for sale.

During the 1960s, the Peruvian state encouraged peasants from the highlands to settle in the eastern Andean lowlands as part of a grand development project – the aim being to integrate the Amazon and expand the agrarian frontier.[4] During the first presidency (1963–8) of Fernando Belaúnde Terry, the area across the peaks was recast as a 'land without men for men without land' – a formulation which erased the many indigenous people who lived there and legitimised large-scale in-migration.[5] State-backed transport projects and colonisation schemes drew thousands of highland families into the opened, previously isolated areas. Though they had no experience of the very different agriculture and lifestyle of the *selva*, these poor migrants were attracted by promises of spectacularly fertile land, and of the full penetration – at some point in the future – of infrastructure and markets. This policy also served to defuse gathering political tensions: amid intensified competition over cultivable land, highland peasants had begun to grab land from large landowners. By sending these communities into the lowlands, the state sought to ease the mounting pressure for land reform without altering existing patterns of land concentration.

The colonisation project accelerated deforestation and soil deterioration. The slash-and-burn clearing technique practised by Andean settlers, combined with poor soil quality and fragile ecological conditions, resulted in low productivity, and settlers needed increasingly large plots to sustain them. This contrasted with indigenous systems, whose smaller-scale shifting cultivation was embedded in a broader subsistence strategy that allowed for forest regeneration. Long-established indigenous groups often found their food systems seriously compromised. Some of these would themselves settle into sedentary farming, while others tried to preserve their lifestyles by withdrawing further into the forest.[6] Ultimately, it would be impossible for these communities to escape the unrest introduced by migrant farmers. Attempts to secure some restoration of their legal rights go on even today, on the whole without success.*

'My parents died together, leaving behind nine children. Our land was too small to feed us. One of my older brothers used to play sport with some farmers who talked to him about this place – here. They said it was beautiful, and there was a lot of food. Two of my brothers came here, they bought land from another farmer, and then they came back to get us.

'We all walked here together. The journey was five hundred kilometres down the mountain. My youngest brother was two years old – we took turns carrying him. We set out with corn and cheese, but eventually it ran out, and we had to knock at the doors of houses and ask for food to eat.

'We were tired, we wanted to stop, and the eldest brothers constantly encouraged us, saying, "You're going to eat beautiful fruit when you arrive. A lot of fruit. Let's keep going!" After many

* In Peru, around 8 per cent of coca cultivation occurs on indigenous lands, particularly those of the Asháninka communities. Typically cultivated on small plots, coca provides income for basic needs such as education and healthcare. At the same time, coca production is embedded within a moral economy that emphasises sustainable land use and cultural values, distinguishing Asháninka practices from those of settlers. However, this involvement also generates tensions, including land disputes, the growing influence of settlers over territory and leadership, and the weakening of indigenous governance, often exacerbated by the state's limited or biased intervention. See 'Monitoreo de la superficie cultivada con arbusto de hoja de coca en producción, en territorios de pueblos indígenas u originarios, 2020' (Lima: DEVIDA, 2021), cited in Maritza Paredes and Alvaro Pastor, 'Illicit Crops in the Frontier Margins: Amazonian Indigenous Livelihoods and the Expansion of Coca in Peru', *Journal of Peasant Studies*, Vol. 51, No. 4 (2024), 960–81.

days, we arrived, late at night, and we said, "Where is the fruit?" My brothers said there were dangerous animals, and we should not go out at night. In the morning, we went and found bananas. That was our first meal in this place. And we began to discuss how we would organise our life. What school we would go to, how we would work, who we would marry.'

The previous farmer had cultivated cocoa, whose secrets were unfamiliar to Carlos and his family. Local Asháninka people showed them how to tend the trees and harvest the pods. They learned the techniques and began to clear surrounding trees to expand their cultivation. Carlos remembers the mystery of the dense forest, filled with jaguars, parrots and fruit. They developed a close relationship with their Asháninka neighbours and helped them regularly on their farms.

When Carlos left school, he wanted to go to university in Ayacucho, but he felt he did not know enough to pass the entrance exam. So he decided to go there to see if any students would help him study for it. He met a young academic who was particularly enthusiastic about mentoring him. That academic would subsequently become the most notorious figure in all Peru. His name was Abimael Guzmán.

'I believed in him initially,' says Carlos, 'because he used to say many good things. He was reading Mao and Marx, and I wanted to be part of that. But my objective was to get into university and to get a higher education. He kept inviting me to political meetings, he showed me maps of the campaigns he was planning, he said, "You can be one of us." I said, "I am not here for that." '

Dismayed that world Communism had become passive and reformist, Guzmán created an organisation whose aim was to occupy Peru – physically and spiritually – and so to open a *sendero luminoso* – or 'shining path' – to global revolution (Figure 21). Inspired by the ideology and military tactics of China's Mao, Guzmán thought of himself as a peasant leader. Promising to confiscate and redistribute the estates of large landowners, to bring down the corrupt state and to put peasants in charge of their own affairs, he found considerable support among small farmers. But Guzmán's vision also had an Andean twist. Appealing to Peru's indigenous peoples, whom he believed to be the true revolutionaries, he held up the pre-Columbian Incan empire as the precursor of the socialist paradise to come. His struggle was intended to undo the Spanish conquest and every vestige of capitalist imperialism.

By 1992, when anti-terrorism agents finally extracted Guzmán from his hideout in Lima, tens of thousands of Peruvians had died in the violence unleashed by his guerrilla organisation.

'Ayacucho was the centre of the movement, and we heard the news from there. They killed anyone who opposed them. They went to villages and said, "I want your hat or your shoes," and they shot you if you refused. They needed soldiers, so they abducted young boys from their families.'

In truth, Guzmán was a poor student of Mao. His forces treated peasants with ruthlessness and contempt, and villages were terrified at their approach.

'The terrorism started in 1981 in Ayacucho, but it took some time to reach here. During that time, I married, and wanted a farm of my own. We bought some land further up the Apurímac River, about forty kilometres from here. We had eighteen hectares there, and we were growing cocoa.* It was there I first met the Shining Path.

'When they came to the village, they called the locals for a meeting in a school. They explained why the government was against us, and what they were going to do. They wanted people from our village to sit on their council. They asked me to be one of the representatives. They said, "You will organise everything. You will be in charge."'

Carlos is smiling as he tells this story. A broad, charismatic smile. It's easy to understand why, as a young man, he would have stood out.

'I knew what kind of people they were. They said they wanted to solve our problems, to give us a better life, to make us equal to everyone else. But their words did not match their actions. They

---

* In Spanish, the crop and the bean used to make chocolate are referred to as *cacao*. I translate this as 'cocoa', following British usage.

were killing people. If you refused to join them, they would take you to the forest and execute you.

'I stood up in the meeting and said, "We want to belong to you. But we need more education about your principles. Could you come later to give us some classes?" That was my strategy. I was lying just to gain time. They went away, and I told my wife we had to leave immediately.

'She didn't want to go. The cocoa was nearly ready to harvest. She was worried we had nothing to eat. She was more concerned about such things than her own life. I said, "We won't be able to say no if they come back again. We have to leave now." '

The couple's first son was twelve years old, prime recruiting age for the Shining Path. Carlos preferred to lose everything rather than compromise their safety. Late that night, they borrowed a small boat from a neighbour, rowed four hours down the Apurímac and moved in with his brother, next door to where we are sitting now.

The terror of Shining Path fighters (Senderistas) arriving in small towns and villages has become a set piece of Peruvian cultural memory.* Their assaults were the spur – in Carlos's life, as in the lives of thousands of other Peruvian peasants – to large-scale coca cultivation.

'We needed to defend ourselves. No one else would defend us. We needed guns. So everybody started growing coca, which was quick to harvest, and the money was good for buying guns. I did the same as everyone else.'

The arrival of the Shining Path coincided with the cocaine explosion in the United States and with the concomitant rise of the Colombian cocaine cartels. As Peruvian peasants sought

---

* Mario Vargas Llosa is only one of many Peruvians to have portrayed the scene. Politically conservative, Vargas Llosa abhorred the movement; his novel *Death in the Andes* likens the bloodletting of the 1980s and 1990s to much more ancient Andean traditions of human sacrifice: 'They came at first light, before the campesinos [peasants] had left to tend their fields . . . They posted guards at all points of egress while synchronised columns walked along the five parallel streets of shacks and cottages . . .' Mario Vargas Llosa, *Death in the Andes* (Spanish: *Lituma en los Andes*), trans. Edith Grossman (London: Faber & Faber, 1996), 60–71.

connections to cash and arms, those cartels extended their networks into the VRAEM. The region's physical inaccessibility, which was one reason the Shining Path were so entrenched there in the first place, made it an ideal location for their activities. By the late 1980s, when Carlos began to cultivate coca, Peru was supplying as much as 70 per cent of the global cocaine industry's raw input.[7]

'In our village, the self-defence league instructed everyone to become coca growers – *cocaleros*. We bought seeds from farmers who were already growing it on the Ayacucho side. There were people who came from other cities, not locals – they used to buy our coca. That was all I knew. I didn't ask who they were. But probably they were from Colombian cartels. With the money, we used to buy weapons from traffickers who turned up here.'

The so-called *rondas campesinas de autodefensa*, or 'peasant self-defence leagues' have become legendary. In places like the VRAEM, they came to symbolise the self-reliance of farmers menaced by ruthless forces and abandoned by the state. For it was soon apparent not only that the army was incapable of providing security but also that it viewed all farmers – since the Shining Path claimed to be a 'peasant movement' – as potential terrorists. Many farmers found themselves in the middle of the struggle which dominated the countryside in the 1980s and 1990s: if they expressed support for the Shining Path, they were killed by the state, and vice versa.

The movement did not end with Abimael Guzmán's capture in 1992. Shining Path factions continued to fight, and there were violent state reprisals throughout the authoritarian presidency of Alberto Fujimori (1990–2000). According to the official Truth and Reconciliation Committee Report of 2003, about 70,000 people were killed or disappeared between 1980 and 2000; state forces were responsible for nearly a third of that number. 'The victims of the violence were primarily poor peasants,' the report says, 'with a high proportion of indigenous identity, living in rural areas distant from the centres of power.' Some indigenous groups, such as the Asháninka, lost more than a tenth of their population.[8]

'We taught ourselves how to use guns,' says Carlos. 'Everyone learned – men and women. We were not very sophisticated. But we were very brave. We were so brave that the army asked us to defend them, which was the opposite of what we expected. When we went out on patrol, our men were in front and the army followed behind.'*

Some peasants became talented military strategists, and the self-defence leagues achieved surprising victories. In a series of bloody battles, they drove the Shining Path back. Those battles entailed lengthy expeditions, which took farmers away from their land for weeks on end. Coca, once again, was the magic ingredient. Coca bushes require little care; coca not only paid for arms, therefore, but allowed coca growers to leave their farms and become soldiers. The crop came to symbolise the spirit of peasants abandoned by the state but surviving nonetheless. Even the Colombian cartels realised they could not fight the peasant leagues and gave up all idea of conquering the region. Instead, they gave cash and weapons to the peasants and relied on their superior force.[9]

Meanwhile, the economy of the VRAEM was becoming entirely criminalised. Shining Path gangs had also turned to coca to fund their operations, and many outside adventurers arrived to profit from the trade.[10] Throughout the forests, people dug maceration pits – *pozos,* in local slang – where coca leaves were stirred with kerosene and sulphuric acid and concentrated into cocaine paste. The region filled up with cocaine processors, traffickers and militias.

'A lot of people from the cities and the highlands came to colonise the land. They started deforesting everything. They dumped great quantities of kerosene and acid on the land. I used to go to the river nearby and catch crabs and fish, but everything became polluted. You couldn't drink the water any more. People were interested in money, they had no interest in nature.

* For a vivid account of how Peruvian peasant communities organised to defend themselves against the Shining Path, see Steven T. Zech, 'Between Two Fires: Civilian Resistance during Internal Armed Conflict in Peru' (PhD dissertation, University of Washington, 2016). The author shows that, while some communities built highly effective self-defence forces, others could not. The variations depended on such factors as local leadership, social cohesion and shared understandings of the conflict.

'In 1994, I stopped growing coca. You need many people to harvest coca, and they used to contaminate my land, throwing trash and plastic bottles. I didn't like that. I switched back completely to cocoa.'

Carlos wants to show me his farm. We walk out into the glorious morning. The land slopes upwards from the house, covered in cocoa trees. The pods are big and ripe – some yellow, some the colour of red wine. Crested chickens are foraging beneath. Carlos strides ahead of me in white wellington boots, which propel him more quickly than my trainers. He turns to wait for me, caressing a tree trunk.

'This is a *cedro rojo*,' he says. 'This is the tree they like to cut down in the forest, because it has the hardest wood. You can see how tall it is. Its canopy spreads over everything else, sheltering the cocoa from the sun. Its leaves fall all over the farm, making natural compost. It's a beautiful tree.'

We walk on the ground of leaves, ducking under the low-standing cocoa trees, whose glossy pods jut out from the trunks. There is a banana tree, a busy wooden beehive.

'There,' says Carlos. 'That is coca.'

There is one coca bush on this cocoa farm. A shaft of light illuminates the bush, whose symmetrical leaves are oval and vibrant green.

'Have you had coca tea?' Carlos asks. 'You're a writer. It will help your concentration.'

Part of the farm is devoted to cocoa processing. Carlos is proud of his installation. He takes me into a plastic tent, where cocoa beans are drying on long racks. He holds the beans up for me to smell: a heady fragrance of earth and chocolate.

'We extract the beans from the pods,' says Carlos, 'and we pour the juice back onto the land. It contains good nutrients.'

We wander back to the house, where we meet Carlos's daughter. Dressed in jeans and a T-shirt, Flora is in her thirties. She is busy packaging glass jars of cocoa powder into boxes.

Flora asks if I would like some coffee, but Carlos wants me to try coca tea. A few minutes later, I am sitting on the terrace with a steaming cup of the green brew.

'It's better than coffee,' says Carlos. 'Coffee gives you energy, but it makes you anxious. This is relaxing.'

I take a sip. The taste is vegetal and agreeably bitter.

'One cup like this when you have to concentrate hard,' says Carlos, 'and you'll see how good it is.'

'This is made from our own bush,' Flora adds. 'You can find the leaves in any market. But you have to be careful. Sometimes they're treated with poisonous chemicals.'

Flora and her father have worked together to process and commercialise their cocoa.

'We were having a hard time with cocoa prices,' she says. 'The lowest point was 2017, when the price went down to about one dollar a kilo. It was impossible to make money at that level. We started transforming the raw cocoa into new products. Pure cocoa powder, and bars of finished chocolate.

'Now the situation has changed again. Cocoa prices have reached eleven dollars a kilo. That's because of global warming in West Africa. Their crop is getting burned. So there is great demand for our cocoa. Our soil is excellent, and we have good local knowledge.'

I begin to feel the effect of the tea. It is very mild, as Carlos promised. My mind feels clearer. As if there were some cloudy glass between me and myself, which has just been cleaned.

I think of what Carlos said at the beginning of our conversation.

'You called yourself an immigrant,' I say. 'You came here when you were fifteen, and you have farmed here all your life. Are you still an immigrant?'

He laughs.

'This is my home,' he says. 'But I have never got used to the food here. You learn your relationship to food and to the earth when you are a little child. It never happens a second time.'

Plants cannot run from their enemies; they must deter them. During their millions of years of defensive experiments, several have independently learned to produce chemicals from the family known as tropane alkaloids, which overstimulate the nervous systems of would-be pests.

Human beings have always been drawn to those plants for their psychoactive properties – using their extracts, variously, as medicines, narcotics and poisons. They have often acquired an occult reputation, as is apparent in some of the names: Angel's Trumpet, Devil's Trumpet, Deadly Nightshade. Dramatic and mysterious, they have also featured regularly in literature: in Shakespeare's *Othello,* Iago declares he will do such things to the hero that not even the mandrake (L. *Mandragora officinarum*) – whose root contains a powerfully hallucinogenic tropane alkaloid – will be sufficient to dull the pain:

> Not poppy, nor mandragora,
> Nor all the drowsy syrups of the world,
> Shall ever medicine thee to that sweet sleep
> Which thou ow'dst yesterday.

One of the reasons the coca bush (L. *Erythroxylon coca*) requires little tending is that its leaves are impregnated with a tropane alkaloid. In humans, cocaine can produce euphoric mind alteration. It also enhances endurance and concentration and boosts the body's capacity to cope with hunger, sickness and altitude. The ability of human beings to live and labour in the harsh Andean region to which it is native has always been tied, in fact, to the coca bush.

Across history, the normal way to consume cocaine has been to chew the coca leaf. The alkaloid agent is not absorbed, however, if it is too acidic; in order for the leaves to deliver their full power, they must be mixed with alkaline. When archaeologists discover coca leaves in close proximity to *llipta* – an alkaline powder manufactured from slaked lime – it is certain evidence, therefore, of coca chewing. Such discoveries have been made in sites as old as 8,500 years.[11]

Most pre-Incan societies seem to have made ritualistic use of coca – as we can surmise from the frequent appearance, in Andean sculpture, of human figures, especially priests, one of whose cheeks bulges with a wad of leaves.[12] Coca was important enough to Wari society (central Andes, 500–1000 CE) that the dead were buried with coca leaves, along with other ritual offerings.[13] Ceramics produced by the coastal Moche nation (100–800 CE) frequently depict coca consumption; the prestige associated with this activity is reflected in the richness of the silver-and-copper containers in which the *llipta* accompaniment was stored (Figure 22).

In the early fifteenth century, the highland society known as the Inca began a process of imperial expansion. Absorbing other nations through a combination of diplomacy and warfare, it soon created the largest political entity ever seen in the Americas until that time. Coca, which was revered both by the Inca and by most of their subjects, became a powerful source of imperial unification.

The expanding Inca state quickly established a monopoly over the coca supply. Broad tracts of the eastern Andean slopes – including the Apurímac and Ene river valleys – were colonised in order to establish state coca plantations; citizens of the empire fulfilled their tax obligations by providing labour to these plantations for set periods each year. As the Inca crossed the Andean peaks and conquered the western valleys, one of their first actions was to take over the coca plantations which already existed there.[14] Provincial populations also paid tribute to the Inca in coca – as well as maize, textiles and other essential supplies.[15]

The distinctive feature of the Inca state was its ability not only to ensure adequate production of essential commodities and to collect them into centralised stockpiles, but also to redistribute those stockpiles over great distances. Just as the classical Chinese and Cambodian empires derived their prestige from irrigation, we might say that the prestige of the Inca was derived from *distribution*. With no money system, the empire did not possess complex markets; instead, the state played the leading role in ensuring supply met demand. To this end, the Inca built a sophisticated transport network, consisting of 40,000 kilometres of imperial highways. These had inns at intervals of twenty-two kilometres, which was equivalent to a day's march – for the empire's goods and information were largely carried by humans on foot. Until the arrival of the

Spanish, there were no horses in the Americas. Llamas were used as pack animals, but they could not be ridden, nor did the Incas use wheeled carts. 'Backpackers' have walked the Andes for centuries.

Each inn was accompanied by a specialised warehouse known in the Inca's Quechua language as *qullqa*.[16] Built of stone and thatched with ichu grass, these buildings were built to a standard size; in busier locations, several units might be arranged side by side. The Inca themselves did not write, but fascinated Spanish invaders sent back detailed descriptions of *qullqa* to their royal sponsors:

> Warehouses full of blankets, wool, weapons, metals and clothing and everything that is grown and manufactured in this realm . . . There is a house where more than 100,000 dried birds are kept, because their feathers, which are of many colours, are used to make garments . . . There are shields, bucklers, beams for roofing houses, knives, and other tools; sandals and breastplates for provisioning warriors in such quantity that it is beyond comprehension.[17]

Because of its essential role in Andean societies, the Inca's distribution of coca established them as lifegivers.* Most religious rituals could not take place without coca; certainly the leaf was indispensable to the Inca's own religion, which was exported all over the empire.[18] Vast quantities of leaves were burned as offerings to gods and ancestors; coca leaves were chewed during religious ceremonies; during burials, they were placed in the mouths of the dead; they were used to tell the future; and they were fed to victims of sacrifice – both animal and human – in their final days.[19]

---

* There has been considerable debate about which classes and communities had access to coca during the Inca period. The traditional view was that coca was distributed among elites as a marker of hospitality and alliance, and that other classes had little access to it. That view was challenged by John Murra in 1986, and subsequent scholars have found coca to have a more general and varied role than previously thought. See John V. Murra, 'Notes on Pre-Columbian Cultivation of Coca Leaf' in Deborah Pacini and Christine Franquemont (eds), *Coca and Cocaine: Effects on People and Policy in Latin America*, Cultural Survival Report No. 23, Cambridge, MA: Cultural Survival Inc. and Latin American Studies Program, Cornell University, 1986.

But coca also had everyday uses. It was an essential energy supplement for physical workers, rather as tea and sugar were essential to Europe's industrial revolution.[20] Among the many groups who received coca supplies from the state were soldiers, the messengers who walked and ran the mountain routes and, crucially, workers in the imperial salt, cinnabar and silver mines, some of which were at an altitude of 4,800 metres.[21] All in all, the Inca's ability to dispense coca sustained the spiritual and physical life of their society and created a reciprocal bond between state and people. We can go this far: the Inca social contract was symbolised in coca, which was given out by the state in exchange for labour, loyalty and religious observance.

The Spanish occupation of the Inca empire began in 1532, under the command of Francisco Pizarro. As they set about exploring their new territory, the invaders were initially perplexed by coca. Pedro Cieza de León, an early traveller, expressed characteristic bemusement at a form of ingestion for which no parallel existed in European tradition: 'The Indians carry this coca in their mouths; from morning until they lie down to sleep, they never take it out . . . It prevents them from feeling hungry, and gives them great vigour and strength.'[22] As the leaf's relationship with ancestor worship and human sacrifice became evident, the Catholic church decided it was an abomination.[23] In 1569, one year before the Inquisition was imported from Spain, the Audiencia Real in Lima – the highest court in the Spanish Viceroyalty of Peru (a vast territory which included all or some of modern Peru, Bolivia, Ecuador, Colombia, Chile and Argentina) – condemned and outlawed the use of coca.[24] That such edicts were to be repeated several times over the years demonstrates how obstinate was local attachment to the leaf. Spanish administrators expressed concern that Peruvian converts, even as they called upon God and Jesus, continued to 'offer secret sacrifices, and carry out other ceremonies with guinea pigs, coca, fat and other things'.[25]

As the Spanish developed their colony, however, they realised coca could bestow enormous practical advantages – precisely those same advantages previously exploited by the Inca. Under Viceroy

Francisco Álvarez de Toledo, who took up his position in 1569, the Spanish abandoned their opposition to coca and instead began to tax it. De Toledo, who supervised the territory's formal industrialisation, developed the silver mines in Potosí into a huge complex consisting of parallel silver and mercury mines – since mercury was necessary for extracting silver from ore – to which long chains of agriculture, manufacturing and transport delivered food and other essential supplies. As he brought slaves and forced labourers to work the complex, it became clear that nothing would function without coca. Silver mining was dangerous and exhausting and took place at a great altitude; coca helped to suppress appetite and boost energy.

Continuing ecclesiastical opposition notwithstanding, the Spanish now became the world's leading coca merchants. Taking over the coca plantations, they organised mule transport up to the mines, where daily supplies were distributed to workers. By the late

Indigenous people working in a mine in Potosí, New Spain (now Bolivia). Engraving by Theodor de Bry, circa 1590.

1500s, the Peruvian coca trade employed about 2,000 Spaniards and generated over 1 million pesos per year – second only to brandy.[26] The mining complex absorbed nearly all this production, generating revenues that excited even Spanish missionaries. 'It seems almost fabulous,' wrote one Jesuit, 'but in truth the trafficke of Coca in Potosí doth yeareley amount to above half a million of dollars.'[27] The significance of this confluence of coca and silver is difficult to exaggerate. Several historians have argued that the fantastic quantities of silver mined by Spain in the Americas – which expanded the European economy and provided the foundation for such emerging financial centres as Antwerp and Genoa – marked the beginning of global capitalism.[28] The inception of the modern world, then, was fuelled by the coca leaf or, more specifically, by its active ingredient: cocaine.

Despite their local success, coca merchants in the Viceroyalty of Peru were unable to develop international markets for their production. Unlike other American discoveries – most famously, chocolate and tobacco – coca failed to find European consumers.[29] There were obvious practical reasons: dried coca leaves tended to lose their potency during the long sea voyage, arriving in Spain as mere botanical trash. But even within Peru the Spanish administrators shunned coca. The ritual of chewing leaves with added lime powder did not correspond to the theatrics of European conviviality. And coca never lost its religious taint: it belonged to the unholy and sacrilegious and could not be incorporated into Christian culture.

It was not until the nineteenth century, therefore, and the advent of a more scientific form of curiosity that Europeans began to experiment with *Erythroxylon coca*. In the 1850s, Paolo Mantegazza, an Italian neurologist and anthropologist, undertook an Andean voyage during which he emulated locals by chewing the leaf. The quasi-mystical reports of his psychedelic explorations helped to establish a literary genre that would become a Western staple over the following century:

> I had full consciousness of myself, yet it seemed I was cut off from the external world, and I saw the most bizarre images, the most

Women gathering coca leaves. Illustration from John R. Jackson, *Commercial Botany of the Nineteenth Century* (London: Cassell & Company, 1890).

> splendid in colour and form, that can possibly be imagined . . . I laughed at those poor mortals condemned to live in this vale of tears, while I, borne on the wings of two coca leaves, went flying through the expanses of 77,438 worlds, each more splendid than the last . . . God is unjust, because he has made man incapable of living forever while chewing coca. I would prefer a life of ten years with coca to one of 100,000 . . . centuries without coca.[30]

A year after Mantegazza's description, a German PhD student at the University of Göttingen became the first to isolate the coca bush's narcotic ingredient.[31] Albert Niemann had access to leaves brought back by the SMS *Novara*, an Austrian steamship which circumnavigated the earth between 1857 and 1859. The leaves were among 22,000 botanical specimens collected on this voyage, and they were carefully stored in airtight containers to permit scientific analysis back home. Calling his discovery 'cocaine', Niemann was struck by another property of the drug: 'Its solutions . . . produce on the tongue a peculiar feeling of numbness, which is accompanied by a sensation of cold.'[32] For a few decades, cocaine was the focus of important experiments in anaesthesia, enabling breakthroughs in ophthalmic and dental surgery.

But in the public imagination cocaine was more exciting for its propensity not to numb but to stimulate. Mantegazza himself had proposed that modern societies might become healthier and more industrious if they would listen to the wisdom of the ancients: 'All [his] feats the Indian accomplishes with coca, and without it he rebels against his master and against life . . . [It is true] that coca sustains life by rendering man capable of a greater expenditure of nervous force . . . I have used coca in all cases of nervous prostration, of general weakness, of hysteria, of hypochondria, and of weariness of life.'[33] Inspired by these words, a French entrepreneur named Angelo Mariani began in 1863 to produce a tonic made of Bordeaux wine and Peruvian coca. His Vin Tonique Mariani contained 250 milligrams of cocaine per litre, and Mariani was able to get leading artists and scientists to testify to its benefits for their work – among them, Sarah Bernhardt, Thomas Edison, Charles Gounod, Jules Verne and H. G. Wells.[34] 'I am obliged to send you a thousand thanks, dear Monsieur Mariani,' wrote the novelist Émile Zola in 1895, 'for this wine of youth which produces life, which conserves energy for those who expend it, and restores it to those who no longer have it.'

Reportedly enjoyed by the queen of England, the tsar of Russia, the shah of Persia, the president of the United States and the pope, Mariani wine helped to incite a cocaine craze (Figure 23).[35] This was an era when there was considerable anxiety, in both Europe and the United States, that modern life was exhausting the human motor. The New York neurologist George Beard devoted a book to what he called 'American nervousness', which he defined as a 'deficiency of nerve-force' caused by 'modern civilisation' with its 'steam-power, the periodical press, the telegraph, the sciences, and the mental activity of women'.[36] Cocaine seemed the ideal antidote to such modern enervation. 'Long-lasting, intensive mental or physical work', wrote Sigmund Freud in his influential 1884 paper

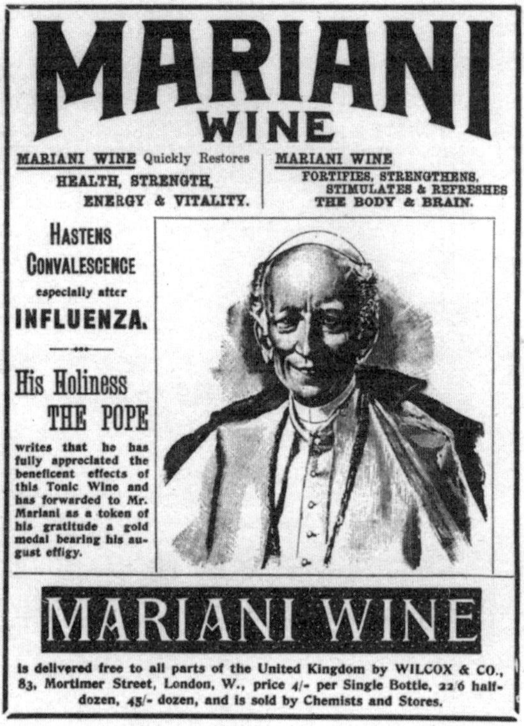

British advertisement for cocaine-laced Vin Mariani.

'On Coca', 'can be performed without fatigue; it is as though the need for food and sleep . . . were completely banished.'[37] Nor did Freud detect anything unnatural or toxic about cocaine. True to its primitive origins, it dispelled the consequences of modern stress and restored him to his natural state: 'The mood induced by coca . . . is due not so much to direct stimulation as to the disappearance of elements . . . which cause depression.'[38] Freud recommended coca as a therapy for all manner of physical and mental ailments.

By the end of the nineteenth century, cocaine was widely available in European and American pharmacies. It was packed as lozenges, tablets, mouth drops and chewing gum; for those who preferred to inhale it, there were snuff, fine powder, nasal sprays and cocaine cigarettes; more dedicated consumers could purchase

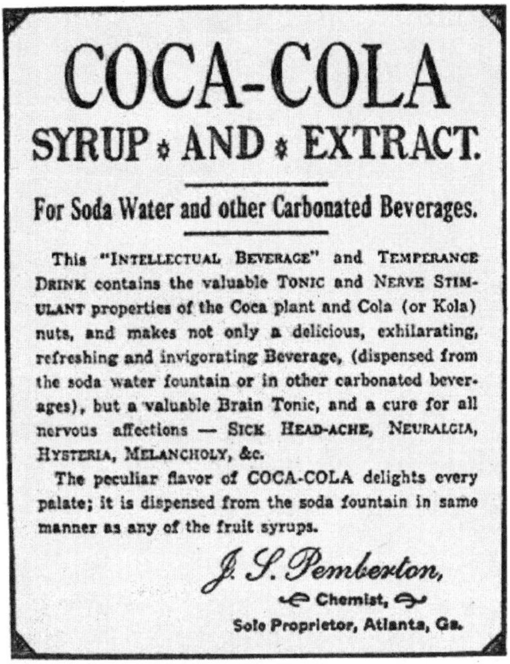

In addition to its health benefits, the 'temperance drink' Coca-Cola was sold as an alternative to alcohol. Trade advertisement, 1890s.

cocaine solution for intravenous injection. Cocaine became a mass-market product – this was the era of Coca-Cola, which was created in 1885, partly in response to the success of Vin Mariani. Combining the therapeutic benefits of Peruvian coca with the arousing power of the West African kola nut – which contained caffeine – Coca-Cola's 'brain tonic' was safe for children and acceptable to the great numbers of Europeans and Americans who shunned alcohol in those years. 'Coca-Cola raked in sales of $519,200 by 1900 . . . and more than $10 million by 1910.'[39]

In 1890, when cocaine was at the peak of its prestige, the British writer Arthur Conan Doyle dramatised its allure in a dialogue between the fictional detective Sherlock Holmes and Watson, his friend and a medical doctor. In response to Watson's disapproval, Holmes expressed his desire for 'mental exaltation' – a desire shared by many real-life intellectuals, celebrities and bohemians of his time:

> Sherlock Homes took his bottle from the corner of the mantelpiece and his hypodermic syringe from its neat morocco case . . . Three times a day for many months I had witnessed this performance, but custom had not reconciled my mind to it . . .
>
> 'It is cocaine,' he said, 'a seven-percent solution. Would you care to try it?'
>
> 'No, indeed,' I answered, brusquely . . . 'Your brain may, as you say, be roused and excited, but it is a pathological and morbid process which . . . may at last leave a permanent weakness . . .'
>
> 'My mind,' he said, 'rebels at stagnation . . . I abhor the dull routine of existence. I crave for mental exaltation.'[40]

In the long term, it was Watson's view that prevailed. The reality of cocaine use was already quite different from Sherlock Holmes's disciplined experiments – especially in the United States, where the drug was cheapest and most heavily promoted. Doctors themselves were among the most vulnerable: a series of hushed scandals broke, in 1898, into a long feature in the *Medical News* entitled 'The Abuse and Dangers of Cocaine', which described the fate of a physician who developed 'an irresistible craving for the drug and abandoned himself entirely to its toxic influence'. Having 'lost his practice [and] squandered his property', he ended up working as an attendant in the asylum where his life had been saved.[41]

By 1902 the American Pharmaceutical Association could estimate that there were 200,000 cocaine addicts in the United States.[42] Most were middle class, but the greatest concerns were raised by working-class, and particularly African-American, addiction. White bosses in the South had discovered – as had Spanish conquerors before them – that cocaine brought significant productivity gains and begun distributing it to black crews on cotton plantations and railway lines. Addiction produced a host of further social diseases, as *Everyday Life* magazine pointed out in 1909: 'Squalor, poverty, starvation, theft, prostitution and murder: these are the inevitable concomitants of cocaine.'[43] 'Cocaine-crazed' was added to the vocabulary of race and class fear. A pharmaceutical trade journal warned of 'the widespread addiction of the coloured and vicious white population of the larger cities to cocaine'.[44] Readers of a 1914 *New York Times* feature – 'Negro Cocaine "Fiends" are a New Southern Menace' – learned that African-American men derived from the drug such superhuman powers that even guns designed for big-game hunting could not arrest their murderous 'cocaine frenzy'.[45]

Legislation was inevitable. A few months after the *New York Times* report, Congress passed the Harrison Narcotics Act, which made cocaine a controlled substance in the United States. Four years later, a Dangerous Drugs Act was passed in the United Kingdom, where London circles had recently been rocked by the media sensation of Billie Carleton – a celebrity actress and singer who, at the age of twenty-two, died of a cocaine overdose in her room in the Savoy Hotel. By the time of the Geneva Opium Convention of 1925, which required national governments jointly to control the production, trafficking and use of opium and cocaine, nearly every major nation had introduced similar legislation. The celebrity tonic Vin Mariani was discontinued in 1914; between 1903 and 1929, all cocaine content was gradually removed from Coca-Cola.

All this had dramatic consequences in Peru, principal engine of the international cocaine boom. In the wake of Freud's endorsement in 1884 and the ensuing experiments with cocaine as a surgical anaesthetic, Peruvian elites began to see their botanical heritage as the means to develop their economy into a modern, scientific, industrial powerhouse. Large landowners, whose coffee and sugar-cane plantations were already connected to merchant houses in Lima, were encouraged to develop commercial-grade coca estates. Investments were also made in industrial processing, where Peru was at a significant disadvantage vis-à-vis the European powers. Two years after Albert Niemann had named the active ingredient in the coca leaf, the Merck company of Germany had developed an industrial process for extracting pristine cocaine hydrochloride. Britain, the Netherlands, France, Germany and the United States quickly embarked on various forms of 'botanical imperialism'; all wanted access to raw coca leaves in order to develop high-value pharmaceutical processing in their countries.[46] The Peruvian chemist Alfredo Bignon (1843–1908) considered the rich history of coca to be his country's gift to the modern world and sought ways to ensure that processing profits benefited Peruvians themselves.[47] In 1885, he developed a process for transforming raw coca into a crude paste known today as *pasta básica de cocaína*: 'an odorous, yellowish, semirefined 50–80 percent sulphate-cocaine cake that shipped easily and retained full potency'.[48] Using easily available inputs such as kerosene, soda ash and sulphuric acid, his low-tech process could be commercialised in the Andean heartlands. Since one kilo of paste held the cocaine content of about 200 kilos of leaves, Peruvian cocaine paste became an essential resource for Germany's pharmaceutical companies.

Physically closer to Latin America, where they also enjoyed deeper political connections, American cocaine manufacturers continued to import coca leaves, bypassing Peru's intermediate production.[49] The American boom was fuelled not by Peruvian industry but by Peruvian landowners, whose annual exports of coca leaves surpassed 1,000 tonnes in the early 1900s. The fact that this enormous volume produced smaller revenues than cocaine paste – whose production never exceeded eleven tonnes – demonstrates how much value was added by industrial processing.[50] That much was clear, also, to well-financed German industrialists who, before long, set up their own factories in Peru, some of which improved Bignon's process so far that their paste was 90 to 96 per cent pure. By the 1890s, German and British interests had displaced Peru's own processors, and the dream of a cocaine-powered national emergence had faded.

At any rate, the global boom, as we have seen, was short-lived. The destruction of the international trading system during the First World War, followed by the criminalisation of cocaine in most major markets, led to the collapse of Peruvian coca. Landowners and factory owners sought ways for the government to protect their commerce, but there was simply no demand – and even Peru's own elites had begun to turn against cocaine. Many farmers left the land

1. Peasants, king and God. In the background is the Sainte Chapelle, private royal chapel and repository of Christ's crown of thorns. From the *Très Riches Heures du Duc de Berry*, 1410s.

2. In 1968, at the peak of 'modernisation', Western children were taught how lucky they were to have been saved from peasant savagery. In this page from an educational magazine, a woman tries to protect a church from peasants brandishing sickles, scythes, hoes and pitchforks.

3. 'The Hongwu Emperor', unknown artist. The founder of the Ming Dynasty was a peasant rebel who restored the age-old Chinese agrarian system.

4. Richard II meeting with the rebels of the Peasants' Revolt of 1381. Illustration from Froissart's *Chronicles*, Paris, early fifteenth century. So formidable were the reports of this assault on power that the French illustrator depicts the rebels not as a hastily assembled peasant band, but as a fully provisioned army.

5. 'The Last of the Clan' by Thomas Faed, 1856. The painting depicts the exodus of the Highland peasants. A group of people watch the departure of an emigrant ship for the colonies, as a man is untying the rope that connects the ship to the shore.

6. 'Voltaire Conversing with the Peasants of Ferney' by Jean Huber, 1770.

7. 'View of the Queen's Hamlet' by Henri Courvoisier-Voisin, c. 1800.

8. 'This won't last for ever', anonymous French engraver, 1789. Harassed by his labours and by the assaults of heraldic beasts, the peasant wears the Phrygian cap of freedom – symbol of the revolution – while self-contented members of the First and Second Estates look on.

9. 'The Angelus' by Jean-François Millet, 1857–59.

10. 'Breton women at the "pardon"' by Pascal Dagnan-Bouveret, 1887.

11. 'Religious Procession in Kursk Governate' by Ilya Repin, c. 1880. Tolstoy was among the few to appreciate this painting, which made clear both the poor condition of the peasantry and the state surveillance accompanying their celebrations.

12. 'A Shy Peasant' by Ilya Repin, 1872. Repin was one of the first to paint an actual portrait of a peasant: an individual human being removed from land and labour.

13. 'Peasants' by Kazimir Malevich, 1930. Painted during collectivisation, the image shows steel-headed figures without gender or history. New humans: *modern* peasants, part of the Soviet economic machine.

14. ‘The Kanheri caves on the island of Salsette, near Bombay, Maharashtra’ by Thomas and William Daniell, coloured aquatint, 1800. Carved into the bare rock of the Borivali Hills, this complex of 109 Buddhist prayer halls and meeting rooms also functioned as a trading hub; on the walls are inscriptions by merchants from Persia and Japan. The purpose of their visits is explained by the sea of sugarcane which still surrounds the caves.

15. 'Digging the Cane-holes' by William Clark, from *Ten Views in the Island of Antigua: In Which Are Represented the Process of Sugar Making, and the Employment of the Negroes, in the Field, Boiling-house and Distillery* (London: Thomas Clay, 1823).

16. 'Cutting the sugar cane', William Clark.

17. 'Grinding sugarcane in a windmill', William Clark.

18. 'The boiling house', William Clark.

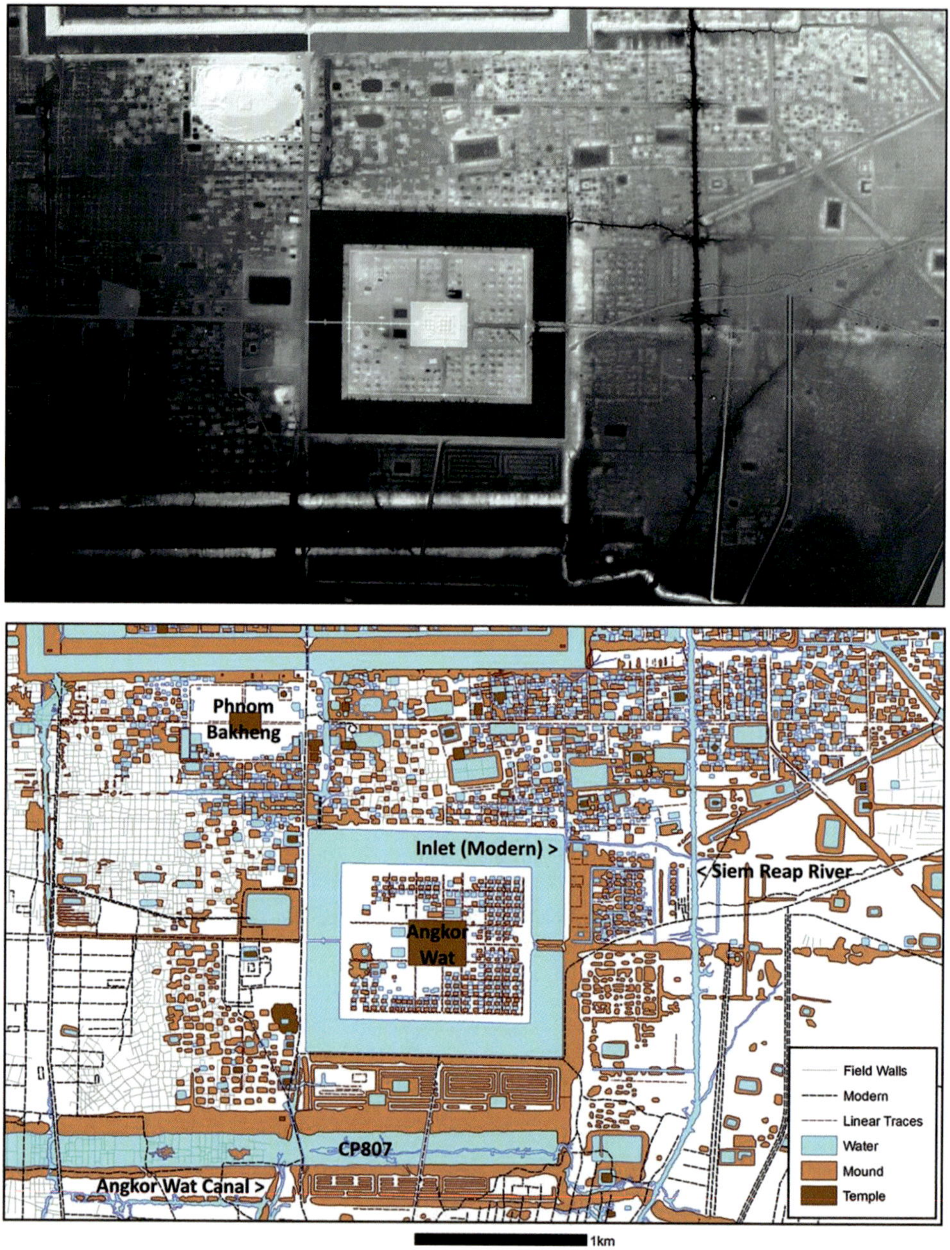

19. In the 2010s, LiDAR imaging able to penetrate the forest canopy transformed the history of Angkor Wat. The temple emerged not as an isolated monument, but as the centrepiece of a vast cityscape of roads, canals, ponds, mounds, fields and suburbs.

20. National crest of Pol Pot's Democratic Kampuchea: dams, canals and geometric rice fields leading to an industrial horizon – all surrounded by rice stalks wrapped in revolutionary flags.

21. 'Workers of all countries, unite!' Shining Path poster from 1985, commemorating five years of the 'people's war'.

22. Ceramic showing Moche priest using a stick to transfer *llipta* from the container to his mouth while he chews coca. Next to the ceramic is an actual Moche lime container.

23. Advertisement for one of Vin Mariani's many imitators. 'Coca of the Incas gives strength and health' – and sends you soaring above the dark urban tumult.

24. Pouring cocoa to froth it. Image from the so-called Tudela Codex, mid-sixteenth century.

25. 'The Chocolate House' by Thomas Rowlandson, 1787. A chocolate pot occupies the centre of the drawing, surrounded by music and flirtation.

26. Advertising poster for Chocolat-Menier, 1860. Many of the company's innovations were in packaging and marketing. It was sold to Rowntree Mackintosh in 1971, which was in turn purchased in 1988 by Nestlé.

or returned to subsistence crops. Coca production reverted to its former state – serving local, traditional demand.

That demand had never gone away: coca retained its place at the heart of Andean life. During his travels in the 1850s, Paolo Mantegazza had seen how coca sustained Peruvians in their poverty; he described, for instance, a small child who was sent into the mountains to watch over a llama herd 'with no other provision than a small sack of coca leaves'.[51] By the 1950s, nothing much had changed. Peru's coca production in that decade was 8,500 tonnes per year, almost all of it chewed by locals, whose consumption was by far the greatest where daily calorie intake was least – such as in the VRAEM.[52] 'Coca chewing is like cigarette smoking or coffee drinking elsewhere,' observed a 1978 report, which also found the habit was closely correlated with altitude: only 3 per cent of adults consumed coca at sea level; at 1,000 metres this increased to 29 per cent, at 3,500 metres to 70 per cent.[53] Despite centuries of Christianisation, meanwhile, Andean communities continued to attribute powerful ritual and magical significance to the coca leaf. In Mario Vargas Llosa's *Death in the Andes*, a village 'witch' tells fortunes in the evenings, 'tossing coca leaves into the air and interpreting the shapes they made when they fell'.[54]

By that time, however, those leaves were gaining new significance as a result of further developments in the United States. American cocaine use had dwindled since the clampdowns of the 1920s, and US policing focused on another drug, also banned but energetically smuggled – heroin. America's relationship with heroin acquired geostrategic importance during the Vietnam War when large numbers of US soldiers found the drug helped them cope better with psychological extremes, and a significant narcotics trade grew up to serve them. President Nixon feared that returning soldiers would unleash a domestic epidemic of addiction and crime; in 1969, he announced aggressive measures against what he believed was now 'a serious national threat'.[55] Another target of the ensuing 'war on drugs' was cannabis, which was even more endemic among soldiers in Vietnam and closely associated with anti-establishment movements at home. Both these were placed in the first schedule of the Controlled Substances Act of 1970; cocaine, on account of its acknowledged therapeutic benefits, was in Schedule II. While the newly created Drug Enforcement Administration went to war on a perceived African-American heroin epidemic, setting up methadone clinics in at-risk urban areas, and while Nixon clamped down on cannabis crossing the Mexican border and began sending aircraft to spray herbicide on Mexican fields, so creating an American narcotics shortage, cocaine was reborn.

Cocaine suffered from none of the urban-underclass associations; in fact, it was remembered as the drug of socialites, jazz musicians and intellectuals. Its brief narcotic cycle made it easily compatible with upscale employment, and even doctors who treated its addiction attached to cocaine none of the moral degeneration associated with Schedule I drugs: 'The drug of aristocrats, kings, high priests and highly articulate and creative men of many eras . . . now, in 1973, cocaine is enjoying renewed popularity among the affluent and the creative . . . Cocaine . . . boosts what we recognise as the highest aspirations of American initiative.'[56] A year later, the *New York Times* declared cocaine 'the most popular drug in America'[57] and, as New York clubs like Studio 54 became famous for their fusion of celebrity and powder, cocaine culture filtered into such films as *Annie Hall* (1977), *American Gigolo* (1980) and *Scarface* (1983).

The early years of this American cocaine boom coincided with a period of political collapse in both Peru and Bolivia. Carlos's was only one of thousands of peasant families who found themselves economically stranded and who responded to official encouragement to migrate to jungle regions. But officials had carried out poor analyses of the soils in those regions, which could not produce anything like the quantities of rice and maize they had anticipated. The newcomers were obliged to clear forest at a great rate, and ecology was quickly degraded.[58] This was all the more the case because highland migrants moved in much greater numbers than planners had anticipated, and by 1981 the population of the VRAEM had tripled.[59] Jungle farming was also very different from the quinoa and potatoes the newcomers were used to, and, in the absence of adequate transport networks, it did not produce cash. Coca, which required relatively little skill, and for which there was rising demand from stronger economies abroad, was the cash crop that allowed these peasants whom failed development policies had left without other options – some have called them 'orphans of development' – to colonise the new regions.[60] According to many scholars, it was failed state planning that created the conditions for a narcotics industry, which turned out to be the only viable antidote to poor public planning and investment.[61]

Even before the rise of the Shining Path in the 1980s, when cocaine took over the VRAEM, migrant farmers had begun large-scale cultivation in the remote jungles of the Huallaga valley, 1,000 kilometres to the north. Using a process similar to that invented by Alfredo Bignon in the 1880s, they processed coca leaves into paste. The upper Huallaga valley saw the emergence of a number of Peruvian family firms, or *firmas* – most of these set up by former farmers – which became specialised in cocaine trafficking.[62] They collected the paste and organised its transport by road, river and air to northern Chile and to Cuba.[63] Chile had developed processing capabilities and pan-American distribution networks in the late 1940s, when political forces had crushed narcotics industries elsewhere; the Cuban revolution of 1959 had dispersed mafia groups already well versed in the illegal drugs and alcohol trade, creating a ready-made network centred on Havana.[64] In those centres, *pasta básica* was refined into cocaine powder and then smuggled via Mexico, Panama, Ecuador and various Caribbean islands to American distribution centres, of which Miami was the most important.

This early distribution was dispersed and fragmented, and its scale remained small by later standards. Each route was run by a different set of individuals and organisations; none acquired the financial power to create an integrated transnational system. That began to change in 1973, when the right-wing dictator General Augusto Pinochet seized power in Chile. The new president ingratiated himself with his American backers by jailing or expelling Chile's drug traffickers, so amputating the cocaine system.[65] A new route opened through Colombia, whose entrepreneurs would, over the ensuing fifteen years, build supply chains leading all the way from Andean fields to New York streets. Not only were these chains equipped with planes and private armies, they were also able to infiltrate national legislatures, police forces and border guards – and they opened corridors for enormously increased cocaine flows. Until the mid-1960s, the volumes entering the United States could probably have been measured in the tens of kilos. In 1977, the Drug Enforcement Administration announced seizures of 200 kilos of cocaine; eleven years later, that number was 60,000 kilos.[66] By the early 1990s, over 200 tonnes of cocaine were entering the United States each year, and Americans were spending about $30 billion annually on the drug. So monolithic were the Colombian organisations that they were able to dominate this revenue. At its peak in the 1980s, Pablo Escobar's Medellín cartel supplied 80 per cent of American cocaine. With the Medellín's decline, and Escobar's assassination by Colombian special forces in 1993, the rival Cali cartel seized a share almost as large, even as it controlled almost the entirety of the European market.[67]

For geographical reasons, the Colombian takeover benefited Peruvian cultivators at the expense of those in Bolivia: Bolivia's closest point was 700 kilometres from the Colombian border. The cartels moved more easily into adjacent Peru, from where as much as 65 per cent of the world's cocaine was sourced until the crackdowns of the 1990s. While the upper Huallaga valley remained a major source of coca leaf, the logistical centre moved to the VRAEM where, as we have seen, state authority was heavily contested during the 1980s. The Peruvian *firmas* moved there too, operating effectively as subsidiaries of the Colombian cartels, which also placed many of their own men on the ground. Even within Peruvian borders, the cocaine economy turned over hundreds of millions of dollars, and it funded both peasant armies and their Shining Path foes. Significant monies also flowed as bribes to every level of the state bureaucracy. All these different parties and alliances were ultimately dependent on the Colombian cartels, which occupied, therefore, the top of the power system.

Migrants like Carlos and his family had been spurred on by state promises of new services, new assistance, new agricultural markets – promises that had evaporated during the 1970s as Peru entered a disastrous debt spiral. Much of the support for the Shining Path emerged from the resulting desperation. But, as we have seen, the Shining Path years also saw peasants not only abandoned by the government, but also harassed, interrogated and killed. Many were enthusiastic, therefore, about the de facto narco-state, whose managers were interested, above all, in their agricultural produce. Peasants who turned to coca in those years had access to loans and administrative support from the cartels and were better paid than ever before.[68] They also developed a sense, before many of their compatriots, of what 'globalisation' would look like. 'Cocaine capitalism'[69] led the way to Peru's integration with the international economy, while the VRAEM became a place of airstrips, dollars and foreign traders.

That era came to an end in August 1995, when President Fujimori's forces fought their way into the VRAEM, defeating most of the remaining Shining Path forces, evicting foreign cocaine brokers, clamping down on coca cultivation and spraying coca fields with herbicide.* Many locals still look back on those events as a tragic defeat. The date of the military incursion, 12 August, has since become a coca festival, when thousands of farmers, many of them in traditional Andean costumes, express their loyalty to the land over the state. Dancing and singing in the streets of Pichari, administrative centre of the VRAEM, festivalgoers hark back to Incan times, when coca provided the basis for a political order they believe was more caring and just. In Spanish and Quechua, their slogans say:

* There was considerable peasant resistance. From that time on, coca-growing farmers organised protests, strikes and marches against Fujimori's forced eradication campaigns, demanding recognition of coca as a livelihood and calling for development alternatives. These mobilisations were the expression of a broader *cocalero* consciousness that had developed alongside the coca expansion in frontier regions from the 1970s. Although long constrained by conflict and the association of coca zones with the Shining Path insurgency, *cocaleros* secured intermittent negotiations with the state and some eradication policies were moderated.

'The coca leaf: tradition, culture, law.'
'Coca: ancient and sacred plant of our Pachamama – goddess of earth and fertility.'
'Long live the coca leaf, eternal sustenance of the poor.'
'Let us harvest our coca.'

I'm chatting to a farmer called Freddy whom everyone calls – I don't know why – *loco*. Crazy or not, Loco Freddy is rotund and about fifty years old, wears an Italian football shirt and hardly stops laughing. Julio, his ageing father, who is also here, is similarly joyful. The two are drinking beer in their front room, while torrential rain falls on the corrugated-iron roof. In preparation for my arrival, they have brought a big plastic shopping bag stuffed with coca leaves.

'From our farm,' says Loco Freddy.

'Take it,' says his father. 'It comes from the ancestors. From the Incas.'

There is no plaster on the interior walls, which show the roughly shaped bricks. A curtain separates us from the bedroom. The floor is piled with cans of herbicide. '*Juntos crecemos bien*,' says the friendly corporate slogan. 'Together we cultivate well.'

Loco Freddy hands me a cold beer.

'I came to this region in the 1950s,' says Julio. 'I came with my father as a child, leaving the women behind. We travelled on a horse across the mountains, walking and riding for four days. Only native people lived here at that time. They grew potatoes and bananas. They grew coca for their own use, not for money. Some landowners had big ranches where they cultivated cocoa and sugarcane. My father and I worked on those farms.

'I used to make some money transporting coca to Ayacucho, which was where the roads came to an end. I went the whole way on foot, two days there, two days back. Then they built another sixty kilometres of road, and the walk was shorter. When I was a young man, they began to extend the highway into the VRAEM. In 1969, we bought a truck. Our transport business did well. We bought one and a half hectares of farmland, which is still with us.

'In the 1980s, you could understand a lot just from driving up and down the highways. The new roads allowed the chemicals to come in for making drugs. We began to see those supplies. Colombian gangs came in and taught people how the process worked.

'One day, I was driving back from Ayacucho when I found the road blocked. They were farmers and herders. That was the first time I met the Shining Path. They used to block the highways and steal food and clothes from passing cars. I saw many of the people who worked on my farm in this group – they had become part of the revolution. They said they knew me and they let me go. But I was afraid, because the Shining Path were taking away young boys to train them. I had six children by then, and I was away all the time on the road. I sent my wife and children to Lima to avoid the risk.'

Loco Freddy makes a comment about the seafood he used to eat in Lima, rubbing his stomach with long-remembered pleasure.

'The army came in to fight the Shining Path,' Julio continues, 'and they were very brutal. They came to my house one day while my family was away and broke down my door. They heard I had been saying things against them, so they arrested me and tortured me. They wanted to know who I was working for. They accused me of trafficking drugs to support the terrorists. They only released me after eighteen months.

'We didn't have any options,' he concludes. 'The terrorists used to kidnap you, so you had to support the terrorists. But if you supported the terrorists, the army kidnapped you. Of course I was not trafficking for the terrorists. But they did not believe me.'

Loco Freddy is concerned I have not touched my beer. It is about 11 a.m. He asks if I would prefer a whisky and bursts again into peals of laughter.

'By 1990, the Shining Path was in decline,' says Julio. 'Freddy came back from Lima to work on the farm. My other children stayed in the capital.'

'All my children have gone to Lima too,' says Loco Freddy. 'One is studying in university. The others are professionals. I will be the last farmer in our family.'

'We cultivated cocoa, banana, papaya, mango, oranges,' continues Julio. 'Mostly local products. But we always grew coca. That is our Incan culture. Those years, the early nineties, we had a great time. The government had no presence, and coca farmers used to produce cocaine. Not just coca paste – there were cocaine plants in the VRAEM too. There was an outdoor market in the city where you could buy cocaine like you buy vegetables. Very cheap. The Medellín cartel was in the VRAEM, protecting the farmers. Farmers were completely integrated with the cartel, and money came easily.

'In 1995, Fujimori sent the army to take over the region and stop production. There was a massive protest. It was very violent – the cartel protected the peasants, and the peasants protected the cartel. But the army won. They shut down the airport at Palmapampa, which was used to send cocaine to Colombia. All our problems started from then. Every year, the coca festival commemorates our protest against the army, changing a sad moment into a celebration.'

The ensuing years saw strenuous government efforts to cut ties with the international cocaine trade. These were closely coordinated with the US, whose escalating aid packages were tied to anti-drugs initiatives. Thousands of hectares of coca plants were destroyed, along with hundreds of cocaine-paste plants and hundreds of tonnes of processing chemicals. The United States also provided radar equipment and training to enable the Peruvian Air Force to shoot down small planes transporting *pasta básica* and cocaine to Colombia. This programme ran from 1995 to 2001, when a Peruvian jet inadvertently shot down a plane carrying American Baptist missionaries. A significant part of America's anti-drugs propaganda was spread, in fact, by such missionaries, and by Protestant churches on the ground.

As far as peasants were concerned, the most conspicuous effort was led by the Comisión Nacional para el Desarrollo y Vida sin Drogas (National Commission for Development and Life without

Drugs), universally known as DEVIDA. Working closely, once again, with the CIA and with USAID, DEVIDA led a comprehensive campaign against the cocaine trade. Its strategy was centred on converting coca farmers to cocoa, bananas, oranges and other crops.

'They come here and lecture us about coca,' says Loco Freddy. 'If we have to grow it, we have to sell it to the government. I will not sell to the government.'

In Peru, it is not illegal to grow coca. Farmers have been growing it, after all, since time immemorial. It is illegal, however, to sell coca to any customer other than the state coca monopoly, Empresa Nacional de la Coca (ENACO), which certifies the quality, distributes it across the country for traditional, medicinal and industrial uses and makes sure there is no leakage.

'There is a legal market and an illegal market,' says Freddy. 'But the only real market is the illegal market. I only sell to illegal buyers. They treat you much better. They come to my farm, take my entire coca production and give me a good price. If I sell to ENACO, I have to transport the coca myself. They don't take everything, because some does not meet their quality standards. On top of all that, they pay half the price. Why would I sell to them?'

'We don't see any sign of DEVIDA's money,' adds his father acerbically. 'A billion dollars has just blown up.'

I have spoken to DEVIDA officials, who struck me as sincere public servants. They were authentically concerned by coca's devastation of the Peruvian environment ('One hundred and twenty thousand hectares of jungle have been cut down for coca,' said one; 'in the VRAEM we have lost twenty to thirty per cent') and above all by the human impact of the drug trade. At the same time, they were under no illusions about the impact of their work. They recognised that illicit coca provided a much better income for many peasants than any alternative. They realised that the brutality of the 1990s invasion, and the ensuing destruction of agricultural livelihoods, had turned many peasants against them. They admitted that only a small minority of coca cultivators in the VRAEM were interested in working with them, that the *firmas* were on the rise again, after years of absence, and that international cartels were moving much more quickly than they could. 'We cannot offer better money,' said a DEVIDA director. 'So our promise is simply, *Viva mejor, viva en paz.*' Live better, live in peace.

'DEVIDA never invested in their objectives,' says Loco Freddy. 'They said, *Grow this, grow that,* but you need a lot of land to benefit. And they never developed markets. The market for those crops is on the coast, but the highways are in bad condition, people can steal my product on the way.'

'We always grew cocoa,' says his father. 'But the price was so low. Coca kept us going.'

'The biggest thing is that the cocoa price has increased because of climate change in Africa. So we're doing more cocoa now. I've planted more trees. Coca needs a lot of people to harvest it, and it needs a lot of chemicals. Cocoa is easier. We extract the beans, dry them and ferment them, and sell them for processing. About a tonne each year.'

The walls are hung with several calendars issued by an evangelical church, showing cute pictures of babies and swan necks intertwined in a heart. Father and son are enthusiastic members, it turns out, of a local congregation.

'Our family converted during the terrorism years,' says Julio. 'Originally, we were Catholics. But the Catholic church abandoned us at that difficult time, as the government did. We got a lot of strength from the Protestant church. That's how we kept our sense of community.'

Many have followed a similar path. The collapse of state institutions in the 1980s and 1990s, and the retreat of the Catholic church, made way for a mushrooming of new evangelical churches. They helped to provide foundations for devastated communities – not only helping people to make sense of violence and to rebuild social ties, but also providing real services, such as care for widows and orphans. There was no single 'evangelical' response to the conflict: some churches encouraged withdrawal and neutrality, while others encouraged armed self-defence against the Shining Path.[70] But in all cases the central position they acquired in these villages of the VRAEM has endured.

During our conversation, the rain has stopped. Bright sunshine enters through the open door. Freddy wants to show me his farm. We pile into the Toyota Hilux, drive out of the village and climb a gravel track. We get out.

I have seen many farms. This is the most beautiful of them all. From where we are standing, the land slopes down to a breathtaking valley. A dramatic quilt of cloud clings to the peaks on the other side. Wet trees glisten and steam under the sun. Flocks of parakeets jet overhead.

The first crop is coca, intense green, blanketing the mountainside. We wander through the bushes, which grow up to my neck. Small oval leaves grow in bunches towards the sky; in this month of March, tiny seed berries are turning red on the stem. Loco Freddy hands me a bunch of fresh leaves.

'These leaves take between two and four months to grow,' he says. 'We get four harvests a year. We keep some for ourselves too, to chew or make tea.'

I inspect the glossy leaves.

'They're sharp,' he observes. 'People who harvest have damaged hands. These days they wear plastic gloves but still they get cut.'

Interspersed with the coca are clumps of coconut and other trees.

'That is *cubé*,' says Loco Freddy, pointing at a broad tree hanging with orange fruit. Many farmers have told me about this tree, which provided one of the first sources of income for early migrants to this region. More widely called barbasco, the tree is prized for its root, which contains a powerful poison. Native peoples discovered long ago that the poison could be used to stun fish, which could then be pulled effortlessly out of the water – and eaten with no ill effects. The practice continues today.

The coca fields extend far down the slope. Beyond Freddy's land, coca lines the valley. Every spur is covered in coca green, as far as the eye can see.

We reach a majestic row of coconut trees, the nuts hanging brown, green and bright orange. The coca gives way to cocoa: Freddy's pods, like Carlos's, are yellow and ripe. The slope gets steeper and steeper as we descend; several times, the mud gives way under my feet. We enter an enchanted land of fruit – endless oranges, mangoes, pineapples. Enormous columns of green papayas. Bananas of every size and colour: tiny purple ones, in bunches of 200 at a time; big orange ones; pale green plantains as long as my forearm. Freddy peels me a yellow banana. Biting into it, I feel as if I have never truly tasted this fruit until now.

I gaze over this magnificent valley. High on a nearby tree, four black vultures spread their wet wings to the sun. Below, I can hear the rush of the river, which runs through Freddy's land. Everywhere, there are plants rushing towards the sky, flowering, spilling fruit. Never have I seen anywhere so powerfully fertile as this.

It is time to return. Freddy has cut down a stalk of bananas with his machete. I offer to carry it for him, but realise I can barely lift it from the ground. He gives me two coconuts to carry. He pulls his football shirt up to his armpits – 'banana skins stain your clothes' – and loads the bananas onto his bare back. We climb the muddy slopes, sweating profusely in the humid heat. We pass the cocoa trees again, the sweeping field of coca, and finally reach the top. Freddy heaves the bananas into the back of the Toyota. I put the coconuts alongside them.

We stand, laughing, out of breath. Freddy's shirt is still hitched over his glistening stomach. I'm impressed by his raw power.

I put the coca leaves he has given me in my jeans pocket. I make a mental note to ensure they are not still there when I embark for John F. Kennedy airport.

'I am a coca farmer, a cocaine trafficker and an arms dealer.'

The man is young and strikingly handsome, with a mass of sculpted black hair and a short goatee. His melancholy face never smiles. His name is Diego.

'The government is not supporting my generation, my people. That's why I do this kind of activity. I started when I was thirteen – now I'm thirty. I grew up in this town. I have to support my old mother and my younger sisters. They are in school, and I pay for their education.'

It is a few days after my arrival in this town. I have come to meet Chacal at his house. Chuzo is also here, the man we gave a ride to on our way. This is not where Chacal lives with his wife and family; it is the house he has maintained since before his marriage and from where he has conducted many kinds of business. Entering from the street through the typical low steel door – two men are posted outside to keep watch on the street – there is a small dark room where a narrow bed is crowded in by every kind of household junk. There are several chests and tables; every surface is piled with knick-knacks, tools and sports trophies. The walls are hung with old photographs falling out of frames.

The second room is littered with dusty balloons, coloured tinsel and garlands, games and children's party costumes. Chacal explains that he once ran a kids' party shop out of this building. Unsurprisingly, it failed. I do not get the impression there is a thriving market in this town for children's birthday parties.

We are sitting in the little garden at the back of the house. Chacal has arranged a circle of plastic chairs, which he dusted carefully before we sat. Above our heads is a huge coconut tree.

'When I was thirteen,' Diego continues, 'some uncles started getting involved in the cocaine business and asked me to join them. I used to wear my school uniform so I would not attract attention. We took public transport from one city to another, and no one would look at me because I was a kid. I transported paste into Bolivia in my school bag. Once I was arrested with several adults but I was in my school uniform and they didn't suspect me. I ran away with my backpack from the police station and escaped.'

He uses a slang word – *pichicata* – to refer to the cocaine paste he carried at that time. Traffickers long ago coined the word – probably derived from Quechua – to disguise their activity, but it has long since entered the public vocabulary.

'Now I transport to Juliaca, which is on the Peruvian shore of Lake Titicaca. From there it is taken by plane or truck into Bolivia. Usually, I go by motorbike with thirty kilos, which pays me seven thousand soles – two thousand dollars. If I go by foot, I carry ten kilos, which pays one thousand dollars. Sometimes, I take a hundred kilos in a car, which pays four thousand dollars. I usually take two trips a month, sometimes three or four. These days, we carry processed cocaine hydrochloride because paste is too heavy.

'We always move at night. If we're walking, we move in groups of twenty or thirty. In front and behind are four men with AK-47s. They are experienced traffickers, who receive the same money as everyone else.

'If we're going by motorbike, we travel in pairs. Before we reach a police checkpoint, one person gets off the bike and walks the drugs through the forest, the other person takes the motorbike through the checkpoint, and we meet up further down the road. Eventually, we load the product into a truck and drive it to the final destination.

'There are so many dangers. If you are arrested, you can spend ten or twenty years in jail. But the biggest threat is other gangs, who follow you to steal your product. The police also try to take your product and sell it themselves. The most vulnerable moment is the journey back, because then you're carrying a lot of cash. The best way to protect yourself is to keep absolutely silent. You can't tell anyone what you're doing because everyone likes to gossip about what is moving where.

'Some time ago, we were transporting two million soles – over half a million dollars. I myself was carrying five hundred thousand soles. A truck started chasing me on my motorbike, and they were shooting at me. It was the middle of the night, and I was on a mountain road with a massive drop into the valley on one side. I was about to be killed, so I jumped off the side of the road into the total darkness. I landed in the thick jungle. I knocked out my front five teeth. My leg was skewered on sharp trees, and the bones were shattered.'

Diego pulls up the right leg of his tracksuit to reveal an ugly scar running from ankle to thigh.

'The men in the truck looked for me in the darkness, but they couldn't find me. They thought I must be dead. Two days later, my friends found me and took me to hospital.

'This is dangerous work. You have to accept it. You can't be negative. Normally I'm OK. It's only when I get a call for a new trip that I start getting anxious. As the day approaches, I wonder what will happen.'

Chacal shakes his head as he listens. The whole subject seems to be heavy for him.

The sun is setting.

'I've bought five hectares of land,' continues Diego. 'I've been farming coca for five years. We harvest four times a year. Each time we get about five tonnes of coca, which I sell for about two thousand dollars. There are a lot of costs, though. Each harvest takes one round of herbicide and two rounds of pesticide. I don't get involved in processing cocaine – the risks of getting caught are very high. I sell to professional organisations who take care of all that.

'DEVIDA asks me to change to cocoa, but there is no profit in cocoa, and it does nothing for the community. Five or six people are enough to harvest cocoa, and there's only one harvest a year. I employ forty or fifty people four times a year, and pay them 1.40 soles per kilo. Coca generates income for the community. I like to help the community. There's no other source of income here.'

This is a new take on an idea we have encountered many times before. Coca as the foundation of Andean society – not just its culture, but also its system of livelihood.

'Farming is in my blood. My grandparents came from the highlands to set up a farm here. They were murdered by the terrorists. I grew up working on the farm with my mother, while my father transported products in his truck.

'The farm covers daily expenses. But it's not enough. My mother has medical bills. My youngest sister is only fifteen. To support the family, I need to do other work. I have no wife, no girlfriend, no children. My life is organised for transporting cocaine. I also traffic guns. I buy them where the prices are low and bring them here to sell.

'Perhaps I will have a different life in the future. I studied as an industrial electrician – maybe I will save money and start a business. But for that I need to go somewhere else. Here, there are only three options: be a coca farmer, transport drugs or go to jail.'

In recent years, the government's efforts to uproot the cocaine trade from the VRAEM have largely failed. Fujimori's assaults on peasants and traffickers resulted in a precipitous decline in Peruvian coca cultivation: from 120,000 hectares at its height in the early 1990s to just 39,000 hectares by the end of the decade.[71] That represented a catastrophic loss of income, and many peasants were obliged to leave the land. Their distaste intensified for the Peruvian state – and indeed for the United States, whose war on their coca fields was prosecuted through Peruvian agencies – and they fought back, often under the banner of Incan culture. Today, the figure exceeds 90,000 hectares once again.[72] This has also been the result of technological innovations by Colombian agronomists, who have developed new, low-altitude strains of the coca plant, allowing for expansion into new regions. Not only that, but Peruvian middlemen have found simpler ways of processing coca into pure cocaine hydrochloride, which previously was carried out only in sophisticated labs.[73] That allows them to capture more of the profit and to support the thriving networks of which Diego is a part.

It is growing dark. In the gloom, I have the impression that the grass is moving. Looking more closely, I see it is covered in giant snails.

'Don't touch them,' Chuzo warns. 'They're African snails. They're poisonous.'

'What my young friend says is true,' says Chacal, nodding towards Diego. 'There is no economy here except the criminal economy. You see, in the 1980s, when Chuzo and I were teenagers, the Shining Path had complete control of this area. The police had fled. That was the beginning of the cocaine dependency. Our livelihood was trapped in cocaine, and still is now.'

'The whole land was converted to coca bushes,' adds Chuzo. 'The gangs came and took advantage of people's poverty. They started offering loans and financial support if people cultivated coca leaves. Many peasants got involved in trafficking to supplement their incomes, and the economy of the town changed.'

We are sitting under fluorescent-tube lights, which begin to attract clouds of mosquitoes.

Chuzo's hair is thin, his manner sweet.

'My parents had a farm here,' he continues. 'They sent me to do military service, to avoid me being kidnapped by the terrorists. I came out of the army when I was twenty, and I had no money. I came back here and met people who had money. They gave me five thousand dollars to carry cocaine to Brazil. Going there took one month. I walked into Bolivia and through the jungle. I travelled across Brazil partly by car and partly on foot. Finally, I arrived in São Paulo. Two girls came to meet me. They swallowed the drugs, and carried them in their stomachs to Europe.'

We said earlier that so much of Andean history, going back to Inca times and before, has been about *moving stuff around*. These men represent the latest stage in that history. Cocaine acquires value when it is moved. Within Peru, a kilo of cocaine is not worth much more than $2,000; in New York or London it may be worth $40,000, in Dubai or Riyadh – where the punishments for trafficking may be death – $250,000. The real money is made, therefore, by foreign networks, whose activity is structured by the differences between national jurisdictions. Brazil is a major cocaine market in itself, as well as a transit point to Europe, but policing is almost as strict as in the United States. Bolivia is regarded as an easier terrain through which to move product eastwards towards the coast.

Chuzo's journey, there and back, was well over 8,000 kilometres.

'Since then, I have taken many long trips. Brazil, Bolivia, Ecuador, Chile. We carry canned food with crackers and basic survival items like salt and sugar. We use pathways that only we know. We carry guns to defend ourselves. There's a great risk of theft. People are waiting to kill us and take our cargo. If someone appears, we don't ask any questions. We just shoot.'

Chuzo's nickname means 'shoe' in local slang. It refers to his speed on foot. Chacal, on the other hand – 'jackal' – is used in the Peruvian drug world to refer to a small boss. Unlike Chuzo, Chacal did not remain at the bottom of the cocaine hierarchy.

'That dark side of my life began in 1990,' Chacal says, 'when I became involved in drug trafficking. I was a teenager, and I realised I could make a hundred dollars very easily. Soon I was making fifteen hundred dollars a week and I began to invest my money in buying more drugs. In three months, I had thirty thousand dollars. I made friends with the bosses and told them, "Don't pay me, teach me." I studied the business around Palmapampa, where the airstrip was. I learned how everything worked, and in one year I made almost half a million dollars. Soon I was buying hundreds of kilos and selling it to Colombian traffickers, who transported it out by plane.

'One day, I met a man who was part of the Medellín cartel. We became friends, and he came to live with me in this house. For a long time, we did business together. When he returned to Colombia, he took me there and I met the Medellín bosses. I started to do deals directly with the cartel.

'The foreign networks were in the VRAEM, but a lot of the product came from the upper Huallaga valley. I worked out ways to bring cocaine from there to the VRAEM so it could be flown out to Colombia. I would fly there with money, landing in illegal airports, and I'd come back with as much as a hundred kilos. I met the pilots who flew these planes. They were fancy guys with aviation companies in Lima. They used to invite me to go there and party with them. They loved cocaine – they used to put half a kilo on the table, and everyone was taking it. I have never taken cocaine. In truth, I am against cocaine.

'In 1995, the army came into the VRAEM, and it became more dangerous. It wasn't so easy to make money. You could be arrested. But my connections to Colombia still gave me a lot of status. This town was very secretive, and no one discussed business, but everyone was involved in cocaine, and they all knew who had power and who didn't. One day a boss from the army asked if he could stay here with his men. I gave him my bedroom, where I had stored four hundred kilos of cocaine. He smelt the cocaine and knew exactly what it was. He said, "I have to leave. I cannot be in this situation." But he did not do anything to me. Cocaine gave you so much power, even the army couldn't touch you.

'In those days I had no problems. That room inside was always full of people queuing to sell me their cocaine. I was transporting tonnes at a time. Of course there were bigger players than me, but I always had more than half a million dollars for myself. I never showed it off, and no one ever saw me spending it. There were always people looking for those who had money. If I went out with friends, I gave them the money, and they changed it into soles and paid for everyone.'

On the other side of the garden wall, a party has started. Speakers are blaring *cumbia*, the local dance music.

'On one occasion in 1998, I bought one tonne of cocaine and transported it to Colombia. I had to go there myself to pick up the money. The deal was for 1.2 million dollars. They gave me the money in a big box. They put fifty thousand dollars on top, but underneath was only fake notes. These exchanges take place in three minutes. By the time I realised, it was too late.

'This kind of thing never happened before, but then I was dealing with fragments of the old Medellín networks – with the leadership gone and everyone out for themselves. They no longer cared about their relationships. It was the breaking point in my life. I knew if I came back to the VRAEM I would have to face all the people who were part of the shipment, who were waiting for their money. They would probably kill me. I waited around in Colombia for months, not knowing what to do.

'I had no choice but to come back. I owed money to many small suppliers. I brought everyone together and said, "They cheated me, this is all the money I have. It is yours." Since I had always been good and loyal to them, nothing happened to me. Everyone wanted to continue working with me, because I was the one with contacts in Colombia. But that was the time I met my wife. And I thought, "Either I continue in the drug business, or I make my family." I changed my life.

'I never liked people who showed off because they had money. I always told them, "It's just money. It comes and goes easily. Your future depends on how good a person you can be, even while you are doing illegal things." But when I lost all my money, I was melancholy. A friend had a taxi company – he asked me to work for him. The first time I drove a passenger, I looked at what he paid me and I thought, "This is not money!" I realised I was just like everyone else – no money, no power. But I cared more about my family, and stopped worrying about those things.

'I also started farming on my parents' land. I never grew coca. I never wanted to have anything to do with it. I grew cocoa. But the prices were so low that I sold the land in 2019. I regret it so much now. That land was the heritage of my parents. With the rise in cocoa prices, it would have given me a handsome income now. Since then I've been doing small businesses to earn money. Selling clothes and other things. All legal. But none has worked. Only cocaine works here.'

We are struggling to hear each other over the party next door, where people are shrieking with excitement. Local music has given way to hip-hop and Bollywood.

Chacal brings out a bottle of lemonade and pours glasses for everyone.

'My wife is constantly anxious about money,' he says. 'Our daughter is studying in Lima, and we are struggling to support her. Every time I am at home, there are arguments.'

'That's why I never got married,' says Chuzo. 'You need money every month to be married. It's easier not to have the extra worries. I live with my mother, I take care of her, and that's it.'

At the beginning, Chuzo was very shy. Now he has lost his inhibitions. He asks me my impressions of him, of them, of this town. He is curious to know what I will write when I leave.

'Have you heard of Vargas Llosa?' he asks. 'He is one of the most famous men of our country. If your book becomes famous, everyone will read about us.'

What I would say to Chuzo is this: in the VRAEM, I witnessed a peasantry subjected by the state to surveillance, militarisation, corruption and crop eradication. That state has not guaranteed rights or livelihoods but constantly disrupted rural life and agriculture. In this vacuum, coca has been more than a crop. It has been a source of economic security, a mechanism of survival and a symbol of autonomy and resistance.

Like peasants in other places, *cocaleros* find it almost impossible to survive on cultivation alone and must look for ways to supplement this income. But the VRAEM contains no significant industries and little formal employment; it possesses weak infrastructure and limited markets for food crops. Nothing else was as reliable as cocaine, for which the *firmas* and cartels built very efficient logistics in the 1980s and 1990s – liquidity, markets and transport. Unlike peasants in parts of India or Cambodia, who can diversify into wage labour, manufacturing or multiple agricultural chains, VRAEM farmers face an economy overwhelmingly organised around coca. Cocaine processing and trafficking remain the primary means by which they can make good their agricultural losses.

According to the state, these are criminal activities, but most of the farmers dismiss any verdict of the state. Peruvian *cocaleros* have therefore created not only a parallel economy but also a parallel moral system, informed by subsistence survival and obligations to family. Each of the three men I have spoken to this evening has his own moral vision, but it can never be reconciled with mainstream morality. Perhaps that is part of the deep anxiety I sense in all of them. But it is difficult for me to see them – as the state does – as 'illicit'.

Their fundamental problem is that they are unable to capture significant revenues from the crop they grow. Though cocaine itself is consumed by some of the world's richest people, who pay more for it – per gram – than gold, almost none of this revenue goes to the farmer. In this sense, Peru's *cocaleros*, far from being unique as we might have imagined, share a predicament with peasants all over the world – producing much-demanded commodities while remaining shut out from most of the profits they generate. Coca farming provides in fact a portrait of the global peasantry in a particularly distilled form.

The criminalisation of these Peruvian lives leads to an additional burden. Wherever we have gone, we have seen that peasant cultivation is tied to the peasant family. Small farmers must have children for the farm to endure; their own reproduction, therefore, is part of their more general commitment to natural fertility. But the anxieties of criminal life make it more difficult to contemplate marriage and children. In renouncing cocaine, Chacal gained a family but lost the possibility of a livelihood. His companions have chosen the opposite route. Because the fertility of the coca farm is preserved by additional, criminal activities, in other words, a fundamental infertility is imposed on the farmer himself.

'I am worried about the future of this town,' says Chacal. 'Crime has become so normalised that no one realises what is going on. This community needs psychological care. I took my daughter out of here because the situation was so crazy. She's in Lima finishing her degree in photography.'

Diego's silence has been brooding and intense. I ask him what he will do if he has children.

'I would never let my children do this work,' he says. 'Never. I will move to another place to make sure that can never happen.'

4

Cocoa: Beneath the Surface

> Their principal and finest drink is called cachanatl and is made from the seeds of a tree fruit that is like a watermelon, but has large grains inside that are almost the size of date pits. The tree bearing this fruit is the most delicate of all the trees . . . They hold this tree in great esteem, because its grains are the principal money circulated in this country.
>
> – DESCRIPTION OF THE COCOA TREE IN THE AZTEC EMPIRE BY THE SO-CALLED 'ANONYMOUS CONQUISTADOR', MID-SIXTEENTH CENTURY[1]

Side by side on the Atlantic coast, the countries of Ghana and Ivory Coast (Côte d'Ivoire) are separated by the Tano River – an opaque brown channel, viscous with topsoil, roiling to the sea. Much of its muddy load has run off the bald land upstream, where miners hack down the forest in their relentless search for gold. Their mercury effluent also hums in these waters, poisoning and depleting the catches of Tano fishing communities, whose young men are surrendering to the inevitable and becoming gold miners themselves.

Ten kilometres short of the ocean, a bridge across the river connects the two nations, and transit towns have grown up at either end. Noé, on the Ivorian side, is not much more than a village; but Ghana's Elubo is a substantial and thriving town. The main roads, wide and well tarmacked, are lined with stalls selling food and drink. Motorbikes and Indian-made autorickshaws speed up and down, as well as the occasional Toyota SUV. Ghana's major banks all have branches here; there are salubrious hotels and thumping bars.

Anyone driving into Elubo at this time of year – it is November – will witness the main cause of all the bustle. The lines of vans and trucks parked along the main arteries into the town are packed with cocoa beans, which have migrated from all over western Ghana to be smuggled across the Ivorian border. Some traffickers will ferry sacks across the river in small boats; many will transport them northwards to remote sections of the land border. Others will simply drive across the bridge, hiding their illicit cargo among other exports or paying bribes to officials, or both.*

The immediate reason for this border frenzy is the condition of Ghana's own cocoa market. In the world's second-largest producer – Ivory Coast is the first – the government has a socialist-style monopoly: every bean must be surrendered to the state cocoa board – known as Cocobod – at a set price. That price is already extremely low. But Cocobod is also disastrously indebted; payment, therefore, is uncertain. Farmers must wait weeks for their money; many accept an even lower price for fear of getting nothing at all.

For those within reach of the border, smugglers provide a better alternative. They arrive with cash up front and pay as much as 50 per cent more than the government rate. After transporting the beans across the border, they sell them to Ivorian buyers and processors, who offer a premium for Ghanaian produce because it is superior in quality.[2] At that point, the beans lose their original nationality: they are absorbed into Ivory Coast's production, which is boosted accordingly. Smuggling alone goes some way to explaining why Ghana's official production fell from two-thirds of Ivory

* The Latin name for the tree at the centre of this chapter is *Theobroma cacao.* In American usage, this is the cacao tree, and its brown seeds are referred to as cacao. From these seeds, processors manufacture cocoa (cocoa powder, cocoa butter and chocolate). Here I follow British usage, from which 'cacao' is absent. Hence: the cocoa tree and its cocoa seeds (or beans). None of this is connected – despite frequent confusion – to the coca bush, protagonist of the previous chapter.

Coast's in 2010 to under one-quarter in 2023. As much as one-third of Ghana's 2023 cocoa output was reportedly smuggled out – much of it into Ivory Coast.[3]

Cocoa smuggling across this border has been going on for decades – in one direction or the other. In Ivory Coast, cocoa pricing is more attuned to global markets than in Ghana. This is partly the legacy of the two countries' inaugural presidents, with their respective capitalist and socialist leanings. So Ivorian farmers have often smuggled their produce into Ghana when world prices are low and when Cocobod's fixed price appears correspondingly attractive. When world prices have surged – as in the 1970s – cocoa has moved in the opposite direction. Today, cocoa prices are at an all-time high; Ghanaian cocoa is moving into Ivory Coast.[4]

High prices should not suggest that everything is well. The reason for the spike is that West African production is collapsing, causing shortages throughout the globe. This has created such extraordinary price differentials between places – in 2024, as the price on the New York futures market hit $12,000, the price paid to Ghanaian farmers hovered just above $3,000 – that smuggling generates unprecedented returns and it has proliferated to all the region's borders. While smuggling across the Ghana–Ivory Coast border was producing returns of 25–50 per cent, smugglers discovered they could earn as much as 100 per cent by moving beans out of both cocoa-producing states into Guinea and Togo and from there directly to Europe.[5]

Large-scale smuggling reduces Cocobod's volumes and therefore its sales on the international market. This further compromises its ability not only to pay farmers but also to solve the problems which have plunged cocoa into this crisis in the first place: ageing trees, endemic disease and climate change. The government has responded with fierce anti-smuggling legislation, as well as moralising speeches and crackdowns. Recently, Cocobod announced it would no longer supply free pesticide to Elubo cocoa farmers, to punish them for their blatant disregard for regulation. But smuggling continues apace. I spoke to some of the farmers affected by the pesticide ban; they seemed almost relieved to be released from this last vestige of a moral contract with the state. 'They do nothing for us,' one farmer told me, displaying a free-market instinct we have encountered before, 'so they have no claim on our cocoa. We can sell to anyone we want.'

In the last chapter, we encountered a cocaine-trafficking town in Peru. This cocoa-trafficking town has a very different atmosphere. Smuggling is normalised, state opposition is feeble – and everything contributes to the gradual unwinding of the system. Paradoxically, perhaps, it is not with cocaine that we encounter the darkest and most dysfunctional peasant experience, but with a crop which, in the West at least, carries sweet and innocent associations: romantic love, Easter bunnies, childish pleasure.

Kwame's machete is a restless extension to his body. As he stands talking under the cocoa trees, the blade fusses in his outstretched hand, slicing a withered pod from a tree, flicking a stone from the path, amputating a dead branch. Locals call this tool a cutlass – and indeed the West African model is unusually long and slim.

Kwame is powerfully built and looks a decade younger than his forty-three years. He wears bright blue wellington boots and a white cloth over his shoulder, with which he periodically wipes his face: it is 32 degrees today, and the humidity is close to 100 per cent.

'This is my mother's farm,' he says. 'I help her take care of it. But I have a small farm of my own too.'

We are in Ghana's cocoa heartlands, just outside the market town of Akim Oda, about 125 kilometres from the capital, Accra.

Kwame is from Ghana's dominant Akan community, whose Twi language has taken over popular culture and everyday commerce. The Akan's idiosyncratic naming system follows the days of the week – Kwame's name reveals he was born on a Saturday. In this community, matrilineal inheritance is the norm. Kwame's mother has three different plots, which will customarily go to her children. His father has his own cocoa farm; this will be inherited not by his children but by his sister's children.

It is harvest season. All around us, fat pods jut out from trunks, yellow, green and red. The unusual appearance of this tree helps explain the powerful mythologies that have arisen around it since ancient times. Its canopy is mostly just that; the flowers and therefore fruit are concentrated on the trunk. Known to botanists as cauliflory, this behaviour has arisen as a response to specific environmental needs. Cocoa trees are relatively small – rarely growing higher than five metres – and they thrive in the damp forest understorey. Their flowers are fertilised by midges which breed in rotting leaf litter and remain close to the ground, which is where the tree positions its flowers.

Each pod contains thirty or forty of the fat seeds known colloquially as cocoa beans. Some of these pods are still pale and immature and will be harvested next year. Some are black with disease.

'We have a mix of trees – Amazonia, Tetteh Quarshie and hybrid. The yellow ones are Tetteh Quarshie. They are the best, but the yield is small. We mix all the different beans together when we harvest.'

The Tetteh Quarshie variety is named after a blacksmith from Accra who, in the 1870s, went to work on a cocoa plantation on the Spanish-owned island of Fernando Po (now Bioko, part of Equatorial Guinea). On his return, he carried some cocoa pods into the kingdom of Akuapem, where a Swiss Presbyterian organisation known as the Basel Mission was running agricultural experiments on model farms. A Christian convert himself, Tetteh had received his blacksmith's training from the Basel Mission. Now he set up a cocoa nursery near the missionary centre in Mampong-Akuapem – about eighty kilometres from where I stand – and began to sell seedlings to local farmers. Much of Ghana's present production is descended from there.

The Amazonia variety was introduced later – direct from Latin America, as the name suggests. Kwame's hybrid is a blend of the other two, engineered for local conditions by the Cocoa Research Institute of Ghana in the 1960s.

We wander through the orchard, whose ground is covered with a thick layer of fallen leaves. Mosquitoes feed on us, gluttonously.

Kwame selects a ripe cocoa pod and slices it open with one expert cut, slightly at an angle to the longitude. He holds it open: I pick out a chunk of white flesh and eat.

The botanist's term for the cocoa tree – *Theobroma cacao* – contains a Greek coinage meaning 'food of the gods' – a reflection of eighteenth-century Europe's fascination with the cocoa seed's traditional role in Mesoamerican ritual offerings. The extraordinary properties of the seeds have caused the heavenly taste of its fruit, however, to be unfairly neglected. I turn the creamy pulp in my mouth, its taste a complex cocktail of sweet and sour, without any hint of chocolate. It is delicious beyond description. I drop the hard cocoa seed on the ground and reach for another chunk. Kwame eats too.

'Where I cut that pod, a flower will come next year, and then another pod. We harvest twice a year – once in May and June, and once in November and December. I employ men to harvest the pods and women to open them and empty them.'

Heaps of old shrivelled pods show where this work has been carried out in the past.

'But the seasons are changing. We are supposed to have two seasons – a dry season from October to March and a wet season from April to September. This year, there was no rain until June or July. So the harvest was delayed, and the yield was very low. Now it is November, and it is still raining.'

The last few days have seen massive rainstorms. I have seen many flooded cocoa farms.

'Water breeds fungus too, which kills the pods. We have many problems! We also have insects which suck the juice out of the pods – we call them *akate.* The puncture marks turn black, and the pods shrivel and die. If you don't have money for insecticide, you will lose your crop – *akate* can spoil everything. But then the insecticide goes into the ground. With the amount of rain and insecticide, the ground is spoiled. That is why our yields are going down.'

With his machete, Kwame scoops our discarded seeds into the cocoa pod. We walk back along the path to the road. He strokes the enormous *Cedrela* trees his mother planted to shade the cocoa. He points out a pineapple tree. He inspects everything as we walk.

'There!' he says suddenly. 'You see?'

He reaches up to a cocoa pod and turns it around so I can see the fat-bodied bug on its surface.

'*Akate*.'

He picks the insect off with his fingers and pulverises it with his boot. I can see he is locked in an endless battle with these little capsids: far too many of his pods bear the black spots of their toxic saliva.

We reach the main road, where a row of plantain trees makes a fence around the orchard. With a deft swipe of the machete, a broad plantain leaf falls to the ground. From the cocoa pod he is carrying, he empties the remaining flesh and seeds on to the leaf, which he folds over them. He fastens the fold with stones.

'This is the principle of fermentation,' he says. 'The beans ferment for five to six days in their pulp, covered with plantain leaves. That gives the flavour. Then we dry them in the sun – another three to six days. Then they are ready to be bagged.'

As cultivators have known since ancient times, cocoa's distinctive taste is brought out by fermentation. When the pod is emptied, the pulp turns to liquid, unleashing chemical reactions which cause the seeds to germinate, releasing their flavour. After two or three days, the high temperatures produced by fermentation kill the germinated seeds. The liquid drains away, leaving the beans covered in a fibrous, sticky mash. After they have matured for some time, they are taken out, the fibres are removed and the beans are dried in the sun. Then they are ready for sale.

We leave the beans fermenting and emerge on to the road. It is mid-morning; we walk into town under a fiery sun.

The tarmac on this road has been washed away at both sides. All that remains is a serrated strip down the middle. Underneath, the mud is red and raw. Three-wheeled vans with motorcycle engines, known locally as tricycles, weave laboriously between flooded ravines, transporting sacks of cocoa. Piled with massive trunks of forest trees, a truck lurches dangerously over the potholes, the words 'Prince of Peace' painted on the side.

'This road is only eight years old,' says Kwame. 'It is so destroyed that it is faster to walk on it than drive.'

On both sides of the road are cocoa farms shielded by clumps of plantain and palm. A few hardwood trees tower over the vista, but all the original forest is gone. The endless expanse of cocoa must be paradise for the *akate*.

'The big problem for cocoa farmers is the price,' says Kwame as we walk. 'The government sells cocoa to buyers at nine thousand Ghana cedis per sack – about eight hundred dollars. But it pays us only three thousand cedis. It's too little. Each sack is sixty-five kilos; from my two-hectare farm I get about three sacks a year. That's nine thousand cedis. I pay about a thousand in costs. And the rest I share with my sister in Accra. It's not enough. I am trying to give a good education to my three children. They are just ten, six and four.'

'Is there no one who will pay you more?'

'No. In the west of Ghana they can smuggle it to Ivory Coast, where the prices are better. But that is too far from here. We can only sell to government buyers.'

The situation Kwame describes arises from the crucial role played by cocoa in the formation of the Ghanaian state, which in turn derives from the extraordinary proliferation of Tetteh Quarshie's first seeds. To understand why Ghana's cocoa farmers must sell on such unfavourable terms, it is necessary to know the transformative role cocoa has played in this region ever since its arrival.

From the seventeenth to nineteenth centuries, the inland belly of what is now Ghana was dominated by the Asante (sometimes rendered Ashanti) empire, which harboured a thriving regional economy built on agriculture, artisanal production and, most conspicuously, gold. The empire possessed plentiful gold reserves, and gold dust – or *sika* – was the only legal currency.[6] The majesty of the emperor – or *asantehene* – was symbolised in dazzling gold regalia, comprising his golden stool, whose significance was like that of the European throne, the jewellery that covered his body and an array of swords, staffs, parasols and palanquins. Slaves played an essential role in the often dangerous work of extracting gold, as well as in agriculture and the army. So did so-called pawns – human beings offered as collateral for loans or favours – whose lives were often not much different from those of slaves. A formidable military machine enabled the empire continuously to expand its territory and so maintain a constant supply of foreign slaves. By the late 1700s, the empire controlled twenty tributary states and employed a large meritocratic bureaucracy to manage its affairs.[7]

The Asante empire played a significant role in the global economy. Gold and kola nuts were exchanged with northern traders for transport across the Sahara, while gold and slaves were exported, through southern intermediaries, to the Gold Coast, as it became known, where European merchants, especially the British, Dutch and Danes, maintained forts and trading posts. Since most slaves fell into that condition as a result of war, some historians have alleged that Europeans deliberately promoted West African warfare by supplying competing states with firearms.[8] If so, the scheme was successful: between 1650 and 1700, as West African states became more ambitious and bellicose, slave exports from the Gold Coast leaped from about 500 to 8,000 per year; for most of the eighteenth century they would exceed gold exports in value, sometimes touching 13,000 per year.[9] Over the course of about three and a half centuries, about 1.2 million individuals were packed into ships at Gold Coast ports for transport across the Atlantic.[10] Europeans paid for slaves, mainly, with cotton cloth and yet more firearms – meagre compensation for the immense evacuation of West African life and labour, whose traumatic consequences for the afflicted communities we can only imagine.

The British slave trade was abolished in 1807, following which the British government began to formalise its control of the Gold Coast under the banner of eradicating slave exports. Efforts to dominate the coastal states brought the naval power into conflict with the Asante empire, which was itself seeking access to Atlantic trade routes. A series of military defeats on both sides culminated in Britain's burning of the Asante capital of Kumasi in 1874 and the proclamation of a British coastal protectorate.

Throughout this period, African smallholders were experimenting with new commodities which could be traded with Europeans, partly to replace the lost commerce in slaves.[11] These developments were led by communities which, because of their enmity towards the Asante, were thrown into convenient cooperation with the British – the Akuapem, for instance, a rival Akan nation, and the Krobo, who belonged to the region's indigenous Guan people. They conducted successful experiments with such cash crops as palm oil, for which there was growing demand in Britain, where it was used for soap and candle manufacture.[12]

The Akuapem had built hillside settlements to give some measure of insulation against the Asante. There they were targeted by European missionaries, who shared similar security concerns. In the 1830s, the Basel Evangelical Missionary Society set up a string of stations in the lush Akuapem hills, before extending into the neighbouring states of Aburi and Krobo. The Basel Mission's objective was the wholesale reconstruction of post-slavery society and economy in West Africa, and while it viewed religious conversion as essential, it also provided training in new trades, new building techniques and, above all, new agriculture.[13] Its model farms featured oranges, mangoes, bananas, beans, groundnuts, coffee, tobacco, cotton, sugarcane and breadfruit. In 1859, the Basel Mission Trading Company was established, under whose auspices the first cotton was exported from the Gold Coast in 1863; by the 1880s, it was exporting rubber.[14]

From this environment emerged a generation of Akuapem farmers accustomed to growing cash crops for international markets. The resulting influx of cash was used to buy new land. ('We do not regard a man as an able man who has succeeded in life', an Akuapem farmer reported to a British anthropologist in the 1960s, 'unless he himself has bought a land for his children.')[15] Much of this land was used for ventures into coffee and – after Tetteh Quarshie's arrival – cocoa. European cocoa demand was exploding at that time – milk chocolate was invented in 1876 – and cocoa proved to be the winning crop. Within a few years, Akuapem farmers had turned their entire state over to cocoa. Within another twenty they had spread northwards and bought up the forest lands of neighbouring Akyem.[16] (These included the region where Kwame's mother's farm lies; indeed, the town of Akim Oda grew up in the early twentieth century as a cocoa transit hub, as well as a missionary centre.) By the outbreak of the First World War, Gold Coast, which exported no cocoa before 1892, was exporting 40,000 tonnes a year, making it the world's largest producer.[17]

Few agricultural explosions in world history are so dramatic, not least because cocoa was a totally exotic crop. Most early adopters, writes one historian, 'cannot have seen a bearing cocoa tree before they themselves began planting cocoa seedlings'.[18] Since the tree takes five or six years to start delivering fruit, those early farmers must have endured prolonged suspense. Cocoa also played no part in local cuisine or rituals; it was grown only to be shipped to unseen buyers for unfamiliar purposes. The fact that it spread so quickly is therefore astonishing, and indeed has stimulated a wide range of scholarly explanations.

The scholars agree on one point: the British had little to do with it.[19] The colonial administrators did create the context – they built train lines to facilitate agricultural exports, and they imposed taxes which pushed farmers towards cash-generating crops. They also elected not to interfere with land customs, which were already complex and tendentious. Europeans were therefore prevented from buying Gold Coast land, and ambitious local farmers faced no external competition. In other respects, however, the extraordinary boom in Gold Coast cocoa was the result of innumerable private decisions by small farmers themselves, who organised land, seeds and labour without direction from the colonial government. In fact, when the Department of Agriculture did try to influence Gold Coast farmers, it tended to be ignored and often for good reason. When it came to such questions as *How far apart should trees be planted?* and *How should capsid infestations be dealt with?*, farmers themselves tended to have the best answers. Farmers rejected the direction to ferment beans in wooden boxes, for instance, inventing an easier and more effective method using plantain leaves.[20] In such ways, West African peasants showed themselves to be better custodians of this sensitive and disease-prone crop than states and corporations. To some extent, this was due to the idiosyncratic behaviour of the cocoa tree itself, which never fared well under the standardised conditions, say, of rubber plantations. Even today, small-scale peasant cultivation remains the cocoa norm.

Profound changes were afoot, meanwhile, in the Asante empire. The eradication of the international slave trade had cut off an important Asante revenue stream. It had also caused slaves to accumulate within the empire: by 1894, perhaps 30 per cent of the population was enslaved.[21] The Asante deployed this labour surplus towards the expansion of their kola production, for which American soft-drinks manufacturers had not yet emerged as principal consumers; those were still to be found in the Sokoto Caliphate (in present-day Nigeria), whose religious strictures prohibited other stimulants. As time went on, they also expanded palm-oil and rubber production for European export, so they too began to develop what one historian calls a 'widespread market-orientation'.[22]

The Asante remained hostile, however, to foreign interference in their internal affairs. Missionaries were treated with suspicion: in 1869, two representatives of the Basel Mission were captured and held hostage for nearly four years.[23] Exotic crops, correspondingly, failed to penetrate the Asante mix. But the empire's seal was breaking as, weakened already by wars with Britain, it began to face raids from rivals on all sides. In 1896 the *asantehene* was exiled and the territory placed under 'indirect' British control. Four years later, a British attempt to seize the golden stool provoked a final Asante uprising, whose suppression led to the annexation of Asante territory in 1901 and the incorporation of both coast and interior into the Gold Coast colony.[24] At that point, missionaries established a formal presence in Asante. Two years later, the railway extension to Kumasi was completed.[25]

Almost immediately, Asante went about implementing its own cocoa revolution. Between 1900 and 1916, vast areas of forests were cleared, and tens of thousands of hectares of cocoa trees planted.[26] Much of the early labour was carried out by slaves and pawns, but soon their number was not enough.[27] By 1910, the first generations of trees were bearing fruit, and farmers had the cash to employ migrant labour; workers from the Ewe community migrated en masse from east of the Volta River in search of this new employment.[28]

With Asante's contribution, Gold Coast cocoa production attained new heights. Output in 1923 was 200,000 tonnes, or five times the 1911 total; in 1936 it passed 300,000 tonnes, which was 40 per cent of the world's total.[29] Between 1897 and 1938, the colony's foreign trade multiplied more than seven times in real terms, thanks mostly to cocoa, whose export value in the 1920s was sometimes five times that of gold.[30] Colonial administrators were astonished at the dynamism of what Gold Coast peasants had achieved. In his 1938 report on the Gold Coast cocoa industry, the British plant pathologist William Nowell observed:

> We found in the Gold Coast an agricultural industry that perhaps has no parallel in the world. Within about forty years, cocoa farming has developed from nothing until it now occupies a dominant position in the country's economy – cocoa being virtually the only commercial crop – and provides two fifths of the world's requirements. Yet the industry began and remains in the hands of small, independent native farmers.[31]

The Gold Coast became a colonial success story, generating a local surplus and attracting waves of migrant labour from what are now Togo, Burkina Faso and Nigeria.

Cocoa worked profound changes in Gold Coast society, particularly when it came to gender relations. As cocoa farming expanded, couples began to move to frontier locations, where men acquired land and trees in their own names, and women lost some of the independence they had previously known, and marriage became a more unequal institution. Traditional systems of reciprocal conjugal production – in which husbands and wives farmed separately and retained independent access to lineage land, but supported one another and helped on each other's land – were gradually displaced. Cut off from their own, inherited land, women channelled their labour into their husbands' estates. Divorce became more difficult, because it meant that women had to walk away from the fruits of years of labour; cash incomes from cocoa also strengthened fathers' claims over children, forcing changes to matrilineal patterns of kinship and inheritance.[32]

Some observers grew concerned about the Gold Coast's sudden dependence on a single crop. As early as 1919, some Asante chiefs were trying to ban new cocoa farms. 'Because the cocoa farmers has maken the cocoa farm in all land,' observed one, 'our children can't get field to make farms for food to support theirself [*sic*].'[33] Given that the chiefs benefited handsomely from cocoa farming, such a chiefly backlash is striking; clearly, food-security concerns were acute. Some British officials shared these concerns. Frederick Gordon Guggisberg, who served as Gold Coast governor from 1919 to 1929, feared that a single-crop colony would be vulnerable not only to violent economic shocks but also to catastrophic infestations. Guggisberg attempted to revive the palm-oil industry and made plans for innovations in groundnuts, shea butter, sisal, corn, sugar, coffee and tobacco.[34] But his efforts had little impact on peasants themselves, who continued to clear forests and to plant cocoa trees.

The most consequential question, for a colony ever more closely integrated with global markets, was the international price of cocoa. That price was especially volatile because of the long lead time associated with the cocoa plant – as opposed, say, to cotton or sugar. When cocoa prices went up, farmers around the world began to plant more trees, but the new stock produced no cocoa for four or five years, during which time the price would continue to rise, encouraging even more tree planting. Inevitably, when all those trees became productive at the same time, prices crashed to a low which lasted several years. During that time, many disillusioned cocoa farmers would replace their trees with other crops, storing up the reverse cycle.[35]

But in a place where colonising foreigners monopolised the connections to global markets, the price of cocoa was also – or especially – political. Farmers constantly suspected Europeans of fixing scales to underweigh; they also believed that foreign buyers colluded to keep prices low, an issue on which all their anti-colonial ire became focused. Such passion was encouraged by their chiefs, who often had a personal, as well as political, stake in the cocoa price. Chiefs played a major role in instigating the so-called hold-ups which rocked colonial relations in the 1920s and 1930s: mass refusals to sell cocoa beans to European buyers, sometimes accompanied by boycotts of European products.[36] The severest hold-up, which lasted for eight months of the 1937–8 season, was triggered by news that Unilever, Cadbury and the other major buyers had agreed to coordinate their activities in West Africa and to pay a pre-agreed, non-negotiable price. At the height of the action, cocoa sales dropped by 80 per cent, and *The Times* of London detected a threat to British power itself: 'the importance of cocoa to the West Coast [of Africa] is so great [that] a growers' strike may be almost synonymous with a semi-rebellious movement throughout the population.'[37]

Under the auspices of the aforementioned William Nowell, the government set up a commission to investigate the crisis, which acknowledged the collusive practices of big companies, declared that cocoa prices were vital to imperial stability and should not be decided by private interests, and recommended the establishment of a state-run marketing board to protect the interests of cocoa producers. The *New York Times* described the commission's proposals in ways that clearly anticipate the structure of Cocobod today: 'Under the plan, all farmers on the Gold Coast would be compelled to pool all cocoa produced by them. Sales then would be made through the association to foreign buyers directly . . . It would be an offense for a local shipper to buy cocoa except from the association.'[38] But the announcement in 1939 of a London-based Cocoa Control Board generated another wave of African opposition, especially when it was revealed that John Cadbury was one of the members.[39] This was just one of many moments in history when peasants have protested against capitalist interests for being *insincerely capitalist* – when they have campaigned not for market abolition but, quite the reverse, for better and more transparent markets. The Cocoa Control Board was eventually replaced by the Gold Coast Cocoa Marketing Board (GCCMB), a state monopoly acting as sole buyer and exporter of the territory's cocoa.

Government oversight provided some relief from previous anxieties; it also introduced new ones. The colonial government had its own motives for price-fixing, after all: surely it was better, colonial officials thought, that cocoa revenues be retained as state profit, which could then be responsibly invested, rather than dispersed into the savings of African peasants?[40] Britain's wartime administrators realised they could generate significant liquidity by buying up West African cocoa production at a price of their own choosing, selling it for more in the market and holding the profit in pounds sterling. They came to rely on this 'forced loan' which could be repaid 'subsequently . . . in much depreciated currency and without interest'.[41] Already by 1951, the cocoa board had accumulated a fund of £76 million – $400 million today. As this fund grew with the new boom in cocoa prices, it was used to finance an ever-wider range of projects and became central to the Gold Coast administration – creating a perennial administrative temptation to depress the price paid to farmers.[42]

This was the background to the conscious strategy by the first president of independent Ghana, Kwame Nkrumah, to use the rechristened Ghana Cocoa Marketing Board – later referred to simply as Cocobod – as a way of redirecting cocoa revenues towards the new country's industrial development. In 1954, three years before independence, Nkrumah sponsored a bill in the Legislative Assembly intended to fix cocoa prices for the next four years, thereby ensuring that the new state, and not farmers, would profit from the ongoing price rises. In his subsequent autobiography, he explained his rationale:

> It became clear to me that further steps were necessary to control the price paid locally to the cocoa farmers . . . Cocoa . . . belongs to the country and it affects everyone . . . By using cocoa funds for development and for providing amenities, it would be possible to improve the general standard of living.[43]

Like other early post-colonial leaders, Nkrumah subscribed to a version of socialism which held industry to be superior to agriculture, and he is especially remembered for his fascination with dams, power plants and factories. Anxious not to give either of the Cold War superpowers excessive influence in his country, he hoped cocoa could pay for industrial development – and indeed, with prices high, and Ghana supplying about half the world's cocoa, it was possible to make wild estimations of future cash flow. But Nkrumah was also desperate, like Guggisberg before him, to diversify the national economy away from a single crop. There was an epidemic of swollen-shoot disease; in many places, this required an entire generation of cocoa trees to be destroyed, at huge cost to the state.[44]

Ghanaian pound note, 1961. On the obverse, the Bank of Ghana; on the reverse, cocoa pods on the tree and on the ground; cocoa pulp fermenting in plantain leaves; cocoa beans drying on a bamboo mat.

No matter how justified his motives, Nkrumah's manoeuvres alienated cocoa farmers – especially those in Asante who, as independence approached, were as sceptical of Accra as they had once been of London. The Asante opposed a Ghana that would use colonial-era cocoa boards to nationalise their chocolate wealth. Proposing a federal system that would keep farming revenues closer to home, Asante chiefs and notables founded a National Liberation Movement to rival Nkrumah's independence campaign. Using a cocoa tree as their symbol, their party manifesto enjoined farmers to 'vote for cocoa', telling them, 'it is your money they want.'[45] Having defeated the NLM, Nkrumah set about crushing Asante resistance in the name of national unity. After independence, he nationalised cocoa revenues to a level unknown during the colonial era. He used those funds, not only for industrial development – especially the fantastically ambitious Volta River Project – but also for vanity projects which became increasingly extravagant and misjudged. As cocoa prices began to fall, whatever financial strategy there had been became fantastical. By 1966, when Nkrumah was ousted in a coup, he had exhausted the country's cash reserves, which at independence – one of the high points of twentieth-century cocoa prices – had stood at £560 million. Foreign debt had increased during the same period from zero to £1 billion.[46]

Ghana's cocoa industry was never able to recapture the promise of the 1950s. Almost no new trees were planted during the first ten years of independence – another result of Nkrumah's industrial emphasis; most of the country's stock dated back to the wild expansion of the 1920s and 1930s. In the 1970s, just as cocoa prices hit unprecedented heights, these trees reached the end of their bearing years, Ghanaian production collapsed and the country was shut out from the boom which so impressed visitors to Ivory Coast during those years. Even so, Cocobod remained the most liquid part of the Ghanaian state, and governments continued to use it to meet their own skyrocketing financial obligations. The 1970s saw even further suppression, therefore, of the prices paid to farmers, and large-scale smuggling into Ivory Coast began for the first time. By the early 1980s, when prices crashed again and Ghana was borrowing desperately against future harvests, cocoa revenues were swallowed by debt repayment, as well as by the enormous inefficiency of Cocobod itself, 10,000 of whose 90,000 employees did not exist.[47] Late-1980s reforms turned things around somewhat – Cocobod was overhauled, cocoa production expanded dramatically and farmers began to take a greater share of overall revenues – but it was not enough. There were always other uses for Cocobod revenues, and successive governments continued to underinvest in new tree stock or disease control.

Kwame and I are entering the outskirts of Akim Oda, which is loud with the music of roadside stalls. Many funerals have been scheduled together this weekend, and the town is unusually full. Women traders are out in force, their wares of fruit and cold drinks on their heads; when a customer approaches, there always seems to be another woman who will step in to help lower the heavy basket to the ground. Dressmaking is another popular trade for female entrepreneurs: I pass a wooden stall where a woman labours at her sewing machine; behind her is a sheet of board on which she has painted repeated Louis Vuitton logos. Next door, a drinks cupboard with a couple of plastic chairs outside has a Union Jack painted on the front and the words 'London Pub'.

Kwame and I, still walking, enter the town. He stops to buy cassava. Bunches of green plantain are laid out on wooden boards, along with dried fish and plastic bowls of tomatoes, onions and bottled drinks. The woman behind the stall wears a brightly patterned yellow dress. Kwame selects his cassava; I buy a bottle of water.

The bottle costs five Ghana cedis, or about fifty US cents. Kwame's annual income could buy about 1,600 of these bottles. I try to imagine how New Yorkers would react if bottles of water were suddenly priced at $50 – though, since tap water in New York is perfectly potable, no one would be *forced* to pay so much. Here piped water is of variable quality; many households also use groundwater, which is increasingly polluted with mining effluent dumped into the Birim River. Bottled water is essential here – as is attested by the ubiquitous plastic waste. Just another way that the poorest pay the most.

I ask Kwame what he will make with the great scaly cassava he has lifted on to his shoulder.

'My wife is making *fufu* at the weekend,' he says. 'With okra stew. The cassava needs a few days to ferment.'

He proceeds to tell me about the evils of uncivilised restaurants which use electric mixers to grind their cassava.

'It tastes of metal,' he says. 'Cassava has to be pounded. Otherwise you can't enjoy it.'

We pass a little church painted with the words 'HELL IS REAL' in capital letters, and then a creaky wooden stand whose cheerful proprietors try to sell us lottery tickets – 'Win Ten Million Cedis!' Finally, we turn into a streetside yard heady with the smell of cocoa.

Raised on bricks are several slatted bamboo mats, about three metres long and a metre wide, covered with a brown mash of fermented pulp and seeds. Men stand at the edges, their hands plunged in, pulling out the seeds and shaking the dried pulp into buckets. It is repetitive, tiring work. Further into the courtyard are more such mats, where previous rounds of seeds are drying in the sun. As they dry, they darken to a beautiful colour of cinnamon bark; they look like pebbles or indeed, as the accepted misnomer has it, beans. Passing children run their hands through them for fun. A couple of crosses woven out of straw have been laid on these beans: benediction for the final product.

At the side of the courtyard are piled plastic sheets to cover the beans if it rains. A couple of chickens run about. A woman fries chopped cassava on a fire of logs and charcoal.

One of the men, old and impressive, waves to Kwame, who greets him with a happy cry. 'He is Yaw Oduro,' Kwame tells me. 'The man who buys our cocoa.'

Kwame summons the old man to join us for coffee. Yaw protests, pointing to his hands, which are covered in dried pulp. Kwame insists, and Yaw goes to wash. He joins us a minute later.

'Come to my office,' he says. We follow him to a small room next door. On the wall is a poster showing a farmer harvesting his cocoa; the text declares in Twi, 'I do not allow child labour.' The room contains very little except a chair, a set of scales and, piled to the ceiling, fat jute sacks stamped with black letters:

GHANA COCOA BOARD
PRODUCE OF GHANA

'Farmers bring their cocoa here,' says Yaw. 'We buy at the official price and deliver the sacks to Cocobod. Cocobod sends them to the port in Tema, where they leave for Europe.'

Not for the first time on this journey, I express my dismay that Ghanaians have so little presence in the truly profitable sectors of this industry: processing and manufacturing. Yaw laughs.

'Politicians don't want to see a thriving chocolate industry in Ghana,' he says. 'It doesn't suit their interests. Many have tried to set up chocolate factories, and they usually fail. Cocobod is not there to help locals. They want to sell to foreigners. They need dollars and euros to pay their debts!'

Only 20 per cent of Ghanaian output is processed in the country – mainly into so-called chocolate liquor, which is the intermediate product required by the confectionery industry.[48] This involves roasting the beans, extracting the nibs or kernels and grinding them into paste. The dominant player is Cargill, a multi-billion-dollar private food conglomerate headquartered in Minnesota. Rumbling behind is Ghana's own Cocoa Processing Company (CPC), which, despite its enormous capacity, generally runs half empty, posts perennial losses and has even begun to have its assets confiscated.[49] The fact that Cocobod is the majority shareholder makes things worse rather than better: CPC is obliged to continue buying beans even when it makes no business sense.

A few small companies persist in making chocolate in Ghana because – despite the ill-will of Cocobod and government, the expensive and frequently interrupted electricity, the difficulties of transport and logistics, the great bureaucratic complexities – they simply believe that Ghanaian chocolate should exist. There is little capital available for such companies, and most subsist at the level of luxury curiosities.[50] None of the dominant firms – Nestlé, Mars Wrigley and so on – even thinks about manufacturing chocolate in a country where afternoons are 30 degrees and refrigeration so onerous. Very little of the ultimate value of these jute sacks, therefore, is realised in this country. And the proportion is going down. The international firms have become expert at playing partners against each other so as constantly to improve their deal; the result has been that every other player in the supply chain has seen their profit share decrease. In the 1970s, farmers earned 40–50 per cent of the retail price of consumer milk chocolate; that figure fell to about 16 per cent in the 1980s. Today it is between 3 and 7 per cent.[51]

Kwame leads us to a little roadside café, where his wife and mother have come to join us. We sit in chairs hammered together out of beautiful planks of wood, straight from the forest. Real wood is so rare in 'rich' countries; here there is no MDF or chipboard, and the meanest little footrest is made from priceless tree trunks.

My companions order Milo, an instant drink manufactured by Nestlé Ghana from malt and cocoa. I order the same.

Kwame's wife wears beautifully styled makeup and a dramatic long dress in purple and yellow. She introduces herself as Dziedzorm.

'It means "happy",' she explains. 'That's why I'm always delighted.'

I ask her what she does. Her face drops in theatrical disappointment.

'Can you not tell I'm in fashion?' she teases, gesturing to her clothes.

'My wife is a dressmaker,' says Kwame.

'I'm a fashion designer,' she corrects him.

'I am sixty-three,' says Kwame's mother. 'I have three children. One is missing. My son is here and helps me with my farm. My daughter lives in Accra with her husband.'

It takes me a moment to understand that one of her children has passed away.

The mother, too, is impressively dressed, with maroon glasses, an elegant black scarf around her head and, cradled in her lap, a small maroon handbag embellished with a YSL logo. This was her outfit for the funeral she attended today.

'My father was chief of a tribe,' she continues. 'I come from a royal family. I dropped out of school at a young age and began farming plantain and cassava. Now I have three cocoa farms. The land came from my mother, and from her mother before her. Cocoa trees have taken care of all my children, fed them and educated them. I have a passion for those trees.'

I ask whether there are any particular difficulties to farming as a woman.

'It makes no difference whether you are a man or a woman,' she says. 'Only if you are hard-working or lazy. There are many female farmers. More than men, in fact. Men farm too, but women are better. Men leave and go to the cities. Women farm.'

'I agree with you,' says Yaw. 'But it is not so easy any more. Whether you are a man or a woman.'

'No,' she says. 'The price is very bad. And the quality has gone down. In my parents' time, they only needed to spray once a year, and the crop was bountiful. They didn't even need to pay attention to the farm. Now you have to spray five times, and if you don't inspect it every day you can lose everything.'

Dziedzorm remonstrates with her in Twi. Kwame laughs dismissively at his wife.

'She is telling my mother she needs to do some magic,' he explains to me.

'Yes,' says Dziedzorm. 'You never know who is doing witchcraft to you. It can be anyone, even your family member. Maybe they did not mean to do you harm, they just summoned a spirit to give them some protection. But once the spirit has done that job it is thirsty for activity and it turns evil. You will never know how it happened. All you know is your farm does not do well, there is no money and your relationships turn bad.'

'So what should you do?' I ask.

'You need to take it to your church. Not an Orthodox church. People just preach there; they can't see spiritual things. You take it to a charismatic church where they can fight the juju.'

The explosion of charismatic churches is one of the most conspicuous features of modern Ghanaian society. It dates back to the early 1980s, when, in response to a profound economic crisis, the government embarked on a programme of sweeping market-oriented economic reforms, which dramatically reduced state welfare and public employment.[52] Jobs became more informal and uncertain, and ordinary Ghanaians had to become more entrepreneurial to survive.

Charismatic churches have played a crucial role in helping people navigate the resulting, high-risk, high-aspiration society.[53] Most preach some version of the 'prosperity gospel', which links spiritual salvation to material success and helps align Christian virtues – such as hard work, discipline and sobriety – with neo-liberal labour conditions.[54] In an era of rapid urbanisation, churches also provide homes and communities to many young people and migrants; often, they offer welfare, mutual aid, professional skills training and health counselling.[55] But, as Dziedzorm reveals, these churches also reinterpret traditional beliefs about witchcraft and spiritual attack, promising protection from everything which might impede personal ambition, intimate relationships and economic success.[56]

Kwame is frustrated by this talk of churches.

'Churches do nothing,' he says. 'They have nothing to offer.'

His mother smiles.

'I am a church elder,' she says. 'In the Presbyterian church. But my son won't come with me. He can't see what is in it for him. But I can tell you we have more than one hundred churches in this town. Akim Oda is on sacred land.'[57]

I ask Yaw what he thinks about church.

'All I know is this,' he says, 'All our politicians go to church on Sundays. They are very faithful to that place. So it cannot be any good.'

He lets out a falsetto scream of laughter, and Kwame slaps him on the back. I laugh too. These people have much to complain about, but whenever two or more are together it is always a party.

The Milo is weirdly tasty, and I tell them so. Kwame tells me it is good for health.

'You should drink it in the morning. Malt and milk and cocoa. All healthy things.'

'Do you eat chocolate?' I ask. 'Do you like it?'

Kwame laughs.

'I have never eaten chocolate,' he says.

The two elders, who have been handling cocoa for the last sixty years, say the same. Dziedzorm is the only one who has eaten chocolate.

'You see what I live with?' she says mockingly. 'I grew up in Tema. The big city, the port. I grew up with many experiences. When I got married, I moved to this jungle.'

'It is a hard life,' I say. 'For all of you. Why don't you sell your land? Try another living?'

'There is nothing else to do,' says Kwame. 'Farming is the only source of living here. If you don't farm, you won't survive.'

'You won't survive,' echoes his wife.

'If you sell your land, you've done a mistake,' says Yaw. 'Because you don't know what will happen in the future. Land is security. I am not just a cocoa buyer, I am a farmer too. I have two plots, seven and three hectares. That land came from my family. I have no choice but to farm it. My children are all in Accra. If I stop farming my land, someone will take it, without my knowledge or my consent.'

'So many have moved to Accra,' I say. 'You could move too.'

'What will we do in Accra?' demands Kwame. 'We don't have a place to sleep in Accra, let alone a job. Have you seen rents in Accra?'

'Have you seen the people on the streets?' says Dziedzorm. 'You see people crazy on marijuana. They take all these pills and mix them with Benylin. Cough syrup. Some of them moved to Accra thinking they would make it in the city.'

Dziedzorm invokes the great universe of urban insecurity which awaits so many of those moving from farming communities to the city. But of course hers is the farmer's perspective. If I were to rove the streets of Accra, many would give me an opposing view. Land flight is one of the reasons, after all, for West Africa's cocoa-production crisis. Even I can spot abandoned and undercultivated farms.

But Yaw's anxieties are real. Still today, the apex landowners, in rural areas at least, are tribal chiefs and the state. Nkrumah did not wish to confront chiefly power any more than the British had, so he left traditional structures broadly intact. This means that the people around this table do not have an absolute title to their land. Thanks to a chiefly grant to their ancestors, they have customary ownership, which is recognised by all as long as they are alive and farming. But if they stop farming, they tell me, others might claim that their land is wasted and petition the chief to reallocate it. Nor is there a developed market for rural real estate, because customary owners are not supposed to sell their land. It is certainly not supposed to pass out of the community. Land cannot easily be turned into cash, therefore, which could be used to start another life. There are real barriers to leaving, and farmers may justifiably feel that they have no way out.

'Who do you hold responsible for all this?' I ask.

Everybody answers together, 'The government.'

Kwame's mother elaborates. 'The government buys cocoa from us at a very low price and sells it at a very high price. They are the only ones who make any money from cocoa. It is not good.'

'The problem is that Cocobod is the only state organisation with any money,' says Yaw. 'So the government uses it to fund all their activities, make sure they get re-elected. They don't have any interest in farmers, and they have no knowledge about cocoa. They use Cocobod like an ATM. They use it to give jobs to their foot soldiers. Cocobod employs thousands of extension officers, who come to your farm to offer guidance. Years ago, those people could look at your trees and your soil and tell you exactly what to do. Nowadays, they know nothing.'

'Many of them are just smuggling fertiliser,' says Kwame. 'They have to give you ten bags of fertiliser but instead they give you five. The rest they sell to Ivory Coast.'

'You will see', adds Kwame, 'that the head of Cocobod is always the president's favourite. It has to be like that. If he doesn't put his favourite there, he can't oil the party machinery. He needs Cocobod to give out favours. Look at Cocobod's scholarships for farmers' children! How many farmers' children get them today? They all go to the children of party members.'

I have no way of verifying their allegations. But clearly, they view the system as broken. 'These days Ghana is a democracy,' I say. 'If things are as bad as you say, you can vote these people out.'

'We *are* a democracy,' says Kwame's mother. 'That's very precious. We don't want to go back to dictatorship. Our young people are becoming very good at campaigning and showing politicians what will happen if they don't take care of the people.'

'But you can't always vote them out,' says Kwame. 'Our local politicians won't be voted out, whatever they do. In this region they know they will be re-elected, simply because they are Akan. People don't vote against their own tribe.'

'We are on our own,' says Yaw. 'It's like this: you plant your trees. For five years you take care of them, and there is no crop. The government doesn't help you. Then the trees start to bear fruit. Suddenly the government is interested, because they want the seeds. Every year, you do all the work, you harvest the pods, you dry the beans, you deliver them in sacks to the government, but the government still gives you nothing. Then you grow old, and your trees are also old. And you are still on your own.'

There are murmurs of assent from around the table.

'Have you heard of Satan?' he adds. 'In the Bible? The government is our Satan. If you are a farmer in Ghana, Satan has sentenced you to do that work.'

He lets out another high-pitched scream of laughter.

Ten thousand kilometres from Ghana, in today's Colombia, Ecuador and Peru, lie the humid lowland forests where *Theobroma cacao* originated. In its native lands, this bizarre and captivating tree has been cherished since ancient times, principally because of the striking qualities of its seeds, which contain traces of caffeine, as well as a mild stimulant called theobromine, both members of a family of compounds called xanthine alkaloids. They also contain the anti-depressive agents serotonin and phenylethylamine, along with the fatty deposits which make up cocoa butter, whose complex chemistry gives it rich nutritional and therapeutic properties.

Three and a half millennia before the tree ever touched African shores, it was already domesticated around what is now Ecuador.[58] From there, cultivation spread northwards into Mesoamerica, where we find the first archaeological evidence of cocoa brews: jars and serving vessels from 1400–1100 BCE with traces of theobromine and caffeine deposited on the interior. In the Olmec society, whose centre was in today's northern Mexico, cocoa became a prestige product. The Olmec gave it the name the Spanish would learn many centuries later: *kakawa*.[59]

That word passed from the Olmec to the Maya, who institutionalised cocoa as the focus of elite celebration and temple ritual – somewhat as champagne is institutionalised today. Even in those regions where it did not grow, cocoa was essential to the conduct of social life, and a substantial system of trade and distribution grew up around it. It would have been quite familiar to the Nahua peoples to the west – the Nahuatl version of the word was *kakawa-tl* – long before they moved in to establish the empire known as Aztec. But the Aztec heartlands were too high and cool for growing cocoa, which was brought by trade and tribute, therefore, from warmer provinces across southern and eastern Mexico, and down through today's Guatemala, El Salvador, Honduras and Nicaragua.[60]

The empire's wealth was symbolised in giant cocoa warehouses, the biggest of which contained, according to one Spanish chronicler, close to a billion beans (40,000 loads – a load containing 24,000 beans, which was the standard quantity carried in the backpack of a cocoa transporter).[61] Tribute in cocoa beans led naturally to formal monetisation, for which they were well suited, being portable and durable, and small enough in value that they could be used for everyday transactions. Anecdotes passed down from

Spanish travellers suggest, for instance, that a small rabbit cost thirty beans, a turkey egg or an avocado three, a tomato or a tamale one.[62] The Spanish were impressed by this exotic currency grown on trees, which was convertible into gold: one gold peso, they calculated, equalled between 4,000 and 4,800 beans, depending on the quantity of the previous harvest.[63] They wanted a part of it: the above estimation for the contents of the emperor Moctezuma's warehouse comes from an account of an all-night heist, during which Spanish raiders carried away 600 loads of cocoa stored in 'large, vat-like containers made of wicker, and so huge that six men could not encircle them, plastered inside and out with clay, all arranged in order, a sight to behold'.[64]

For Mesoamerican societies – as for nearly everyone until the nineteenth century – cocoa was consumed as a *drink*. Fermented beans were roasted and ground, usually mixed with maize, and then boiled. Since they contained a great deal of insoluble fat, the drink was frothed to prevent separation, usually by pouring it repeatedly from a height between clay vessels (Figure 24). The resulting decoction was rarely sweet – it was bitter, rather, and hearty – but it was flavoured with a range of fruits, flowers, spices and herbs. Different tones were accentuated by selecting beans of different varieties and from different regions, some of which were particularly prestigious. Cocoa was also brewed as a medicine; the recipes that have survived from pre-Columbian times, which involve a dazzling array of plant and animal additions, are all medicinal.[65]

The first detailed accounts of cocoa brewed for feasting and pleasure come from Spanish travellers. The Franciscan friar Bernardino de Sahagún, for instance, who travelled widely in Mesoamerica in the middle decades of the sixteenth century, lists a variety of cocoa drinks served to the Aztec emperor: 'green, made of tender cacao; honeyed chocolate made with ground-up dried flowers – with green vanilla pods; bright red chocolate; orange-red chocolate; rose-coloured chocolate; black chocolate; white chocolate'.[66] Served in elegant pots and drinking vessels, the extravagance of these decoctions was an important expression of the Aztec power system – as is obvious from Díaz's courtly descriptions:

> [Servants of the emperor Moctezuma] brought some of every kind of fruit that grew in the country, but he ate very little of it. Sometimes they brought him . . . a drink made from the cocoa plant, which they said he took before visiting his wives . . . I saw them bring in a good fifty large jugs of this chocolate, all frothed up, of which he would drink a little. They always served it with great reverence.[67]

In regions where cocoa was farmed and therefore plentiful, however, it was not the sole preserve of elites. Ordinary people also consumed it; cocoa traces have been found in many household grinding stones. Cocoa was expensive but not inaccessible: as a luxury drink, it supplied a festive spirit to weddings, births and funerals. The general population also used both seeds and pulp to produce medicines and ointments; they probably also used cocoa infusions to flavour maize, fish and meat.[68]

During the many centuries of cocoa's centrality to Mesoamerican societies, it acquired extraordinary symbolic power. These societies shared a sense that the cosmos was made of elemental substances, which had their counterpart in human flesh, blood, semen, faeces. Maize was the most primordial of these substances. A Mayan myth transcribed in the eighteenth century by a Dominican priest describes how the gods decided to create human beings to 'nourish and sustain' themselves; at that point four symbolic animals were sent to discover which food should 'enter into the flesh of man'. The animals found maize: 'And thus they found the food, and this was what went into the flesh of created man, the made man; this was his blood; of this the blood of man was made.'[69] Maize was the essence of the human, and it was the essence of the cosmos. The Maize God stood at the centre of all things – and the first food to grow from his body was cocoa.[70] His fertility was often symbolised, in fact, by cocoa pods growing from his body.

Partly as a result of its connection with birth and fertility, cocoa became powerfully identified with blood. In both Mayan and Aztec carvings, cocoa pods are shown spurting blood when pierced.[71] In one Aztec tale, the cocoa tree first emerged from the blood of a virtuous princess, who was slain by her husband's enemies for refusing to betray his treasure ('And so it was that Quetzalcóatl gave to humans the gift of the cocoa tree').[72] Prepared cocoa drinks had some physical resemblances to blood; sometimes they were stained red with *achiote*, a flower pigment. Blood was often added to cocoa: one historian notes that in Cholula, Mexico, a special cocoa beverage was made 'from water in which knives used in human sacrifices had been washed'.[73] Spanish inquisitors encountered many women who had mixed their menstrual blood into a cocoa drink in the belief it could make a man fall in love with them.[74] Naturally, for cultures so preoccupied by blood offering, this connection heightened cocoa's ritual significance. Both Mayan and Aztec societies believed in the importance of feeding blood to the gods, and cocoa was offered as a botanical analogue – a 'food of the gods' which would nourish the presiding spirits, allowing them to sustain the fertility of agricultural systems.

The Spanish were curious about cocoa – which they would later refer to as *chocolate* – an adaptation of another, unrelated Nahuatl word, *chokola:tl*, whose root is mysterious but which presumably refers to some kind of drink ('*a:*' = 'water').[75] Its evident importance for pagan ritual certainly gave them pause, but they quickly realised it had very attractive properties. For a start, since they had not tasted tea or coffee, cocoa provided their first encounter with the pleasures of alkaloids.[76] Cocoa was also made by boiling water, which eradicated pathogens, and, though tasty and stimulating, it produced no intoxication. Most intriguingly, cocoa in its sixteenth-century form was fatty, rich and nutritious, which meant it could substitute for food. The account of the so-called Anonymous Conquistador emphasises that advantage:

> To drink it one must open the mouth wide, for since it has a froth it is necessary to make room for it to dissolve and go in gradually. This drink is the most wholesome and substantial of any food or beverage in the world, because whoever drinks a cup of this liquor can go through the day without taking anything else even if he is on a journey.[77]

This quality made chocolate very desirable to a class of hard-travelling invaders and missionaries whose religion prohibited them from consuming nourishing food from every midnight until Communion the next morning, whatever time that was – in addition to the forty-day fast of Lent.[78] Chocolate could provide a loophole in these restrictions, hence the extraordinary attention devoted by Catholic theologians to a seemingly trivial question: was chocolate a drink or a food? Conservatives pointed to its full-bodied constitution and the rush of energy it supplied, arguing it was a food and therefore infringed fast restrictions. Often, they also invoked the persistent idea that chocolate stimulated sexual desire. The debate was not fully resolved until well into the seventeenth century, when a Spanish jurist formulated a pragmatic solution: cocoa could be considered a drink and therefore consumed at times of fast, as long as it was made only with water and not with substantial additions.[79]

The very fact that this debate was taking place demonstrated that ecclesiastical authorities were in agreement about one thing: chocolate drinking did not violate any fundamental Christian principle. Unlike coca consumption – repeatedly outlawed, and regarded as incompatible with Christian faith and practice – cocoa gained rapid religious acceptance. A celebrated 1685 treatise on chocolate includes eyewitness accounts from 'the Indies' to suggest that 'people drink chocolate in churches while the divine office is being celebrated.'[80] Native converts in Mexico City were encouraged to bring their traditional cocoa offerings into the cathedral and to place them at the wooden feet of the so-called Christ of the Cacao (the cathedral's motives were certainly financial as well as spiritual). Cocoa was incorporated without hesitation, therefore, into the culinary repertoire of Spanish colonists, who rapidly set about producing it themselves. They took over Mesoamerican tribute networks and extended existing cocoa groves along today's Mexican Pacific coast, and through Guatemala and El Salvador.[81] Within a couple of decades of their first encounter with the crop, they were clearing forest for new cocoa plantations in Ecuador and Venezuela – source of the 'Caracas cacao' that would be prized around the world until the nineteenth century. These were originally worked by coerced native Americans; by the mid-seventeenth century, the dwindling numbers of natives were being reinforced by transported African slaves.[82]

Cocoa arrived in Spain at some point in the mid-1500s, and over the following century it acquired a central position in Spanish courtly life. Though the Spanish preferred their chocolate sweet – adding large quantities of Caribbean cane sugar – they remained faithful in other respects to the fatty, foamy drink they had discovered in Mexico, even respecting the original marigolds, vanilla, ear-flowers and *achiote*. They did however develop their own vessels for whisking and serving chocolate, making of it a spectacle that impressed such visitors as the Comtesse d'Aulnoy, a French writer and traveller who visited Madrid in 1679:

> Then they brought out chocolate, each porcelain cup on a small agate saucer trimmed with gold, with sugar in a matching box. There was iced chocolate, hot chocolate, and chocolate with milk and eggs. It is eaten with biscuits, or with small rolls as dry as if they had been roasted, which are made especially for this purpose. There are women who drink up to six cups in a row, and often two or three times a day.[83]

The drink later began to spread to the great houses of France and Italy – though Spain remained its acknowledged home. In Italy, the doctor and polymath Francesco Redi (1626–97) declared that, by adding jasmine flowers and lemon peel to the traditional cinnamon, amber, musk and vanilla, his native Florence had improved upon Spain, 'where it is [nonetheless] made in all perfection'.[84] French aristocrats began to drink chocolate under Louis XIII (r. 1610–43) and Louis XIV (r. 1643–1715), both of whom were married to Spanish infantas. In France too, the most prestigious and extravagant recipes were for a long time labelled 'in the Spanish style'. It was in Versailles, however, that chocolate ultimately shed its Spanish flavour – along with the heavy associations 'of Jesuitical gloom [and] the Inquisition' – and became the centrepiece of rococo chic.[85] Eighteenth-century French aristocrats would not only drink their chocolate but also enjoy an ever-expanding range of chocolate desserts.

An advertisement in the *Publick Advertiser* suggests that in June 1657 Londoners were still on the whole unfamiliar with chocolate:

> In Bishopsgate Street in Queen's Head Alley, at a Frenchman's house, is an excellent West India drink called chocolate, to be sold, where you may have it ready at any time, and also unmade at reasonable rates.[86]

Chocolate was more urbane in England than in France, a drink of the commercial elite. Accounts by the London diarist Samuel Pepys suggest that, in the 1660s, chocolate was becoming a staple of well-to-do officials such as himself. At one point, he notes that someone left him a gift of chocolate, presumably a hard cake of processed nibs, which could then be mixed into water; at another, he records that a friend served him chocolate to dispel a hangover.[87] The importance of chocolate (as well as coffee and tea) to the emerging system of London clubs is reflected in such names as the Cocoa Tree and White's Chocolate House. These houses also appealed to discerning clients by promising chocolate 'in the Spanish style'.[88]

Chocolate was a costly and elaborate ritual, and, wherever it travelled from its American home, it found itself in competition with alternatives. In those parts where tea or coffee was already well established – which is to say almost all of Asia and North Africa – it rarely made inroads (Spain's colony of the Philippines was a conspicuous exception).[89] But in Europe all three of these products arrived around the same time – as did tobacco – and jostled together for a place alongside existing alcohol practices. Naturally, these exotic agents were subjected to intense medical scrutiny. Seventeenth-century Europeans imagined the human body as a system of fluids, hot and cold, and wet and dry. The near-simultaneous appearance of three new brews, respectively from America, Asia and Africa, containing unfamiliar and stimulating alkaloids, naturally caused people to ask what influence they would have on the existing balance of 'humours'.[90] Apothecaries studied them and observed their effects on the well and the sick. An apothecary from Lyon, Philippe Dufour, was one of many

Europeans to try to sum up existing knowledge on the subject: his *New and Curious Treatises on Coffee, on Tea and on Chocolate – a Work Equally Necessary for Doctors as for Those who Appreciate Their Health* (1685) debated each of the products in turn.* Open-minded and an admirer of Asian art, Dufour ultimately endorsed all three

Frontispiece to Dufour's book: a Turk drinks coffee, a Chinese drinks tea and an American drinks chocolate.

* The section on chocolate began: 'The use of Chocolate has become so common in Europe, first in Spain and then in England, in France and in Italy, that we should no longer consider it to belong to America, where it was born, but as a drink that has become naturalised among us. That obliges me to examine its composition and virtues . . . in order to know if it truly deserves all the praises we give it, and to which kinds of people it is suited.' Dufour, *Traitez nouveaux & curieux du café, du thé et du chocolate*, 305–6.

drinks, though he did not neglect the harmful consequences of excess. In the case of chocolate, he worried it might produce weight gain and lethargy in those already of a 'hot' disposition and warned against excessive flavouring.

Ultimately, all three brews became wildly popular in Europe; but their relative importance differed from place to place. Chocolate was associated with a pleasure principle that was quintessentially Catholic and aristocratic. Such was the import of the drink's most famous on-stage appearance – in Mozart's *Così fan tutte* (1790), set amid the palaces of the Neapolitan aristocracy. As a maid came onstage complaining about her princess employers, for whom she was simultaneously whisking chocolate, Da Ponte's libretto treated audiences to an endless stream of sexual double entendres:

È mezza ora che sbatto;	I've been beating it for half an hour;
Il cioccolatte è fatto, ed a me tocca	The chocolate is made, and I'm left to stand here
Restar ad odorarlo a secca bocca?	And smell it without my mouth (/vagina) getting wet?
Non è forse la mia come la vostra,	Isn't mine [my mouth/ vagina] just like yours?
O garbate signore,	Oh gracious ladies
Che a voi dèssi l'essenza,	Why should the essence fall to you
E a me l'odore?	And to me only the smell?
Per Bacco, vo' assaggiarlo: cospettaccio!	By Bacchus, I want to try it! Good heavens!
Com' è buono!	It's so good!
[Si forbe la bocca.]	*[She wipes her mouth.]*[91]

For those most incensed by stories of Catholic decadence, real life made things even worse. In 1772, rumours – most of them invented – reached Paris that a famously depraved aristocrat, the

Noël Le Mire (1724–1800), 'La Crainte' ('Fear'), engraving after a painting by Jean-Baptiste Le Prince (1734–1781). A noise startles the room: the noblewoman and her dog look towards the door as her lover leaps to hide behind the bed. After a night of frolics – which have overturned a chair – the couple were about to recharge themselves with a cup of chocolate before they were disturbed. Prominent on the table – and symbolising the erotic action – is a silver *chocolatière*: a specially designed pot with a hole in the centre of the lid, into which a whisk was inserted and agitated.

Marquis de Sade, had held a ball at which, under cover of chocolate, he had lured the town of Marseille into infernal excess:

> Into the dessert he slipped chocolate *pastilles* . . . He had mixed [an aphrodisiac] into these *pastilles*. The virtue of this medication is well known: it proved to be such that all who ate it, burning with immodest ardour, abandoned themselves to the excesses to which the most amorous frenzy leads . . . And so it was that M. de Sade enjoyed his sister-in-law, with whom he fled to avoid the punishment he deserves. Several persons died of the excesses in which they indulged . . . and others are still very sick.[92]

Two years later, a chocolate scandal penetrated the Vatican itself. The English politician Horace Walpole received the news from his friend Sir Horace Mann, who wrote to him from Italy. 'The murder of the Pope has been proved to the clearest evidence,' declared Mann, 'a slow poison was given to him . . . in a dish of chocolate last Holy Thursday at the Vatican, where he assisted at the ceremonies of that day.'[93] In truth, the fate of Clement XIV was no more than a rumour, but Mann's certainty did much to flatter Walpole's well-known anti-Catholic feeling.

Even back in England, a whiff of aristocratic scandal attached to chocolate houses, for their obvious purpose was – as the *Tatler* put it in 1709 – 'Gallantry, Pleasure and Entertainment', and gambling and prostitution were frequently part of the fun (Figure 25).[94] For the good middle classes of London, Amsterdam or Hamburg, therefore, who sought a morning boost to their labour power rather than to their libido, the obvious destination was the tea or coffee house. Few institutions could be more *productive*, after all: as hubs of newspaper consumption, artistic discussion, political debate and business dealing, tea and coffee houses incubated an energetic and profit-minded Protestant modernity.[95]

There was also the question of price. Throughout its era of baroque elegance, European chocolate was grown on slave-worked plantations that were not only spectacularly cruel in human terms but also poorly adapted to the job at hand. Rationalised plantations did not suit this delicate and whimsical crop, and over time they produced lower and lower yields. Partly as a result, chocolate remained, by the early nineteenth century, significantly more expensive than tea and coffee, which found many new consumers and came to seem more democratic and modern. Britain's was a tea empire, the United States was dominated by coffee, as was much of continental Europe. While Europe's cocoa imports remained under 10,000 tonnes per year at the end of the eighteenth century – more than half of that going to Spain – tea imports exceeded 20,000 tonnes, and coffee imports came close to 100,000.[96] Even Latin America learned the love of the foreign brews.

'Slaves harvesting cocoa in Mexico', 1864. Illustration from Louis Figuier's *Le Savant du Foyer*, a French introduction to science for children. The artist, who had clearly never seen cocoa trees, made the common European mistake of imagining the pods grew from the branches and not the trunk.

But as the eighteenth century tipped over into the nineteenth, as the pleasure-loving French aristocracy was destroyed and Protestant Britain became the supreme capitalist power, commercial energy and profit would also transform chocolate. The beginnings were small: England's largest manufacturer, Fry's of Bristol, employed sixteen workers in 1835, while Rowntree's was little more than a York grocery store, and Cadbury operated out of a Birmingham shop.[97] But important innovations were taking place. In 1828, the Amsterdam chocolate maker Casparus van Houten patented a machine for pressing cocoa butter out of chocolate, so eliminating the high fat content which had always limited its solubility and made it heavy on the stomach.[98] The Van Houten press took some time to travel, but once it did it unlocked other advances. Fry's began to offer eating chocolate in the 1840s, an eccentric product which became far more palatable after the company acquired a Van Houten press in 1868.[99] In the 1870s, the Swiss company Lindt discovered conching – a technique for producing a highly aromatic 'melting chocolate' – which proved a revolution for the baking and confectionery industries.[100] Another Swiss, Daniel Peter, reduced the bitterness of eating chocolate by combining it with Nestlé's sweetened condensed milk, resulting in a milk-chocolate empire later acquired – like so many of the other Swiss firms – by Nestlé. Enhanced product ranges allowed all these companies to invest in larger factories, to develop striking packaging and advertising and, importantly, to establish direct connections to cocoa suppliers – which were still almost exclusively in Latin America. When he inherited his family firm in 1853, for instance, Émile-Justin Menier was concerned to extend his control over the supply chain. He purchased cocoa estates in Nicaragua, and sugar beet farms and refineries in France, along with his own ships and branch railway. By the 1870s, his factory in the Paris suburbs produced 4,000 tonnes of chocolate a year; with another factory in London and a distribution centre in New York, Menier claimed to be the biggest chocolate company in the world (Figure 26).[101]

Such large companies were able to offer their products at affordable prices, which coincided happily with the sudden increase in spending power of Western industrial workers. 'A Belgian male labourer needed to work sixty hours to buy a half-kilo bar of chocolate in 1893,' writes one historian, 'but only just over an hour in 1913.'[102] The power of modern chocolate was not in luxury items, but in products for the mass market. These products depended on many further technical innovations, mostly aimed at making the product lighter, more digestible and more aesthetically pleasing. A partial list of the enduring chocolate snacks developed at the beginning of the twentieth century gives a sense of the range of experiments being conducted: Cadbury Dairy Milk (1905), Hershey's Kisses (1907), Toblerone (1908), Cadbury Flake (1920), Milky Way (1923), Cadbury Fruit & Nut (1926), Reese's Peanut Butter Cups (1928), Snickers (1930), Mars Bar (1932), KitKat (1935), Maltesers (1937), Smarties (1937).

The complexity of the industrial processes, and the extravagance of the accompanying marketing campaigns, meant that big, established firms tended to oust all others. The companies driving the chocolate boom of the turn of the century were the incumbents of

France, Britain, Germany, the Netherlands and Switzerland – most of which were founded before 1840 – with the addition of some American late entrants: Hershey's (1894) and Mars (1911). Each of the leading chocolate nations was dominated by one or two companies, which faced little competition. In the early twentieth century, Menier accounted for one-quarter of France's bean imports, the Walter Baker Company one-half of those into the United States. Britain's Cadbury's, Fry's and Rowntree's – which were inter-related by marriage, and sometimes operated in concert – together consumed two-thirds of England's bean imports. Van Houten employed one-fifth of Dutch chocolate workers; in Switzerland, Suchard was the outstanding giant until Nestlé acquired a consortium of Swiss chocolate manufacturers in 1928.[103]

There were other reasons why scale mattered. The first was that chocolate executives needed to invest far more in their workers than their peers in textiles or steel, say. The work was delicate and skilled, the raw materials expensive and perishable, the costs of worker lateness or inattention high. To attract skilled employees, and to ensure they could devote themselves fully to their labour, manufacturers offered salaries and benefits that were unknown in other sectors. In the case of Menier, Cadbury and Hershey, workers were provided with dedicated company towns equipped with schools, hospitals, churches, parks and even theatres.[104]

The prerequisite for such lavish investment, obviously, was profit – and profit depended, in turn, on state protection and support. This was the second reason chocolate companies had to be big: they needed political influence. Many chocolate moguls were actively involved both in national politics and in the administration of the towns that were home to their factories and workers.* Many chocolate companies benefited greatly from

* Menier and his sons had distinguished careers as mayors, members of Parliament and senators. The English Quakers were active as thought leaders, lobbyists and local officials; the Cadbury family pursued political campaigns through the pages of its newspaper, the *Daily News*. Outside Britain and France, chocolate executives were more discreet, but Stollwerck, Suchard, Lindt, Cailler, Nestlé and Van Houten all fielded mayors, councillors and chamber-of-commerce leaders.

political protection. At the turn of the century, Germany's tariffs on imported chocolate were ten times greater than those on wheat and nearly three times those on high-value cheeses, such as Italian Gorgonzola or Parmesan.[105] The United States charged duties on chocolate imports of 50 per cent, France about 90 per cent.[106] Only in Britain, the free-trade superpower, were tariffs on imported chocolate a mere 5 per cent – and British consumers consequently enjoyed a wide choice of international brands. The main benefit to the companies was not that Menier in France was protected from imports from Switzerland; it was that the industrialised nations were protected from competition from cocoa-growing countries. One of the reasons no chocolate giant arose in Latin America or the Caribbean was that they were prevented from selling in the rich consumer markets. Cruger and Leotaud, for instance, 'a model chocolate manufactory'[107] in Trinidad, failed for this reason: the island could not place tariffs on British imports – that was the point of the imperial system – while Trinidadian exports to core consumer markets were highly taxed.[108]

But the most important reason chocolate companies had to be big was this: they needed sufficient political and financial power in order to ensure that their cocoa imports – along with their imports of sugar, nuts and flavourings – remained cheap. Producing millions of low-cost, low-profit, cocoa-based items required companies to have sufficient clout to manipulate prices – by influencing colonial policy or colluding with their competitors. In 1906, for instance, the powerful cocoa planters of São Tomé decided they would take advantage of the fact that they were now the world's biggest supplier and would form a cartel to hoard stocks and keep prices high. Such measures necessitated a powerful corporate response: German and Swiss chocolate companies reacted by setting up a cocoa-buying 'pool' (the Kakao-Einkaufsgesellschaft) to coordinate prices and so resist the offensive. Menier also joined the society; the British firms had suggested they would join in too when, in 1908, the planters' cartel collapsed.[109] The fact that chocolate firms had to be powerful enough to wage such political battles established a structure for the global industry: a small number of very large buyers and millions of small sellers. This is where this historical overview begins to rejoin our experiences in Ghana.

Let us return to the Latin American cocoa fields of the nineteenth century, which were in a turbulent state. The colonial cocoa order was shaken by wars of independence – which had sometimes destroyed cocoa estates – and the abolition of slavery. Wherever ordinary people, including ex-slaves, were able to buy or squat land, there was a burst of peasant cultivation. This was the case in Venezuela, whose independence war ignited the internal divisions between slaves and creole planters; it was the case in parts of the Brazilian Amazon and some of the Caribbean islands.[110] But more usually large landowners were able to turn the new conditions to their own advantage, sometimes expanding to a scale never seen before or since.

Large planters presented themselves as ideal partners for big chocolate, promising labour discipline and consistent brand quality. But they were often not as stable as their size suggested. Many planters were viewed as politically illegitimate and had constantly to fight off land claims from traditional owners and squatters. Others had incurred enormous debts to acquire their land and collapsed into bankruptcy when cocoa demand and prices collapsed in 1914. All faced the perennial problems of sizeable plantations: endemic disease and, after four or five decades, declining yields.[111]

Both the Spanish and Portuguese reacted to the loss of their Latin American possessions by exploiting equivalent ecologies in Africa. The Spanish began cultivating cocoa on Fernando Po. Leading up to the independence of Brazil in 1822, the Portuguese transferred seedlings from Bahia to their West African islands of São Tomé and Príncipe.[112] The abolition of New World slavery, and the exhaustion of many old estates, accelerated this shift. During the later nineteenth century, colonial banks, investors and politicians converted São Tomé and Príncipe into vast cocoa plantations; in 1905 they briefly became the biggest cocoa producers in the world.[113] The Dutch, meanwhile, tried to establish cocoa plantations in Java, but without much success.

The landscape of large cocoa plantations was conspicuously cruel. The powerful landowners of Bahia expanded their lands with considerable violence, and worked their labourers into the cycle of fatigue, malaria, debt and death which features so prominently in the novels of Jorge Amado, himself the son of a cocoa planter.[114] Conditions in São Tomé and Príncipe were even worse. Estate owners continued to use slave labour until slavery was abolished in 1875, after which 'free' workers were sent to the plantations from Portugal's colony of Angola. Their condition in turn deteriorated quickly into slavery, since they were forced to sign themselves over to their employer, who could then sell them on. After 1908, this system was replaced by one of indentured labour, which drew in tens of thousands from Cape Verde, Angola and Mozambique; many were tricked or kidnapped, some had been previously enslaved. Around 8 per cent of workers died each year on São Tomé, double that on Príncipe, mostly because of fatigue and disease.[115]

Chocolate manufacturers were not entirely complacent. They were among the first companies to possess what we now call global brands, and their promise was one of wholesome products suitable for the young and pure in heart. Nor could they keep a lid on what was happening. From 1905 to 1906, a British journalist, Henry Nevinson, ran a series of hair-raising first-hand reports of the slave routes leading from Angola to São Tomé; under the title 'The New Slave Trade', he offered descriptions of slave markets and ships, and photographs of human remains and shackles dangling from trees.[116] For most large manufacturers, the Portuguese islands were the biggest single source of cocoa at that time, and many journalists, especially in the English-speaking world, wrote bitter attacks. No companies were more susceptible than the British Quaker firms, which were famous for their moralising tone. 'Messrs Cadbury, Fry and Rowntree are men of deservedly high reputation,' sneered the satirical *John Bull* in June 1908. 'Is it worthy of such men to buttress up a horrible system of slavery?'[117] The following year, as public pressure built, Cadbury, Fry and Rowntree announced a boycott of 'red [i.e. bloodstained] cocoa'.[118] Within a few days, the

German firm of Stollwerck joined their action, to be followed by Epps in England, Suchard in Switzerland and Van Houten in the Netherlands.

Initiated by William Cadbury, who had just returned from a voyage of inspection, first to São Tomé and Príncipe and then to Angola, the boycott was not merely cosmetic. The Cadburys had a genuine horror of slavery and had for many years used their London newspaper to criticise forced-labour regimes all over the world. Theirs was a very Victorian conception of ethical capitalism, in which individuals transact freely in the labour market. They wanted a world in which all large plantations would disappear, along with their slaves and their indentured labourers, to be replaced by free peasants in charge of their own destinies. This was a moral and ideological position; it was also the policy of clear-sighted chocolate executives. The Cadburys did not like sourcing from the rival – and Catholic – Spanish and Portuguese empires, which they regarded as corrupt, cruel and turbulent. Like Rowntree's, they had also tried to run plantations themselves – mostly in the Caribbean – and had learned first-hand the many problems they faced; all those experiments were coming to a miserable end by this point. By that time, many British officials, too, had come to believe that 'smallholders [were] the most effective cocoa growers'.[119] Inspired by memories of the English 'yeoman', the Quakers believed in the honesty and ingenuity of the small landowner who, in the case of cocoa, could give the necessary attention to individual trees and would not simply abandon ageing groves and fell more forest – as colonial planters often had – but would continually care for and replenish ancestral land.

The Gold Coast was the answer to all their problems. Recently annexed in its entirety by the British government, it was a territory of smallholder farmers rushing to cultivate cocoa (and converting in droves, not incidentally, to Protestantism). By the time of the Portuguese boycott, as we have seen, the Gold Coast already had very substantial capacity, and the quality was as good as anywhere in the world. Significantly, after his visit to the Portuguese territories, William Cadbury decided to return to England via the

Gold Coast. He already had a significant team there; together, they decided to create a model plantation at Mangoase, an Akuapem town just east of Accra. He also visited Emanuel Mate Kole (1860–1939), paramount chief of the Manya Krobo people, who had trained as a teacher at the Basel Mission Seminary and favoured modernisation and parliamentary rule. Mate Kole presented Cadbury with some cocoa beans from his own groves, which the latter pronounced excellent. Cadbury later sent him a gift of 'two cocks and four hens'.[120]

We can now see that the explosion of Gold Coast cocoa we described earlier was funded by some of the biggest corporations in the world. England's three Quaker firms acted in concert in this matter; having voluntarily forgone their principal cocoa source, they were suddenly channelling millions of pounds into new supplies. During the year prior to the São Tomé boycott, Cadbury Bros bought forty-one tonnes from Gold Coast and Asante. That number leapt to 696 tonnes the following year, to 1,222 in 1910–11 and to 2,768 tonnes in 1914–15.[121]

The relationship between the British chocolate firms and West Africa would become the global norm after 1914, as the world's major cocoa estates, many of which were still run more or less as they had been under the conquistadors, collapsed under their own decadence and contradiction, giving way to more democratic landholding. The large firms had done much to 'peasantise' West Africa; they would play a role, also, in 'peasantising' parts of Latin America. All this was good for the companies' public relations, but it was also good for their commerce. Peasants did not, as big planters did, form cartels; their negotiating power was significantly weaker than that of multi-million-dollar corporations.

In that sense, the chocolate industry settled into its comfort zone: very large corporate interests resting on peasant foundations. It is worth pointing out that, one century after these events, many Ghanaian cocoa farmers possess resources identical to those their ancestors had: five hectares of land, a few hundred cocoa trees. The same corporations they dealt with in 1910, however, are immeasurably larger. In 1910, Cadbury's turnover was in the low millions, as was Nestle's – equivalent, today, to a few hundred million dollars. Today, Nestle's revenues are in excess of one hundred *billion* dollars, while Cadbury is just one of the many chocolate brands owned by the US giant Mondelez, which turns over $40 billion per year.

I am in the back of a little taxi heading out of the town of Obuasi. The car is not old, but its suspension is destroyed, and I am thrown around by each bump in the road. The feeling of disorientation is increased by the rap music pounding from the speakers behind my head.

> I heard a young nigga had to sell his soul
> For a new Bugatti and a ton of gold . . .

His eyes hidden behind sunglasses, the young man in front watches videos on his phone as he drives. He wears a black hoodie and baggy jeans; as he steers the car, his wrists jangle with gold-plated jewellery. His music rhapsodises about American drug culture – infinite wealth, expensive cars, contempt for systems and authority:

> I just fired my banker, now I just rubber-band it . . .

I am travelling with a woman named Akosua. Uncowed by the driver's gangster performance, Akosua, who is in her fifties, shouts directions at him and slaps him mercilessly on the shoulder when he takes a wrong turn.

Outside, the streets are packed with Hyundai vans, chosen vehicle of the town's private bus operators. Their roofs piled with cargoes of plantain and cassava, the vans keep their sliding doors open, so passengers may skip in and out. In the slow-moving traffic, women vendors crowd around these open doors, hoping to find buyers for the vegetables and water bottles they carry in drums on their heads. I see adverts for Chinese trucks and excavators: Sinotruk, Hangcha, Lonking.

Situated about 130 kilometres north-east of Akim Oda, Obuasi lies in the Asante heartlands, not far from Kumasi. The town exploded from a small village after the British-owned Ashanti Goldfields Corporation opened a gold mine here in 1897. Under Nkrumah, the Ghanaian government bought a majority stake in the mine, which began to languish from lack of know-how and investment. In the 1990s, the state sold off its stake, and the company was eventually merged with a South African mining firm to form AngloGold Ashanti. Having moved its headquarters once again to the UK in 2023, AngloGold Ashanti is today a $40 billion giant active across Africa, Latin America and Australia. In 2024, according to the company's annual report, it extracted 14.3 tonnes of gold – then worth roughly $900 million – from its two Ghanaian installations. It also paid a total of $159 million to the Ghanaian government in taxes, royalties and fees, making AngloGold Ashanti one of the state's single biggest taxpayers. Altogether, international companies mined about ninety tonnes of gold in 2024, raising the former Gold Coast to the level of sixth-largest producer – and paid $1.2 billion in fiscal revenues to the Ghanaian government.[122]

That number far exceeds revenues from cocoa, for so long the country's primary revenue source. In 2024, in fact, when cocoa prices were at record highs, the state's cocoa revenues were deep in the red. Cocobod had sold cocoa long in advance, committing itself to delivering certain volumes at a certain price.[123] It could not benefit from the sudden price spike, therefore; more seriously, as Ghanaian production crashed and sizeable quantities were smuggled out of the country, its deliveries fell 370,000 tonnes short of its contractual commitments.[124] Cocobod was forced to roll the contracts over to the next year, or to buy cocoa on the open market at exorbitant prices. One of the country's leading business newspapers outlined the consequences: 'Cocobod itself is drowning in debt, with its balance sheet showing total liabilities of [US$ 2.4 billion] . . . The International Monetary Fund has identified Cocobod's recurring annual losses as a significant threat to the sector and Ghana's broader fiscal stability.'[125] It is not difficult to understand why, as revenues from gold mining continued to soar, the government turned increasingly away from agriculture. It seemed the country's future liquidity would come not from Cocobod, a vestige of colonial times, but from Goldbod – a brand-new state agency with the exclusive right to buy Ghanaian gold set up in 2025.

The problem was that corporate mining did little to support the population at large. In 2024, the international mining companies had only 11,300 people on their Ghanaian payrolls, plus a couple of tens of thousand contract workers.[126] Cocoa farming, by contrast, directly supported about 5 million people. As cocoa hit a crisis, this became a critical issue: 57 per cent of Ghana's population was under twenty-five; every year, nearly a million people reached working age. As in other places where the disintegration of peasant economies enjoyed no corresponding industrial boom, youth unemployment was rampant: 32 per cent, compared to 13 per cent for the population at large.[127] This is why such considerable numbers of young Ghanaians were beginning to dig for gold themselves – a practice known as artisanal and small-scale mining, or ASM. Today, between 1 and 2 million Ghanaians currently work as informal gold miners; many more are involved in processing, trading and security.[128] Most of these are ex-farmers, or sons and daughters of farmers – Ghana's gold deposits are located on cocoa lands so it is easy to switch from one activity to the other. This is particularly the case among the Asante, whose forefathers mined gold while women took care of the farms, and to whose culture gold remains central even today.[129]

At a traffic light, a man proffers a bundle of *kotsa* twigs through the open window, which Akosua tells me locals use to clean their teeth. We drive through streets of Asante houses, which are quite different from the open family homes of Akim Oda. Here, big clan compounds present blind walls to the street and open onto central courtyards. Nearly everyone here is connected to mining in some way or another; whole dynasties have built up their fortunes on the back of gold. In the centre of a roundabout, we pass a gold-painted statue of a miner holding a pneumatic drill – symbol of the large-scale mining that built this town.

Finally, we reach the outskirts and find ourselves on a country road. Our speed increases. I grip the seat in front of me to prevent myself being thrown around with every bump. Not fifteen minutes after leaving Obuasi, Akosua signals to the young driver to stop. It is a relief to get out of the car. As we walk away, I can still hear the blasting music:

Being dead broke is the root of all evil
Get money, my nigga, do good with your people.

We set out along a dirt track with forest trees on either side. Akosua is taking me to see the cocoa farm she sold to gold miners four years ago. At that time, her cocoa trees were infected with swollen-shoot disease.

'There is no cure,' she says. 'You have to dig out the trees, treat the soil and replant. So you have to wait six years to harvest again.'

Infected trees turn yellow and start to produce less fruit; all die within five years. The disease has been the perennial bane of Ghanaian cocoa cultivation: prevention and cure both require state management of the kind that has mostly been absent. Recent studies have found that the virus is endemic to all Ghana's cocoa-growing regions. In some, more than 80 per cent of trees are affected.[130] This is another major reason for the collapse of West African cocoa and for the migration to gold mining.

The trees come to an abrupt end. I realise these few metres of forest were just a cosmetic screen, to hide the devastation from the road. We emerge into a moonscape of sand and flooded craters. Discarded water bottles and plastic bags litter the area. Nothing grows here, not even grass; the pools of water are acid green. This is the signature of ASM.

Akosua gestures wordlessly at the hellish prospect.

Without her knowledge, gold prospectors went to the local chief to offer money not only for her farm but for all the farms around. The chief, who was the true owner of the land, and the main financial beneficiary, struck a deal. Many farmers refused to leave their land, but Akosua knew she could not resist.

'I had lost my husband in a road accident,' she said, 'and I had teenage daughters. I was worried what they might do to us. My trees were sick, and it was not worth the fight. My compensation was twenty thousand dollars: ten thousand up front, and two further payments of five thousand dollars. Even if I farmed for the rest of my life, I would not have that much money. So I left the land that had supported us. I gave it to people who would poison it. I committed that sin.'

The emotion has not left her. She turns her back to me and climbs to a sandy outcrop; from there she can see the corner where her farm once lay. Her purple headcloth shines sapphire-like in the dull light. Her wrapped clothes are pocketless; she carries her mobile phone in her armpit, which does not seem to impair her gesticulation.

'All the other farmers eventually left too,' Akosua says, turning back to me. 'Some held out, but the miners dumped chemical slurry on their land, and eventually their trees died. All these stories end the same way. If there is gold under the land, it will win.'

After the land had been secured, mechanical diggers were brought in to level the cocoa trees – which were burned – and to open pits in the earth. Diesel pumps were sunk in the river, to power the high-pressure hoses used to blast the soil and turn it into slurry; the slurry was directed downhill to a washing station installed on the riverbank. Over the course of several months, every last grain of Akosua's farmland, and of all the surrounding farms, passed through this washing station, where it was broken down into individual particles, and where the heaviest particles – including gold – were separated from the rest. To this residue was added mercury, which binds to gold, allowing everything else to be washed away. Finally, the mercury was burned off – leaving behind, at the end of every day, a few small pellets of gold. These pellets would have added up: on gold-rich land like this, artisanal mining can extract 200 grams or more per hectare; from Akosua's ten-hectare farm, that equates to about $300,000 worth of gold. Most of the revenues from artisanal mining are taken, of course, by landowners and bosses, but even workers can clear $70 per day.

'My two sons have become gold miners,' Akosua says. 'They have lost respect for farming. I think they are happy to spread poison on all these farms. They say mining is the only way they can survive.'

Of all the assaults unleashed on Ghanaian cocoa – climate change, disease, chronic underinvestment and mismanagement – ASM is by far the most serious. The land in front of me has been lying barren for years, converted by mining from orchard and forest into desert. So extreme is the washing process that all organic material is flushed out; miners leave behind massive heaps of white sand where once there was rich dark soil. Cocoa farms dug up for gold are definitively exhausted and cannot be returned, afterwards, to farming: mining is the end of the line. This is why it feels so apocalyptic, to people like Akosua, when her children turn to mining – they are forced into destroying the conditions for their own existence. Ghanaian cocoa production plummeted from over 1 million tonnes in 2020–1 to just over 500,000 in 2023–4.[131] Looking at carved-up landscapes like this one, many farmers wonder whether Ghana will be producing cocoa at all in a few years' time – or whether the entire country will be reduced to a chewed-up infinity of sand and stagnant water.[132]

The greatest damage is to the underlying hydrology. Most washing stations empty directly into rivers, which become dark with sediment. This 'turbidity' itself kills the riverine ecosystem, blocking light and so eradicating plant life, and clogging everything from fish gills to water-treatment plants. But the real threat is mercury. Plants absorb mercury, which damages root systems and inhibits photosynthesis. The metal is deposited throughout the organism, and shows up in crops such as cassava, plantain, maize and indeed cocoa beans. In rivers, mercury is absorbed by small organisms and concentrated through the food chain, causing reproductive failure in big fish and deformities in fish-eating birds. Chronic mercury exposure can cause severe nerve and kidney damage in humans; even small traces can stunt brain development in foetuses and young children.

As one academic study declares, 'mercury-dependent artisanal and small-scale gold mining is the largest source of mercury pollution on earth' – and in Ghana this has become a national crisis.[133] Mercury pours out of thousands of washing stations into rivers. The final stages of the process also produce mercury vapour, which is not only hazardous to unprotected workers but subsequently condenses and ultimately enters the water system too. There is widespread concern among Ghanaians that staple foods, especially vegetables and fish, contain mercury. In 2025, the European Union and Japan, concerned about the interaction between gold mining and cocoa farming, imposed mandatory testing of Ghanaian cocoa for heavy-metal contamination – a serious blow to its public relations.[134] This is inevitable: most water sources are contaminated, and small farmers can barely afford to truck in water from distant river systems.

'We do not even have uncontaminated water to drink,' says Akosua. 'That's why there are plastic bottles everywhere.'

In 2024, the national water company announced that it could not process the amount of waste and pollution miners were flushing into Ghana's rivers, and that it would be forced to reduce its delivery of drinking water to some regions by 75 per cent.[135] Astonishingly, for a country endowed with the grandest river basin in West Africa – the Volta River, which was dammed to create Lake Volta, one of the largest artificial lakes in the world – Ghana is in danger of running out of uncontaminated water. According to one NGO, it will be forced to import fresh water by 2030 if current trends continue.[136]

By and large, ASM is illegal. The pidgin word used almost universally to describe the activity is *galamsey* – a contraction of 'gather them and sell', which conveys the criminal overtone. It is true that some artisanal miners – perhaps 15 per cent of the total[137] – possess licences for their work and are theoretically subject to environmental and tax regulations. But most ASM is illicit, from beginning to end: from the empty contracts with farmers to the unlicensed felling of trees and extraction of essential national resources, to the release of contaminants into land and soil. It fundamentally undermines the state's ability to manage Ghana's land, water and mineral resources. It conflicts not only with cocoa farming but also with corporate miners, which sign up to strict environmental regulations, especially regarding the clean-up and restoration of exhausted mines (even though, in practice, pollution from big mines, which includes arsenic as well as mercury, is a major problem too). So why is it not better controlled?

'Who controls galamsey?' asks Akosua. 'The people who are supposed to prevent it. The politicians and the chiefs. They hide behind other people, they do not want to be identified. But the money goes to them.'

As gold prices rose and galamsey miners became better equipped and more productive, there was an enormous escalation in ASM licences issued. An estimated ninety licences were issued in the twenty years prior to 2017; in the following eight years, the authorities granted 2,000.[138] This was facilitated by a 2022 law allowing licences to be allocated to forest areas of exceptional biodiversity, which had previously been protected. Most people could see what was going on even before the leaking, in 2023, of a confidential report by the former environment minister, which found that 'many [ruling] party officials . . . their friends, personal assistants, agents, relatives' were beneficiaries of these licences.[139] The report described how a prominent businessman, and relative of the president, had used his political influence to interfere with planned raids on illegal miners. By 2024, the entire Ghanaian power system was falling into crisis: in August of that year, the *asantehene* removed three of his chiefs for their involvement in galamsey. 'I gave the town to you,' raged Otumfuo Osei Tutu II, but 'you could not take care of it. If I still keep you in charge, you will destroy my communities and ruin the lives of our people.'[140] Four months later, amid widespread accusations that revenues from illegal ASM were funding the ruling party, the government fell.*

---

* For a discussion of the growing entanglement between artisanal and small-scale mining and agriculture in Ghana, see Daniel Siaw, George Ofosu and David Sarpong, whose interviews in Ghana's cocoa-growing regions demonstrate how the spread of small-scale gold mining is transforming rural life. Miners often pressure farmers into selling their land,

The incoming president made galamsey his core issue. 'I assure you,' he declared, 'as your President, that I will never give up this fight against illegal mining.'[141] But stories of raids on illegal mining continued to arouse scepticism.

'I know how this works,' Akosua continues. 'My sons tell me everything. The miners pay the police to warn them about raids. They pay every level in the police force, including the bosses in Accra. It is obvious who the police work for. The miners are tearing down forest, they have chainsaws and massive machines – the police can easily find them if they want. Why is it the only people who get punished are poor boys no one cares about? That's why I worry for my sons every day. Anything can happen. You heard about the shooting in Obuasi? Until then, we didn't know the government could use guns on our own people.'

She is referring to the fatal shooting of seven miners who entered the AngloGold Ashanti premises on 18 January 2025.[142] In a sign of its strategic importance, the location was guarded by Ghana's state military, who later claimed the miners had been armed and that the soldiers had fired in self-defence.

'They were *not* armed,' declares Akosua. 'They were just ordinary miners. The company had stopped mining on that site, so those men wanted to move in to take anything that remained. Seven people died, but several others were wounded. Very pointless deaths.'

All this explains why the government has been far more focused on capturing the revenues from galamsey than stopping it. Since ASM accounts for a full 40 per cent of Ghana's annual gold production – some sixty tonnes, or $8 billion at 2026 market rates – it can potentially help to improve the country's financial standing, and the government has introduced several reforms to prevent this

---

creating a growing class of landless rural workers forced to seek work elsewhere. Daniel Siaw, George Ofosu and David Sarpong, 'Cocoa Production, Farmlands, and the Galamsey: Examining Current and Emerging Trends in the ASM–Agriculture Nexus', *Journal of Rural Studies*, Vol. 99 (2023).

value leaking away.[143] During the currency crisis of 2022, a 'gold-for-reserves programme' was introduced, under which the state would buy domestically mined gold with Ghanaian cedis in order to increase its own gold reserves. In 2025, withholding taxes on ASM gold were removed in the hope of bringing down the vast quantity smuggled out each year, mostly to the UAE, with Turkey and Switzerland following behind. In that same year, Goldbod was created as the only legitimate buyer of Ghanaian gold.

A band of egrets flies overhead, brilliant white against the rain-heavy sky. The sky is the only part of this landscape, in fact, that remains beautiful and unchanged.

Akosua wears gold earrings herself. Her face is beaded with sweat.

'Even our richest politicians are not really in charge of galamsey,' she continues. 'Galamsey is run by foreigners. Foreigners cannot lease land in Ghana – they need the local chiefs and politicians. But the gold goes out of the country, and the money too. You know who my sons work for? Chinese people. They don't speak English, they don't speak Twi. But they have everyone working for them. They bring in big Chinese excavators – so big they can divert a river, mine the riverbed and then put the river back again. They have enormous machines to wash the soil. That's why the pollution has gone up so much.'

Chinese involvement in galamsey is widely reported.[144] As Akosua suggests, this is where the Ghanaian government finds itself subject to greater forces. Under such arrangements as the $2 billion Sinohydro road programme, China is building significant infrastructure in Ghana; it has also made grants of money and equipment to the Ghanaian police.[145] Local journalists tell me this places Chinese companies and nationals in a generally advantageous position.

'The Chinese use Ghanaian workers, but they always bring them from a different region, so they can't be influenced by locals. My sons are not here, they are in the Eastern Region, on the Birim River. And they are surrounded by soldiers with guns. Even the police cannot go there because they have better weapons.'

Akosua cannot bear the sight of this place any more. We turn back along the forest path. I ask her what she has done with her money.

'Twenty thousand dollars is a lot of money, right?' she says. 'I left behind this life and I went to Kumasi. Kumasi is a big city, not like here. I got my ten thousand dollars up front. I bought land on the edge of the city and began to build a little house. And I set up a new business. A water sachet business. I rented a spot on a main street from a shopkeeper. I have a stand on the street with a cooler and ice. I buy the water sachets from the company – they have their own well, the water is really good. One sachet is five hundred millilitres – I sell it for one Ghana cedi. I have customers all day.

'I spent three thousand dollars on the land and I used up the rest of the ten thousand building the ground floor. When I went to collect the second instalment of five thousand, they pretended they did not know me. I went to the local chief and told him they were not paying, but he took the company's side. I never saw any more money. I live with my unmarried daughter in that little ground-floor room. I don't know if I will ever build another storey.'

I have seen so many of those houses in Ghanaian towns. Where the money has run out halfway through. The roof bristles with rusty rebars, in expectation of future concrete.

In Peru, we saw the rush of farming activity stimulated by high cocoa prices. Ghana has once again failed, of course, to benefit from the boom, which is substantially caused by the collapse of its own production – by its sick and ageing trees, by the disillusionment of farmers, by the takeover and poisoning of farmland by galamsey. So this grand tale ends here: of Latin America and Europe and Africa, of Aztec gods and French princesses and Valentine's Day lovers, of slavery and plantations and peasants. It ends in a small room on the outskirts of Kumasi, which was intended to be a kitchen and living room, but has now become a bedroom and bathroom too. It ends with a peasant family forced off the land, sidetracked into temporary, precarious work and having only toxic waste to return to. The story ends here.

5
The Future

> [T]he subsistence ethic is not only a given of peasant economics . . . it has a normative or moral dimension as well.
>
> – JAMES SCOTT, 1976[1]

Thinkers of every hue continue to proclaim, as the natural consequence of capitalist modernity, the extinction of the global peasantry. For thinkers on the left, global capitalism concentrates money and opportunities in cities and leads inexorably to 'global depeasantisation'.[2] For those on the right, anyone who even refers to peasants today is lost in some romance of the past. The global countryside, they imagine, is taken over by industry and commerce to the extent that 'there *are* no "peasants" in the world of contemporary capitalist globalisation'.[3]

The idea that peasants are quietly evaporating in the face of modern life – like a bird whose forest habitat is disappearing, perhaps – ignores the fact that a full-blown war has been waged against them for most of the last century. Peasants are in crisis today not because they are somehow unsuited to modern conditions but because they have been hunted to the limits of possibility.

In the decades following 1945, this war was crude and overt. Policies of collectivisation and resettlement killed tens of millions of peasants in Communist states. By far the greatest number were in China, but the Soviet Union, Cambodia, Ethiopia and North Korea all saw significant death tolls. Simultaneously, in other places, peasants were the primary victims of campaigns against insurgents and subversives – as in Vietnam, Indonesia, Algeria, Guatemala, El Salvador, Peru and Colombia – and of superpower-backed civil wars – as in Afghanistan, Mozambique, Angola and Sudan. As the Cold War came to an end, rural communities continued to bear the brunt of terrifying ethnic struggles and resource wars: they were the prime victims *and* perpetrators in the continuing civil violence in Sudan, as well as in the Rwanda genocide and the Congo wars. Peasants are the primary victims of ongoing land conflicts, battles over resources and frontier violence. In various regions today, peasants are victimised and killed by their former co-peasants, who have turned, precisely because of the collapse of the countryside, to religious militias: the Taliban has killed large numbers of peasants in Afghanistan and Pakistan, as did ISIS in Iraq and Syria and Al Shabaab in Somalia.[4] Boko Haram has killed as many as 50,000 people, a great many farmers and herders, and displaced 2 million more; many more peasant communities were targeted by the Nigerian government's campaigns against the militant group.* The total peasant death toll is impossible to calculate, but it is certainly in the tens of millions: more than any nationality or ethnic group, they have been the primary victims of post-1945 violence.

The drop in peasant numbers that is so often presented as simple 'progress', therefore – gentle, benign and inevitable – is in reality far more complicated. And that remains the case. Violence against peasants is less militarised today than in the 1960s and 1970s, but that is because today's world is controlled primarily by virtual systems of law and finance. The war we are in today is a class war between humanity's urban and rural factions – with the urban faction controlling politics, markets, money, law, media and the military. The purpose of this war is to force the global peasantry to absorb all the costs of their activity – and of the wider capitalist

* Similar changes are happening in other parts of the world. For a fascinating account of the relationship between the Taliban and the Afghan peasantry, see Anand Gopal, *No Good Men Among the Living: America, the Taliban, and the War through Afghan Eyes* (New York: Metropolitan Books, 2014).

system – while relinquishing the profits. Long-term underinvestment by states in soil, water, botanical stock and climate-change preparation means that peasants must either make this investment themselves or live with declining yields, or both. On top of all that, financial and legal systems are designed to force peasants to make large-scale subsidies to industry and consumers – by imposing low prices on agricultural commodities, by illegalising non-corporate seeds and chemicals and by blocking the exits to farming, so that the cycle must continue. The consequences of this war are what we have seen throughout this book. Peasant farmers have weaker and weaker claims on the financial value generated from their crop; they carry enormous volumes of debt, often at exceedingly high interest; they must adopt extreme lifestyles in order to survive, and suicide is never too far away; and often they are obliged to watch the slow – or even rapid – collapse of the ecological systems on which their activity depends.

This war has been internalised by the industrial system as if it is 'natural': corporations and consumers alike have come to depend on the subsidies they receive, for instance, from sugarcane or cocoa farmers. But as a grand strategy it is irrational. If peasants are the most enduring class of humanity, it is because they have always been able to keep land fertile and productive for generations. The corporate plantation can exhaust the soil and then leave; the peasant cannot. She must deploy her knowledge of natural systems to ensure her farm will still be productive for her children, and for their children. The peasant family is organised around the eternal fertility of a particular piece of land: it must sustain soils, water systems, biodiversity and diverse farming landscapes. Peasants therefore act as dependable custodians of natural systems and form a crucial buffer against ecological breakdown. The fact that a substantial proportion of the world's cultivable land is controlled by peasants protects us enormously against the final exhaustion of natural systems. 'Sustainability' is not just a nice concept, in other words; it is the principle without which peasant life breaks down. Peasant societies have therefore built an entire ethical system around it – and, in today's 'unsustainable' world, they offer an essential corrective.

If we destroy the conditions of peasant existence, the first thing we will realise is that the cities cannot absorb their vast numbers. We will understand that, in the absence of exceptional industrialisation, nothing sustains large populations as reliably as the land. China's industrial growth has been enormous enough to absorb hundreds of millions of peasants into factories. But that cannot be repeated everywhere. In much of Africa, and even in parts of Latin America and Asia, there will never be enough jobs in industry or services to absorb peasants forced off the land. Well over a billion people in those regions already live in a structural limbo – no longer supported by smallholder agriculture nor absorbed into stable industrial or service employment. Many fall into abject poverty; other choices range from informal labour to criminality to militancy – or crossing international borders in the hope of making a better life elsewhere. Any of these scenarios carry great risks for peasants themselves, as well as threats to already fragile social and political systems.

How can we end the war against peasants? Not by perpetuating the condescending assumption that peasants are too fragile or primitive to be exposed to modern markets. Peasants are highly attuned to markets, and many would like to benefit much more from the demand for their products. But they are special kinds of producers, who do need protection from excessive price fluctuations, or from downward pressure applied by powerful buyers. They also need iron-clad protection for their land, and forms of credit that are quite different from other kinds of business. And all that assumes states which place a priority on their peasant populations, rather than – which has been the story of this book – expropriating them, selling them out to big business and abandoning their principal interests.

We need to bring peasants back into the global conversation. They are the makers of the modern world, which continues to depend on their production. But, more than that, we depend today on the new ways of living and adapting they are creating. Peasants are the custodians of an ethos that has not been, and can never be, folded into that of twenty-four-hour industrial capitalism – an ethos which, more than any technocratic programme, has the potential to turn our global system back from the precipice.

I give the last words to a young farmer from Maharashtra, who had this message for the world: 'We farmers are the only people who can produce ten grains out of one, and allow the rest of you to survive. All you who work in offices, who do not farm yourself: think again about your attitude towards farmers. Living correctly with nature, and growing enough food – this is not only our job, it requires everyone in the world to work together. If you design everything to punish farmers, we will all perish.'

Notes

EPIGRAPH

1 Nezami Ganjavi, *Khosrow and Shirin*, ed. and trans. Dick Davis (London: Penguin Classics, 2025). *Khosrow and Shirin* is one of five narrative poems in the *Khamsa* ('Five Treasures') of the twelfth-century Persian poet Ganjavi.

PART ONE: HOW WE FORGOT

CHAPTER 1: THE PEASANT WITHIN

1 James C. Scott, *Against the Grain: A Deep History of the Earliest States* (New Haven, CT: Yale University Press, 2017).
2 This point is made in detail in David Graeber and David Wengrow's magisterial *The Dawn of Everything: A New History of Humanity* (London: Allen Lane, 2021).
3 James C. Scott, *Seeing Like a State: How Certain Schemes to Improve the Human Condition Have Failed* (New Haven, CT: Yale University Press, 1998).
4 From the *Chronicle* by Jean le Bel, written in the 1360s (Paris: Société de l'Histoire de France, 1905), 255–60.
5 P. Chidambaram, interview in *Tehelka*, 31 May 2008, quoted in Bharat Dogra, 'Denial of the Rural', *Down to Earth*, 15 September 2008.
6 Eric Hobsbawm, *The Age of Extremes: The Short Twentieth Century, 1914–1991* (London: Abacus, 1994), 289.

CHAPTER 2: PEASANTS IN THE CHINESE SYSTEM

1 This process is described in detail in Mark Elvin, *The Retreat of the Elephants: An Environmental History of China* (New Haven, CT: Yale University Press, 2004).

2 This is my retelling of a story from the *Huainanzi*. See John S. Major, Sarah A. Queen, Andrew Seth Meyer and Harold D. Roth (eds), *The Essential Huainanzi: Liu An, King of Huainan* (New York: Columbia University Press, 2012), 193.
3 John Berger, *Pig Earth* (London: Pantheon, 1979), xv–xvi.
4 Angus Maddison, *The World Economy: A Millennial Perspective* (Paris: Development Centre of the Organisation for Economic Co-Operation and Development, 2001).
5 Michael Wood, *The Story of China: A Portrait of a Civilisation and Its People* (London: Simon & Schuster, 2020), 116.
6 R. Bin Wong, 'China before Capitalism', in Larry Neal and Jeffrey G. Williamson (eds), *The Cambridge History of Capitalism*, Vol. 1 *The Rise of Capitalism: From Ancient Origins to 1848* (Cambridge: Cambridge University Press, 2014), 150.
7 See James C. Scott, *In Praise of Floods: The Untamed River and the Life It Brings* (New Haven, CT: Yale University Press, 2025), 70.
8 Robert B. Marks, *China: An Environmental History* (Lanham, MD: Rowman & Littlefield, 2012), 151, and R. Barker, 'The Origin and Spread of Early-Ripening Champa Rice: Its Impact on Song Dynasty China', *Rice*, Vol. 4, No. 3–4 (2011), 185.
9 See Robert M. Hartwell, 'A Revolution in the Chinese Iron and Coal Industries during the Northern Sung, 960–1126 AD', *Journal of Asian Studies*, Vol. 21, No. 2 (1962), 153–62; Robert M. Hartwell, 'Markets, Technology, and the Structure of Enterprise in the Development of the Eleventh-Century Chinese Iron and Steel Industry', *Journal of Economic History*, Vol. 26, No. 1 (1966), 29–58; Donald B. Wagner, 'The Administration of the Iron Industry in Eleventh-Century China', *Journal of the Economic and Social History of the Orient*, Vol. 44, No. 2 (2001), 175–97; Hans Ulrich Vogel, 'Gas: Exploitation and Use of Natural Gas in Premodern China', in Helaine Selin (ed.), *Encyclopaedia of the History of Science, Technology, and Medicine in Non-Western Cultures* (Dordrecht: Kluwer Academic Publishers, 1997), Peer Vries, *State, Economy and the Great Divergence: Great Britain and China, 1680s–1850s* (London: Bloomsbury, 2015), 298.
10 Quoted in Peter Frankopan, *The Earth Transformed: An Untold History* (London: Bloomsbury, 2023), 321.
11 Imperial Tomb Tablet of the Great Ming, stele inscription in Fengyang, Anhui Province, erected in 1378. Translation by Laurie Dennis, published at lauriedennis.com, 2023.

12 Elvin, *The Retreat of the Elephants*, 141.
13 See Robert B. Marks, *China: An Environmental History*, 2nd ed. (Lanham, MD: Rowman & Littlefield, 2017), 272–74; Elvin, *The Retreat of the Elephants*, 127–30; James Carter, 'When the Yellow River Changes Course', *The China Project*, 29 June 2022; David A. Pietz, *The Yellow River: The Problem of Water in Modern China* (Cambridge, MA: Harvard University Press, 2015), 65.
14 Isaiah 1:7.
15 Charles Desnoyers, 'The Killing Fields of Jiangnan: Genocide and China's Taiping Rebellion, 1851–1864', in Ned Blackhawk, Ben Kiernan, Benjamin Madley and Rebe Taylor (eds), *The Cambridge World History of Genocide*, Vol. 2: *Genocide in the Indigenous, Early Modern and Imperial Worlds, from c.1535 to World War One* (Cambridge: Cambridge University Press, 2023), 566.
16 *New York Times*, 24 February 1878.
17 Figures from Mike Davis, *Late Victorian Holocausts: El Niño Famines and the Making of the Third World* (London: Verso, 2000).
18 Quoted in Elizabeth J. Perry, *Rebels and Revolutionaries in North China, 1845–1945* (Stanford, CA: Stanford University Press, 1980), 176.
19 Quoted in *ibid.*, 181.
20 Pietz, *The Yellow River*, 88.
21 Perry, *Rebels and Revolutionaries in North China.*
22 Mao Zedong, 'Report on an Investigation of the Peasant Movement in Hunan', in *Selected Works of Mao-Tse-Tung*, Vol. 1 (London: Lawrence & Wishart, 1954), 23.
23 Hans van de Ven, *China at War: Triumph and Tragedy in the Emergence of the New China* (Cambridge, MA: Harvard University Press, 2018), 137.
24 Perry, *Rebels and Revolutionaries in North China*, 214.
25 Stanley Rosen, 'The Chinese Communist Party and Chinese Society: Popular Attitudes toward Party Membership and the Party's Image', *Australian Journal of Chinese Affairs*, Vol. 24 (1990), Table 1.
26 Mao Zedong, *On Guerrilla Warfare* (Washington, DC: US Marine Corps, 1989), 92.
27 Marks, *China*, 345.
28 *Ibid.*, 344.
29 Van de Ven, *China at War*, 240.
30 Marks, *China*, 312.

31 Viola Rothschild, 'State Repression and Selective Expression: Communal Canteens and the "Collective" Memory of China's Great Leap Famine', *China Quarterly*, Vol. 265 (2025), 146–64. According to the author, the 'dismantling of the family unit and concentration of power and resources into official hands gave the state unprecedented control over village life'.

CHAPTER 3: WHY BRITAIN DESTROYED THE PEASANT

1 See Katharina Pistor, *The Code of Capital: How the Law Creates Wealth and Inequality* (Princeton, NJ: Princeton University Press, 2019).
2 Gregory Clark and Anthony Clark, 'Common Rights to the Land in England, 1475–1839', *Journal of Economic History*, Vol. 61, No. 4 (December 2001), 1009–36.
3 Christopher Dyer, *Peasants Making History: Living in an English Region, 1200–1540* (Oxford: Oxford University Press, 2022), 98.
4 Peter Linebaugh, *The Magna Carta Manifesto: Liberties and Commons for All* (Berkeley, CA: University of California Press, 2008), 39. Such principles were biblical and were therefore enshrined in much of European law until the modern period. The books of Deuteronomy and Leviticus, for instance, forbade farmers from harvesting to the edges of their fields, ordered that some grapes be left on the vines and allotted to the poor whatever was dropped or still unharvested on a certain date.
5 Dyer, *Peasants Making History*, 52–3.
6 John Hatcher, *The Black Death: An Intimate History* (London: Weidenfeld & Nicolson, 2008).
7 Dan Jones, *Summer of Blood: The Peasants' Revolt of 1381* (London: HarperPress, 2009), 96.
8 Thomas Walsingham, *The Chronica Maiora of Thomas Walsingham, 1376–1422*, trans. David Preest (Woodbridge: Boydell Press, 2005), 133.
9 *Ibid.*, 153.
10 Lyndal Roper provides a spectacular account of this episode in her *Summer of Fire and Blood: The German Peasants' War* (London: Basic Books, 2025).
11 Dyer, *Peasants Making History*, 94–5.

12 Gerrard Winstanley, 'A Declaration to the Powers of England', in Thomas N. Corns, Ann Hughes and David Loewenstein (eds), *The Complete Works of Gerrard Winstanley*, Vol. 2 (Oxford: Oxford University Press, 2009), 5.

13 Rana Dasgupta, *After Nations: The Making and Unmaking of a World Order* (London: William Collins, 2026), ch. 5.

14 For a fuller account of this 'dictatorship of property', see *ibid.*

15 James Horn, 'British Diaspora: Emigration from Britain, 1680–1815', in P. J. Marshall (ed.), *The Oxford History of the British Empire*, Vol. 2 (Oxford: Oxford University Press, 1998), 28–52.

CHAPTER 4: REVOLUTION: ARE PEASANTS MODERN?

1 Voltaire, 'Essai sur les mœurs et l'esprit des nations', in *Œuvres complètes de Voltaire*, Vol. 11 (Paris: Garnier Frères, 1963), 23. Translation by the author.

2 *Ibid.*

3 Eugen Weber, *Peasants into Frenchmen: The Modernization of Rural France, 1870–1914* (Stanford, CA: Stanford University Press, 1976), chapter 1; Amy S. Wyngaard, *From Savage to Citizen: The Invention of the Peasant in the French Enlightenment* (Newark, DE: University of Delaware Press, 2004), 34. One historian notes that, in the 1790s, 'roughly 12 million out of the 26 million inhabitants constituting the population of the Republic were ignorant of French or had trouble understanding it'. Roger Dupuy, *La République jacobine: Terreur, guerre et gouvernement révolutionnaire, 1792–1794* (Paris: Seuil, 2005). Translation by the author.

4 Hilton L. Root, *The Fountain of Privilege: Political Foundations of Markets in Old Regime France and England* (Berkeley, CA: University of California Press, 1994), 67–8.

5 For more detail, see John Markoff, *The Abolition of Feudalism: Peasants, Lords and Legislators in the French Revolution* (University Park, PA: Pennsylvania State University Press, 1996).

6 *Ibid.*

7 *Ibid.*

8 Alfred Cobban, *The Social Interpretation of the French Revolution* (Cambridge: Cambridge University Press, 1999), 39.

9 Quoted in Markoff, *The Abolition of Feudalism*, 444.

10 Simon Schama, *Citizens: A Chronicle of the French Revolution* (New York: Alfred A. Knopf, 1989), 694.
11 Quoted in Timothy Tackett, *The Coming of the Terror in the French Revolution* (Cambridge, MA: Belknap Press of Harvard University Press, 2015), 293.
12 Peter McPhee, 'A Vicious Civil War in the French Revolution: "The Vendée", 1793–1795', in *The Cambridge World History of Genocide*, Vol. 2 (Cambridge: Cambridge University Press, 2023), 312–34.
13 The electorate would not expand substantially again until the revolution of 1848, after which universal male suffrage returned. See '1792: le suffrage universel est introduit pour l'élection de la Convention nationale', Assemblée Nationale website; 'Statistique électorale de la France de 1815 à 1877', *Journal de la Société statistique de Paris*, Vol. 22 (1881), 323.
14 Weber, *Peasants into Frenchmen*, 4.
15 *Ibid.*
16 Henry Heller, *The Bourgeois Revolution in France, 1789–1815* (New York and Oxford: Berghahn Books, 2006), 7.
17 Letter of 20 February 1888 to Émile Schuffenecker. Quoted in Victor Merlhès (ed.), *Correspondance de Paul Gauguin*, Vol. 1: *1873–1888* (Paris: Fondation Singer-Polignac, 1984), 172.
18 Karl Marx, 'The Eighteenth Brumaire of Louis Bonaparte', in *Karl Marx and Frederick Engels: Collected Works* (London: Lawrence & Wishart, 1979), Vol. 11, 187.
19 Karl Marx and Friedrich Engels, *The Communist Manifesto*, trans. Samuel Moore (London: Penguin, 2002), 235.
20 Orlando Figes, *Natasha's Dance: A Cultural History of Russia* (London: Penguin, 2003).
21 Quoted in Tibor Szamuely, *The Russian Tradition* (London: Fontana, 1974), 201.
22 Fyodor Dostoevsky, *A Writer's Diary*, trans. K. Lantz (Evanston, IL: Northwestern University Press, 1997), 160.
23 Figes, *Natasha's Dance*, 224.
24 V. I. Lenin, 'Socialism and the Peasantry', *Proletary*, No. 20 (1905), https://lenin.public-archives.com/en/L1371en.html.
25 *Ibid.*
26 *Ibid.*
27 Scott, *Seeing Like a State*.

28 R. W. Davies and Stephen G. Wheatcroft, *The Years of Hunger: Soviet Agriculture, 1931–1933* (Basingstoke: Palgrave Macmillan, 2004), 413–14; Andrei Markevich, Natalya Naumenko and Nancy Qian, 'The Political-Economic Causes of the Soviet Great Famine, 1932–33', NBER Working Paper no. 29089 (2021), 8 n. 12.
29 Scott, *Seeing Like a State.*
30 Michael Gold, 'Is the Small Farmer Dying?', *New Republic*, 7 October 1931, quoted in James C. Scott, *Seeing Like a State.*
31 Scott, *Seeing Like a State*, 198.
32 Davis, *Late Victorian Holocausts*, 37–8.
33 Inderjeet Parmar, 'The "Big 3" Foundations and American Global Power', *American Journal of Economics and Sociology*, Vol. 74, No. 4 (2015), 676–703.

CHAPTER 5: THE QUESTION OF THE PEASANT

1 See Eric R. Wolf, *Peasants* (Englewood Cliffs, NJ: Prentice-Hall, 1966).
2 For much more on this aspect of peasant attitudes, see James C. Scott, *The Moral Economy of the Peasant: Rebellion and Subsistence in Southeast Asia* (New Haven, CT: Yale University Press, 1976).
3 Berger, *Pig Earth*, xi.
4 Jan Douwe van der Ploeg, *The New Peasantries: Struggles for Autonomy and Sustainability in an Era of Empire and Globalization* (London: Earthscan, 2008), xiv.
5 Maryam Aslany, 'The World Needs Peasants', *Aeon*, 23 September 2025.
6 S. K. Lowder, J. Skoet and T. Raney, 'The Number, Size, and Distribution of Farms, Smallholder Farms, and Family Farms Worldwide', *World Development*, Vol. 87 (2016), 16–29.
7 See Eric Vanhaute, *Peasants in World History* (London: Routledge, 2021) for an expansion of this history.
8 Liyao Wang et al., 'Insights into the Environmental–Economic Sustainability of Rice Production in China', *Journal of Cleaner Production*, Vol. 498 (2025).
9 World Bank, *Urban Population (% of Total Population) – China* (2024).
10 Government of India, 'Economic Survey Highlights Thrust on Rural Development', Press Information Bureau, Ministry of Finance, 31 January 2023.

PART TWO: PEASANTS IN THE TWENTY-FIRST CENTURY
CHAPTER 1: SUGARCANE: REBELS FROM THE FIELD

1 *The Book of the Discipline (Vinaya-Pitaka)*, trans. I. B. Horner, Vol. 4 (Lancaster: Pali Text Society, 2007), 285.

2 James Walvin, *Sugar: The World Corrupted: From Slavery to Obesity* (New York: Pegasus Books, 2018), 44–5.

3 For the origin of sugarcane, see Tsugitaka Sato, *Sugar in the Social Life of Medieval Islam* (Leiden: Brill, 2014).

4 Lallanji Gopal, 'Sugar-Making in Ancient India', *Journal of the Economic and Social History of the Orient*, Vol. 7, No. 1 (April 1964), 57–72.

5 *The Book of the Discipline (Vinaya-Pitaka)*, Vol. 4, 307–8.

6 Gopal, 'Sugar-Making in Ancient India'.

7 Khodadad Rezakhani, 'Continuity and Change in Late Antique Irān: An Economic View of the Sasanians', *International Journal of the Society of Iranian Archaeologists*, Vol. 1, No. 2 (2015), 93–106; Robert McC. Adams, 'Agriculture and Urban Life in Early Southwestern Irān', *Science*, Vol. 136, No. 3511 (1962), 109–22.

8 Willem M. Floor, 'Sugar', *Encyclopaedia Iranica*, 20 July 2009.

9 Marco Polo, *The Travels*, ed. and trans. Nigel Cliff (London: Penguin, 2016), 231.

10 Ibn Battuta, *Travels in Asia and Africa*, ed. and trans. H. A. R. Gibb (London: Routledge & Kegan Paul, 1953), 282.

11 One of Alexander's admirals, Nearchus, quoted two centuries later in the *Geographica* of Strabo, https://penelope.uchicago.edu/Thayer/E/Roman/Texts/Strabo/15A1*.html.

12 Pliny the Elder, *Natural History: A Selection*, ed. and trans. John Healey (London: Penguin, 2004), 209. Pliny adds, 'Although Arabia produces cane-sugar the Indian variety is more esteemed.'

13 Sidney W. Mintz, *Sweetness and Power: The Place of Sugar in Modern History* (New York: Penguin, 1985), 82.

14 Clive Ponting, *World History: A New Perspective* (London: Pimlico, 2001), 487.

15 Ulbe Bosma, *The World of Sugar* (Cambridge, MA: Harvard University Press, 2023), 26.

16 Ponting, *World History*, 658.

17 Quoted in Melanie Alexxann Koskella, 'A Universal Approach to Plague Epidemics in Fifteenth Century Mamluk Egypt and Syria' (PhD dissertation, University of Utah, 2014), 29.

18 N. Shehadeh, 'The Climate of Jordan in the Past and Present', *Studies in the History and Archaeology of Jordan*, Vol. 2 (1985), 25–37.
19 Bethany J. Walker, 'Mamluk Investment in Transjordan: A "Boom and Bust" Economy', *Mamluk Studies Review*, Vol. 8, No. 2 (2004), 133; also Sato, *Sugar in the Social Life of Medieval Islam*. For a micro-historical account of sugar production in later, Ottoman Egypt, see Nelly Hanna, *Making Big Money in 1600: The Life and Times of Isma'il Abu Taqiyya* (Syracuse, NY: Syracuse University Press, 1998).
20 Bosma, *The World of Sugar*, 29.
21 *Ibid.*, 28.
22 Ponting, *World History*, 659.
23 Quoted in Martin Page, *The First Global Village: How Portugal Changed the World* (Alfragide: Casa das Letras, 2002), 102.
24 Ponting, *World History*, 659.
25 R. H. Major (ed.), *Select Letters of Christopher Columbus* (London: Hakluyt Society, 1870), 81.
26 David Aworawo, 'Bitterness on a Sugar Island: British Colonialism and the Socio-economic Development of Jamaica (1655–1750)', *Lagos Notes and Records*, Vol. 16, No. 1 (2010), 199.
27 See the SlaveVoyages database compiled by Emory University and partners: www.slavevoyages.org. A total of 37 per cent of slaves disembarked in British, French, Dutch and Danish possessions in the Caribbean. A large number certainly arrived in the Spanish Caribbean too – so the total is almost certainly larger than 40 per cent – but we have data only for the Spanish empire as a whole.
28 Sidney Mintz, 'Labor and Sugar in Puerto Rico and in Jamaica, 1800–1850', *Comparative Studies in Society and History*, Vol. 1, No. 3 (1959), 274.
29 Aworawo, 'Bitterness on a Sugar Island', 199.
30 Dale W. Tomich, *Slavery in the Circuit of Sugar: Martinique and the World-Economy, 1830–1848* (Albany, NY: State University of New York Press, 2016), 51.
31 Matthew Parker, *The Sugar Barons: Family, Corruption, Empire and War in the West Indies* (New York: Walker & Co., 2011), 350.
32 Quoted in Richard B. Sheridan, *Sugar and Slavery: An Economic History of the British West Indies, 1623–1775* (Baltimore, MD: Johns Hopkins University Press, 1974), 60.

33 Elizabeth Abbott, *Sugar: A Bittersweet History* (London: Duckworth, 2009), 68.
34 Compiled from statistics in Mintz, *Sweetness and Power*, 67.
35 John Gladstone, letter to Sir George Grey, assistant secretary at the Colonial Office, 25 March 1837, UK National Archives, TNA CO 111/161.
36 Daniel North-Coombes, 'Slavery, Emancipation and the Labour "Crisis" in the Sugar Industry of Mauritius, 1790–1842', *Tanzania Zamani*, Vol. 3, No. 1 (1997), 27.
37 Bosma, *The World of Sugar*, 143.
38 See Ulbe Bosma, *The Sugar Plantation in India and Indonesia: Industrial Production, 1770–2001* (Cambridge: Cambridge University Press, 2013).
39 G. R. Knight, 'From Plantation to Padi-Field: The Origins of the Nineteenth Century Transformation of Java's Sugar Industry', *Modern Asian Studies*, Vol. 14, No. 2 (1980), 192.
40 See for instance Bouissou and El Sayed, 'Brazilian Plantations Accused of Forced Labour Supply Europe with Sugar'.
41 Bosma, *The Sugar Plantation in India and Indonesia*, 228.
42 Bosma, *The World of Sugar*, 93–95.
43 Mala Lalvani, 'Sugar Co-operatives in Maharashtra: A Political Economy Perspective', *Journal of Development Studies*, Vol. 44, No. 10 (November 2008), 1474.
44 Bosma, *The Sugar Plantation in India and Indonesia*, 252.
45 Donald W. Attwood, *Raising Cane: The Political Economy of Sugar in Western India* (London: Routledge 1992).
46 S. J. Kamath, *The Political Economy of Suppressed Markets: Controls, Rent-Seeking and Interest Group Behaviour in the Indian Sugar and Cement Industries* (Delhi: Oxford University Press, 1992).
47 Pawar's own memoir contains a fascinating account of his rise. Sharad Pawar, *On My Terms: From the Grassroots to the Corridors of Power* (New Delhi: Speaking Tiger, 2016).
48 Quoted in Patrick Joyce, *Remembering Peasants* (New York: Scribner, 2024), 67.
49 See Maryam Aslany, *Contested Capital: Rural Middle Classes in India* (Cambridge: Cambridge University Press, 2020), ch. 4.
50 See *ibid.*, ch. 3.
51 Muthukumara Mani, Sushenjit Bandyopadhyay, Shun Chonabayashi, Anil Markandya and Thomas Mosier, *South Asia's*

Hotspots: Impacts of Temperature and Precipitation Changes on Living Standards (Washington, DC: World Bank, 2018); Maryam Aslany and Shannon Brincat, 'Class and Climate-Change Adaptation in Rural India: Beyond Community-Based Adaptation Models', *Sustainable Development*, Vol. 29, No. 3 (2021), 571–82.

52 Maryam Aslany and Rana Dasgupta, *Harvest: The True Cost of Cotton*, podcast series produced by Plan B Entertainment and Amazon Audible (2025).

53 The government of India's announcement of the 2022–3 FRP was typical: 'This FRP . . . [ensures] the promise of giving the farmers a return of more than 50% over their cost.' See 'In Another Farmer's Friendly Step, Government Approves Fair and Remunerative Price of Sugarcane Payable by Sugar Mills to Sugarcane Farmers for Sugar Season 2022–23', Ministry of Food Processing Industries press release, 3 August 2022.

54 Amar Habib, *Anti-Farmer Laws*, trans. Sagar Pilare (Ambajogai: Parisar Prakashan, 2018).

55 Government of India, Ministry of Agriculture & Farmers Welfare, Directorate of Economics & Statistics (DES), *Agricultural Statistics at a Glance 2020*, and Government of India, Press Information Bureau (PIB), 'Final estimates of crop production for 2024–25 released . . .' (posted 20 November 2025).

56 Aslany and Dasgupta, *Harvest: The True Cost of Cotton* podcast.

57 *Ibid.*

58 Government of Maharashtra Public Health Department survey, 2019.

CHAPTER 2: RICE: STRUGGLING ECOSYSTEM

1 Henri Mouhot, *Travels in the Central Parts of Indo-China (Siam), Cambodia and Laos during the Years 1858, 1859 and 1860*, Vol. 1 (London: John Murray, 1864), 270.

2 Francis Garnier, *Voyage d'exploration en Indo-Chine* (Paris: Librairie Hachette, 1885), 12. Translation by the author.

3 Rüdiger Gaudes, 'Kaundinya, Preah Thaong, and the "Nagi Soma": Some Aspects of a Cambodian Legend', *Asian Folklore Studies*, Vol. 52 (1993), 333–58.

4 Zhou Daguan, *A Record of Cambodia: The Land and its People*, ed. and trans. Peter Harris (Chiang Mai: Silkworm Books, 2007), 54.

5 Kenneth R. Olson and Lois Wright Morton, 'Tonle Sap Lake and River and Confluence with the Mekong River in Cambodia', *Journal of Soil and Water Conservation*, Vol. 73, No. 3 (2018), 66.

6 Hydrology data in this paragraph from Mekong River Commission, *Overview of the Hydrology of the Mekong Basin* (Vientiane: Mekong River Commission, 2005), 63; Mekong River Commission, 'Geographic Regions', Mekong River Commission website; UNESCO, 'Angkor Water Crisis', UNESCO website, 18 April 2017.

7 Louis de Carné, *Voyage en Indo-Chine et dans l'Empire Chinois* (Paris: E. Dentu, 1872), 54. Translation by the author.

8 A. C. Bhaktivedanta Swami Prabhupāda (trans.), *Śrīmad Bhāgavatam* (Los Angeles: Bhaktivedanta Book Trust, 1976), 30.

9 *Rig Veda* 1.32. See H. H. Wilson, *Rig-Veda Sanhitá: A Collection of Ancient Hindu Hymns*, Vol. 1 (London: N. Trübner & Co., 1866), 45.

10 Michael Sullivan, 'The Lake that Feeds the Mekong Basin is Facing a Shortage of Fish', NPR.org, 9 November 2019.

11 Zhou Daguan, *A Record of Cambodia*, 62.

12 David Chandler, *A History of Cambodia* (Boulder, CO: Westview Press, 2008), 7.

13 Marks, *China*, 30–31; Cristina Cobo Castillo, 'Development of Cereal Agriculture in Prehistoric Mainland Southeast Asia', *Man in India*, Vol. 95, No. 4 (2017), 335–52; Dorian Q. Fuller and Cristina Cobo Castillo, 'The Origins and Spread of Cereal Agriculture in Mainland Southeast Asia', in Paul Sidwell and Mathias Jenny (eds), *The Languages and Linguistics of Mainland Southeast Asia: A Comprehensive Guide* (Berlin: De Gruyter Mouton, 2021), 45–59; Fabio Silva, Alison Weisskopf, Cristina Cobo Castillo, Charlene Murphy, Eleanor Kingwell-Banham, Ling Qin and Dorian Q. Fuller, 'A Tale of Two Rice Varieties: Modelling the Prehistoric Dispersals of Japonica and Proto-Indica Rices', *The Holocene*, Vol. 28, No. 11 (2018), 1745–58; Peter Civáň, Sajid Ali, Riza Batista-Navarro, Konstantina Drosou, Chioma Ihejieto, Debarati Chakraborty, Avik Ray, Pierre Gladieux and Terence A. Brown, 'Origin of the Aromatic Group of Cultivated Rice (*Oryza sativa* L.) Traced to the Indian Subcontinent', *Genome Biology and Evolution*, Vol. 11, No. 3 (2019), 832–43.

14 Damian Evans, Christophe Pottier, Roland Fletcher, Scott Hensley, Ian Tapley, Anthony Milne and Michael Barbetti, 'A Comprehensive Archaeological Map of the World's Largest Preindustrial Settlement

Complex at Angkor, Cambodia', *Proceedings of the National Academy of Sciences*, Vol. 104, No. 36 (2007), 14279.

15 Friar Gabriel Quiroga de San Antonio, *Brève et véridique relation des événements du Cambodge*, trans. Antoine Cabaton (Paris: Ernest Leroux, 1914), 94.

16 Richard A. Engelhardt, 'Two Thousand Years of Engineering Genius on the Angkor Plain', *Expedition*, Vol. 37, No. 3 (1995), 24.

17 Chandler, *A History of Cambodia*, 17, 27.

18 From the *Book of Liang*, a compilation of historical texts completed in 635 CE. Quoted in Lawrence Palmer Briggs, *The Ancient Khmer Empire* (Philadelphia, PA: American Philosophical Society, 1951), 28.

19 Chandler, *A History of Cambodia*, 23; William Dalrymple, *The Golden Road: How Ancient India Transformed the World* (London: Bloomsbury, 2024), 244–5.

20 Chandler, *A History of Cambodia*, chapter 3; Roland Fletcher et al., 'The Water Management Network of Angkor, Cambodia', *Antiquity*, Vol. 82 (2008), 658–70.

21 Chandler, *A History of Cambodia*, 22.

22 Colin Poole, *Tonle Sap: The Heart of Cambodia's Natural Heritage* (Bangkok: River Books, 2006), 10–13; Chandler, *A History of Cambodia*, 39; UNESCO World Heritage Centre, 'Phnom Kulen: Archeological Site/Ancient Site of Mahendraparvata'.

23 Radhakrishna Choudhary, 'Slaves and Serfs in Medieval Cambodia (circa 400–1300 AD)', *Proceedings of the Indian History Congress*, Vol. 28 (1966), 520–31; Chandler, *A History of Cambodia*, 29–30.

24 Zhou Daguan, *A Record of Cambodia*, 77.

25 Dan Penny, Jean-Baptiste Chevance, David Tang and Stéphane De Greef, 'The Environmental Impact of Cambodia's Ancient City of Mahendraparvata (Phnom Kulen)', *PLOS One*, Vol. 9, No. 1 (January 2014), 2–3.

26 Evans *et al.*, 'A Comprehensive Archaeological Map of the World's Largest Preindustrial Settlement Complex at Angkor, Cambodia', 14279.

27 Chandler, *A History of Cambodia*, 75.

28 Roland Fletcher, Damian Evans, Christophe Pottier and Chhay Rachna, 'Angkor Wat: An Introduction', *Antiquity*, Vol. 89, No. 348 (2015), 1388–1401; Brian Fagan and Nadia Durrani, 'The Secrets

of Angkor Wat: How Archaeology Is Rewriting History', *Current World Archaeology*, July 23 2016.

29 Roland Fletcher interviewed by Fagan and Durrani, 'The Secrets of Angkor Wat'.

30 Damian Evans and Roland Fletcher, 'The Landscape of Angkor Wat Redefined', *Antiquity*, Vol. 89, No. 348 (2015), 1402–19.

31 Maurice Glaize, *Les Monuments du Groupe d'Angkor* (Paris: Jean Maisonneuve, 1993), 167–9; Chandler, *A History of Cambodia*, 69–79.

32 Zhou Daguan, *A Record of Cambodia*, 101.

33 Chandler, *A History of Cambodia*, 80.

34 See Ian Harris, *Cambodian Buddhism: History and Practice* (Honolulu: University of Hawai'i Press, 2005).

35 Yoneo Ishii, *The Junk Trade from Southeast Asia: Translations from the Tosen Fusetsu-gaki, 1674–1723* (Singapore: Institute of Southeast Asian Studies, 1998), 170.

36 Memorial regarding Cambodian harvest failure and imperial famine relief quoted in 'Đại Nam thể hiện vai trò cường quốc trong khu vực', National Archives of Vietnam website (posted 22 August 2024; Google translate).

37 Chandler, *A History of Cambodia*, 187.

38 *Ibid.*, 181.

39 Philippe Preschez, 'Le Cambodge depuis 1941: État des travaux', *Revue Française de Science Politique*, Vol. 11, No. 4 (1961), 909. Translation by the author.

40 See David P. Chandler, *The Tragedy of Cambodian History: Politics, War, and Revolution since 1945* (New Haven, CT: Yale University Press, 1991).

41 Ben Kiernan, *The Pol Pot Regime: Race, Power, and Genocide in Cambodia under the Khmer Rouge, 1975–79* (New Haven, CT: Yale University Press, 1996).

42 James A. Tyner, *From Rice Fields to Killing Fields* (Syracuse, NY: Syracuse University Press, 2017), 106.

43 Chandler, *The Tragedy of Cambodian History*, 253.

44 See David DeVoss, 'Religion: Buddhism under the Red Flag', *Time*, 17 November 1980.

45 Chandler, *The Tragedy of Cambodian History*, 7.

46 Tyner, *From Rice Fields to Killing Fields*, 110.

47 See Kiernan, *The Pol Pot Regime*.

48 See David Chandler, *Voices from S-21: Terror and History in Pol Pot's Secret Prison* (Berkeley, CA: University of California Press, 2000).

49 Kiernan, *The Pol Pot Regime*; Ben Kiernan, *How Pol Pot Came to Power* (New Haven, CT: Yale University Press, 2004); Peter Swift, 'Changing Ethnic Identities among the Kuy in Cambodia: Assimilation, Reassertion and the Making of Indigenous Identity,' *Asia Pacific Viewpoint*, Vol. 54, No. 3 (2013), 296–308.

50 Cambodia Office of the High Commissioner for Human Rights, *Economic Land Concessions in Cambodia: A Human Rights Perspective* (Phnom Penh: OHCHR Cambodia, 2007), 3.

51 Global Witness, *Taking a Cut: Institutionalised Corruption and Illegal Logging in Cambodia's Aural Wildlife Sanctuary* (London: Global Witness, 2004).

52 United Nations General Assembly, *Report of the Special Rapporteur on the Situation of Human Rights in Cambodia, Surya P. Subedi* (New York: United Nations General Assembly, 10 October 2012); Ratana Pen and Phalla Chea, *Large-Scale Land Grabbing in Cambodia* (Phnom Penh: Heinrich Böll Stiftung Cambodia, 2015); Global Witness, 'Cambodia's Family Trees: Illegal Logging and the Stripping of Public Assets by Cambodia's Elite, June 2007.

53 United Nations General Assembly, *Report of the Special Rapporteur on the Situation of Human Rights in Cambodia*; Chang Hang Saing, Socheth Hem, Chandarany Ouch *et al.*, 'Foreign Investment in Agriculture in Cambodia', CDRI Working Paper Series No. 60, June 2012.

54 United Nations General Assembly, *Report of the Special Rapporteur on the Situation of Human Rights in Cambodia*; Global Witness, 'Country for Sale: How Cambodia's Elite has Captured the Country's Extractive Industries', 5 February 2009.

55 Will Tucker, 'Lifting the Veil: Deforestation Disguised as Agriculture in Cambodia', *Viewpoints* (Washington DC: Forest Trends), 13 August 2015.

56 Global Forest Watch, Cambodia report, Globalforestwatch.org.

57 Global Forest Watch, 'Cambodia Deforestation Rates & Statistics', World Resources Institute. GFW reports that Cambodia lost approximately 3.0 million ha of tree cover between 2001 and 2025; 1.7 million ha, or 57 per cent, took place after 2016.

58 See for instance Sopeng Cheang, 'Ten Cambodian Environmental Activists Receive Prison Sentences', Associated Press, 2 July 2024, or,

by the same writer, 'A Prominent Cambodian Environmentalist is Arrested While Investigating Illegal Logging', Associated Press, 24 November 2024.

59 Global Witness, 'Death of a Comrade', 26 April 2012.

60 See Mathieu Guérin, *Paysans de la forêt à l'époque coloniale: La pacification des aborigènes des hautes terres du Cambodge (1863–1940)* (Rennes: Association d'histoire des sociétés rurales, 2008).

61 United Nations General Assembly, *Report of the Special Rapporteur on the Situation of Human Rights in Cambodia*, 12.

62 Sullivan, 'The Lake that Feeds the Mekong Basin is Facing a Shortage of Fish'.

63 Olson and Wright Morton, 'Tonle Sap Lake and River and Confluence with the Mekong River in Cambodia', 66.

64 W. Nathan Green, 'Placing Cambodia's Agrarian Transition in an Emerging Chinese Food Regime', *Journal of Peasant Studies*, Vol. 49, No. 6 (2022), 1249–72.

CHAPTER 3: COCA: THE ILLICIT PEASANT

1 Paolo Mantegazza, 'Sulle virtù igieniche e medicinali della coca e sugli alimenti nervosi in generale', *Annali Universali di Medicina*, Vol. 167 (1859), 463, 469–70, 476. Translation by the author.

2 Pablo Neruda, *The Heights of Macchu Picchu*, trans. Nathaniel Tarn (London: Jonathan Cape, 1966), 37–9.

3 Mario Vargas Llosa, *Death in the Andes* (Spanish: *Lituma en los Andes*), trans. Edith Grossman (London: Faber & Faber, 1996), 31.

4 Maritza Paredes and A. Pastor, 'Illicit Crops in the Frontier Margins: Amazonian Indigenous Livelihoods and the Expansion of Coca in Peru', *Journal of Peasant Studies*, Vol. 51, No. 4 (2024), 960–81; Maritza Paredes and Hernán Manrique, 'Ideas of Modernisation and Territorial Transformation: The Case of the Upper Huallaga Valley of Peru', in Paul Gootenberg and Liliana M. Dávalos (eds), *The Origins of Cocaine: Colonisation and Failed Development in the Amazon Andes* (New York: Routledge, 2018), 54.

5 Maritza Paredes and Hernán Manrique, 'The State's Developmentalist Illusion and the Origins of Illegal Coca Cultivation in Peru's Alto Huallaga Valley (1960–80)', *Journal of Latin American Studies*, Vol. 53, No. 2 (2021), 245–67.

6 Paredes and Pastor, 'Illicit Crops in the Frontier Margins'.

7 United Nations Office on Drugs and Crime, Peru country profile, 2003, 16.
8 *Hatun Willakuy: Abbreviated Version of the Final Report of the Truth and Reconciliation Commission, Peru* (Lima: Comisión de Entrega de la CVR, 2004), 139.
9 My interview with investigative journalist Gustavo Gorriti, founder of IDL-Reporteros and author of *La calavera en negro: El traficante que quiso gobernar un país* (Barcelona: Editorial Planeta, 2006), provides much of the background to this early development of coca cultivation in the VRAEM.
10 *Ibid.*
11 T. D. Dillehay, J. Rossen, D. Ugent, A. D. Karathanasis, V. Vásquez and P. J. Netherly, 'Early Holocene Coca Chewing in Northern Peru', *Antiquity*, Vol. 84, No. 326 (210), 939–53.
12 Lidio M. Valdez, Juan Taboada and J. Ernesto Valdez, 'Ancient Use of Coca Leaves in the Peruvian Central Highlands', *Journal of Anthropological Research*, Vol. 71 (2015), 231–58.
13 *Ibid.*, 246–7.
14 María Rostworowski de Diez Canseco, *Pachacamac y el Señor de los Milagros: Una trayectoria milenaria* (Lima: Instituto de Estudios Peruanos, 2002), 90.
15 Valdez, Taboada and Valdez, 'Ancient Use of Coca Leaves in the Peruvian Central Highlands'; Catherine J. Julien, 'Coca Production on the Inca Frontier: The Yungas of Chuquioma', *Andean Past* 5 (1998); Terence N. D'Altroy and Timothy K. Earle, 'Staple Finance, Wealth Finance, and Storage in the Inka Political Economy', *Current Anthropology*, Vol. 26, No. 2 (1985).
16 Terence N. D'Altroy, *The Incas* (Malden, MA: Blackwell Publishing, 2003), chapter 11.
17 Pedro Sancho de la Hoz, 'Relación para Su Majestad de lo sucedido en la conquista y pacificación de estas provincias de la Nueva Castilla' (1534), in Horacio H. Urteaga (ed.), *Los Cronistas de la Conquista* (Paris: Desclée de Brouwer, 1938). Translation by the author.
18 See Valdez, Taboada and Valdez, 'Ancient Use of Coca Leaves in the Peruvian Central Highlands'.
19 Joseph Kennedy, *Coca Exotica: The Illustrated Story of Cocaine* (New York: Cornwall Books, 1985), 26; Valdez, Taboada and Valdez, 'Ancient Use of Coca Leaves in the Peruvian Central Highlands'. See also the

chronicle of Bernabé Cobo, a sixteenth-century Jesuit priest: 'Among the sacrifices of plants, vegetables, and fruits of the land, none was as highly esteemed as coca. It was offered in many ways. Sometimes the whole [leaf] was offered, and other times the leaf was offered after it had been chewed and the juice sucked out. Sacrifices were made to the earth by scattering coca on it . . . at the time of ploughing, sowing and harvesting the crops; this was accompanied by much dancing and drinking.' Bernabé Cobo, *Inca Religion and Customs*, trans. Roland Hamilton (Austin: University of Texas Press, 1990), 116.

20 Valdez, Taboada and Valdez, 'Ancient Use of Coca Leaves in the Peruvian Central Highlands', 232.

21 W. Golden Mortimer, *History of Coca: 'The Divine Plant' of the Incas* (New York: J. H. Vail, 1901), 47.

22 Pedro Cieza de León, *The Discovery and Conquest of Peru* [*La Crónica del Perú*], ed. and trans. Alexandra Parma Cook and Noble David Cook (Durham, NC: Duke University Press, 1998), 221.

23 Joseph A. Gagliano, *Coca Prohibition in Peru: The Historical Debates* (Tucson: University of Arizona Press, 1994), 49. The author captures the mood with this outburst from Spanish missionaries: 'God only knows how many idolatries and how much witchcraft would cease if there were no coca.'

24 Mortimer, *History of Coca*, 108.

25 Anonymous, 'Los errores y supersticiones de los indios sacadas del Tratado y averiguación que hizo el licenciado Polo [de Ondegardo]', in *Confessionario para los curas de indios* (Lima: Antonio Ricardo, 1585), 275.

26 Gagliano, *Coca Prohibition in Peru*, 43.

27 José de Acosta, *The Natural and Moral History of the Indies*, trans. E. Grimston, ed. C. R. Markham (Cambridge: Cambridge University Press, 2010), 245.

28 Immanuel Wallerstein, Andre Gunder Frank and, more recently, Giovanni Arrighi are particularly associated with this viewpoint.

29 Paul Gootenberg, 'A Forgotten Case of "Scientific Excellence on the Periphery": The Nationalist Cocaine Science of Alfredo Bignon, 1884–1887', *Comparative Studies in Society and History*, Vol. 49, No. 1 (2007), 205.

30 Mantegazza, 'Sulle virtù igieniche e medicinali della coca e sugli alimenti nervosi in generale', 493–4.

31 Gootenberg, 'A Forgotten Case of "Scientific Excellence on the Periphery"', 205.
32 Albert Niemann, 'Über eine neue organische Base in den Cocablättern' (PhD dissertation, University of Göttingen, 1860).
33 Mantegazza, 'Sulle virtù igieniche e medicinali della coca e sugli alimenti nervosi in generale', 476, 501.
34 Kennedy, *Coca Exotica*, 84–6.
35 *Ibid.*
36 George M. Beard, *American Nervousness: Its Causes and Consequences: A Supplement to Nervous Exhaustion (Neurasthenia)* (New York: G. P. Putnam's Sons, 1881), vi.
37 Sigmund Freud, 'Über Coca', *Centralblatt für die gesammte Therapie*, Vol. 2 (1884). This quotation is from the English translation published in *Journal of Substance Abuse Treatment*, Vol. 1 (1984), 211.
38 *Ibid.*
39 Paul Gootenberg, *Andean Cocaine: The Making of a Global Drug* (Chapel Hill, NC: University of North Caroline Press, 2008), 62.
40 Arthur Conan Doyle, *The Sign of Four* (London: Smith, Elder & Co., 1908), 1–4.
41 William Scheppegrell, 'The Abuse and Dangers of Cocaine', *Medical News*, Vol. 73, No. 14 (1898), 417–22.
42 Jill Jonnes, *Hep-Cats, Narcs and Pipe Dreams: A History of America's Romance with Illegal Drugs* (New York: Scribner, 1996), 25.
43 C. W. Collins and J. Day, 'The Demon in the Bottle', *Everyday Life* (August 1909), 4–5.
44 Anonymous, 'Cocaine Alley', *American Druggist and Pharmaceutical Record*, No. 37 (10 December 1900), 337, cited in J. M. DeSilva, G. Hamilton and S. Kidder, 'Cocaine Alley Queens: Gender, Race and Drug Use in American Midwestern Cities, 1890–1920', *Urban History* (2025), 1–34 at 32.
45 Edward Huntington Williams, 'Negro Cocaine "Fiends" are a New Southern Menace: Murder and Insanity Increasing among Lower Class Blacks Because They Have Taken to "Sniffing" since Deprived of Whisky by Prohibition', *New York Times*, 8 February 1914.
46 Gootenberg, *Andean Cocaine*, 30.
47 Gootenberg, 'A Forgotten Case of "Scientific Excellence on the Periphery"', 202–32.
48 Gootenberg, *Andean Cocaine*, 58.

49 *Ibid.*, 142.

50 *Ibid.*, 351, and Paul Gootenberg, 'Cocaine's Long March North, 1900–2010', *Latin American Politics and Society*, Vol. 54, No. 1 (2012), 162.

51 Mantegazza, 'Sulle virtù igieniche e medicinali della coca e sugli alimenti nervosi in generale', 475.

52 Vicente Zapata Ortiz, 'The Problem of the Chewing of the Coca Leaf in Peru', United Nations Office on Drugs and Crime, 1 January 1952.

53 Juan C. Negrete, 'Coca-leaf Chewing: A Public Health Assessment', *Bulletin of the Pan American Health Organization*, Vol. 12, No. 3 (1978), 211.

54 Vargas Llosa, *Death in the Andes*, 28.

55 Special Message to the Congress on Control of Narcotics and Dangerous Drugs, 14 July 1969.

56 George R. Gay, Charles W. Sheppard, Darryl S. Inaba and John A. Newmeyer, 'An Old Girl: Flyin' Low, Dyin' Slow, Blinded by Snow: Cocaine in Perspective', *International Journal of the Addictions*, Vol. 8, No. 6 (1973), quoted in Jonnes, *Hep-Cats, Narcs and Pipe Dreams*, 305–6.

57 Ann Crittenden and Michael Ruby, 'Cocaine: The Champagne of Drugs', *New York Times*, 1 September 1974.

58 Paredes and Manrique, 'The State's Developmentalist Illusion and the Origins of Illegal Coca Cultivation in Peru's Alto Huallaga Valley', 245–67; Paredes and Pastor, 'Illicit Crops in the Frontier Margins', 960–81.

59 Paredes and Manrique, 'The State's Developmentalist Illusion and the Origins of Illegal Coca Cultivation in Peru's Alto Huallaga Valley', 260.

60 Paul Gootenberg, 'Introduction: Orphans of Development: The Unanticipated Rise of Illicit Coca in the Amazon Andes, 1950–1990', in Gootenberg and Dávalos (eds), *The Origins of Cocaine*, 1.

61 F. Thomson, 'Escaping Capitalist Market Imperatives: Commercial Coca Cultivation in the Colombian Amazon', *Journal of Peasant Studies*, Vol. 51, No. 4 (2024), 826–60.

62 My interview with investigative journalist Gustavo Gorriti.

63 Mirella van Dun, 'Cocaine Flows and the State in Peru's Amazonian Borderlands', *Journal of Latin American Studies*, Vol. 48, No. 3 (June 2016).

64 Eduardo Sáenz Rovner, *The Cuban Connection: Drug Trafficking, Smuggling and Gambling in Cuba from the 1920s to the Revolution* (Chapel Hill, NC: University of North Carolina Press, 2008), ch. 8; Gootenberg, *Andean Cocaine*, 261ff.
65 Gootenberg, *Andean Cocaine*, 324.
66 Figures from DEA website.
67 Elaine Shannon, 'The Cali Cartel: New Kings of Coke', *Time*, 1 July 1991.
68 Based on my interview with Gustavo Gorriti.
69 Gootenberg, *Andean Cocaine*, 299.
70 See Cecilia Tovar Samanez, 'Being a Church in a Time of Violence: Peruvian Church during the Armed Internal Conflict 1980 to 2000', *Religions*, Vol. 11, No. 11 (2020); and Brenda Tatiana Paredes Guerrero, *Two Quechua Protestant Villages and Terror in Huanta, Peru 1980–1991* (MA thesis, University of North Carolina at Charlotte, 2018).
71 Gino Costa, 'Security Challenges in Peru', *Americas Quarterly*, 19 October 2010; United Nations Office on Drugs and Crime (UNODC), *Coca Cultivation in the Andean Region* (Vienna: UNODC, 2006).
72 UNODC, *Peru: Monitoreo de Cultivos de Coca 2023* (Lima: UNODC, 2024).
73 My interview with investigative journalist Gustavo Gorriti.

CHAPTER 4: COCOA: BENEATH THE SURFACE

1 Quoted in Patricia de Fuentes (ed. and trans.), *The Conquistadors: First-Person Accounts of the Conquest of Mexico* (Norman, OK: University of Oklahoma Press, 1993), 172.
2 My interview with investigative journalist Kent Mensah provides much of the background to gold mining and cocoa smuggling.
3 Ghana Cocoa Board, 'Ghana's New Cocoa Price: Sustaining Incomes, Livelihoods and the Environment'. Published 1 October 2024.
4 My interview with investigative journalist Kent Mensah.
5 Susannah Savage, 'Chocolate Cartels: The Rise of Cocoa Smuggling', *Financial Times*, 2 August 2025.
6 Gareth Austin, 'Vent for Surplus or Productivity Breakthrough? The Ghanaian Cocoa Take-Off, c. 1890–1936', *Economic History Review*, Vol. 67, No. 4 (2014), 1054.

7 Helen Ludlow, 'Ghana, Cocoa, Colonialism and Globalisation: Introducing Historiography', *Yesterday & Today*, No. 8 (December 2012), 6.
8 D. E. K. Amenumey, *Ghana: A Concise History from Pre-Colonial Times to the 20th Century* (Accra: Woeli Publishing Services, 2008), 106.
9 Paul E. Lovejoy, *Transformations in Slavery: A History of Slavery in Africa* (Cambridge: Cambridge University Press, 2011).
10 David Eltis, Stephen D. Behrendt, David Richardson and Manolo Florentino (eds), *Voyages: The Trans-Atlantic Slave Trade Database.*
11 John Iliffe, *Africans: The History of a Continent*, 2nd edn (Cambridge: Cambridge University Press, 2007), 154–5.
12 William Gervase Clarence-Smith, *Cocoa and Chocolate, 1765–1914* (London and New York: Routledge, 2000), p. 113.
13 Juliet Oppong-Boateng, *Economic Enterprises of the Basel Mission Society in the Gold Coast: A Study of the Basel Mission Trading Company from 1859 to 1917* (MPhil thesis, University of Ghana, 2014), 9.
14 Austin, 'Vent for Surplus or Productivity Breakthrough?'.
15 Polly Hill, 'The Migrant Cocoa Farmers of Southern Ghana', *Africa: Journal of the International Africa Institute*, Vol. 31, No. 3 (1961), 217.
16 *Ibid.*, 210–11.
17 Austin, 'Vent for Surplus or Productivity Breakthrough?', 1035.
18 *Ibid.*, 1060.
19 Gareth Austin, 'Capitalists and Chiefs in the Cocoa Hold-Ups in South Asante, 1927–1938', *International Journal of African Historical Studies*, Vol. 21, No. 1 (1988), 65–6.
20 Clarence-Smith, *Cocoa and Chocolate*, 136.
21 Austin, 'Vent for Surplus or Productivity Breakthrough?', 1055.
22 Austin, 'Capitalists and Chiefs in the Cocoa Hold-Ups in South Asante', 66.
23 Friedrich A. Ramseyer and Johannes Kühne, *Four Years in Ashantee* (London: James Nisbet & Co., 1875).
24 S. C. Ukpabi, 'The British Colonial Office Approach to the Ashanti War of 1900', *African Studies Review*, Vol. 13, No. 3 (1970).
25 Iliffe, *Africans*, 210.
26 Gareth Austin, 'The Emergence of Capitalist Relations in South Asante Cocoa-Farming, c. 1916–33', *Journal of African History*, Vol. 28 (1987), 260.
27 *Ibid.*, 262.

28 Austin, 'Vent for Surplus or Productivity Breakthrough?', 1048.
29 *Ibid.*, 1035.
30 *Ibid.*, 1061.
31 Quoted in Órla Ryan, *Chocolate Nations: Living and Dying for Cocoa in West Africa* (London: Zed Books, 2011), 14.
32 See Jean Allman and Victoria Tashjian's fascinating study of the impact of the cocoa economy on colonial Asante, *I Will Not Eat Stone: A Women's History of Colonial Asante* (Portsmouth, NH: Heinemann, 2000).
33 Chief of Adanse in southern Asante quoted in Austin, 'Vent for Surplus or Productivity Breakthrough?', 1050.
34 Amenumey, *Ghana*, 191.
35 Clarence-Smith, *Cocoa and Chocolate,* 2–3.
36 Austin, 'Capitalists and Chiefs in the Cocoa Hold-Ups in South Asante', 79.
37 *The Times*, 25 October 1938.
38 'Britons Urge Pool of Cocoa in Africa; Commission's Plan Calls for Compulsory Growers' Union on the Gold Coast', *New York Times,* 25 October 1938.
39 Shashi Kolavalli and Marcella Vigneri, *The Cocoa Coast: The Board-Managed Cocoa Sector in Ghana* (Washington, DC: International Food Policy Research Institute, 2017), p. 18; W. E. B. Du Bois, 'A Cup of Cocoa and Chocolate Drops (1946)', in *W. E. B. Du Bois: International Thought* (Cambridge: Cambridge University Press, 2022), 221–3.
40 Shashi Kolavalli and Marcella Vigneri, *The Cocoa Coast: The Board-Managed Cocoa Sector in Ghana* (Washington, DC: International Food Policy Research Institute, 2017), 21.
41 Olisa Godson Muojama, 'Cocoa Marketing Board and the Sustainable Cocoa Economy in Colonial Nigeria', *African Economic History*, Vol. 47, No. 1 (2019), 12.
42 Kolavalli and Vigneri, *The Cocoa Coast*, 23.
43 Kwame Nkrumah, *Ghana: The Autobiography of Kwame Nkrumah* (New York: International Publishers, 1957), 216.
44 *Ibid.*, pp. 151–3; Hill, 'The Migrant Cocoa Farmers of Southern Ghana', 224.
45 Quotes from Ryan, *Chocolate Nations*, 14.
46 *Ibid.*, 15.

47 Amenumey, *Ghana*, 278.
48 United States Department of Agriculture Foreign Agricultural Service, 'Ghana – Cocoa Sector Overview, 2025', 31 March 2025.
49 Ecorys, *Cocoa Processing Study: Final Report*, commissioned by the Netherlands Enterprise Agency (RVO), 5 March 2023.
50 Based on my interviews with small-scale chocolate producers in Accra (November 2025).
51 Fairtrade International, *Promoting Living Incomes in the Cocoa Sector: Policy Options for Consumer Countries* (Bonn: Fairtrade International, 2020); Food and Agriculture Organisation of the United Nations, *Comparative Study on the Distribution of Value in the European Chocolate Chains* (Rome: Food and Agriculture Organisation, 2020), accessed online.
52 Paul Gifford, *Ghana's New Christianity: Pentecostalism in a Globalising African Economy* (London: C. Hurst & Co., 2004).
53 *Ibid.*
54 Based on my observation of Sunday services at charismatic churches in Accra, as well as conversations with pastors.
55 Birgit Meyer, '"Make a Complete Break with the Past": Memory and Post-Colonial Modernity in Ghanaian Pentecostalist Discourse', *Journal of Religion in Africa*, Vol. 28, No. 3 (1998), 316–49.
56 Birgit Meyer, 'Pentecostalism and Neo-Liberal Capitalism: Faith, Prosperity and Vision in African Pentecostal-Charismatic Churches', *Journal for the Study of Religion*, Vol. 20, No. 2 (2007), 5–28.
57 For women, Pentecostal participation can create opportunities for leadership and income generation, even as churches promote conservative ideals of marriage and family life. See Meyer, '"Make a Complete Break with the Past"'.
58 Louis Evan Grivetti and Howard-Yana Shapiro (eds), *Chocolate: History, Culture and Heritage* (Hoboken, NJ: John Wiley & Sons, 2009), 99.
59 Terrence Kaufman and John Justeson, 'The History of the Word for "Cacao" and Related Terms in Ancient Meso-America', in Cameron L. McNeil (ed.), *Chocolate in Mesoamerica: A Cultural History of Cacao* (Gainesville, FL: University Press of Florida, 2006), 118.
60 Martha J. Macri, 'Tempest in a Chocolate Pot: Origin of the Word Cacao', and Gabrielle Vail, 'Cacao Use in Yucatán Among the Pre-Hispanic Maya', in Grivetti and Shapiro (eds), *Chocolate*;

Frances F. Berdan et al., *Aztec Imperial Strategies* (Washington, DC: Dumbarton Oaks, 1996), 115ff.

61 Francisco Cervantes de Salazar, *Crónica de la Nueva España* (Madrid: Hispanic Society of America, 1914), 374.

62 Manuel Aguilar-Moreno, 'The Good and Evil of Chocolate in Colonial Mexico', in McNeil (ed.), *Chocolate in Mesoamerica*, 275.

63 Grivetti and Shapiro (eds), *Chocolate*, 765.

64 Cervantes, *Crónica de la Nueva España*, 374.

65 Grivetti and Shapiro (eds), *Chocolate*, 100.

66 Bernadino de Sahagún, *The Florentine Codex: The General History of the Things of New Spain*, ed. and trans. Arthur J. O. Anderson and Charles E. Dibble (Santa Fe, NM: School of American Research; Salt Lake City: University of Utah Press, 1954), Book 8, 39.

67 Bernal Díaz, *The Conquest of New Spain*, trans. J. M. Cohen (London: Penguin, 1973).

68 Cameron L. McNeil, W. Jeffrey Hurst and Robert J. Sharer, 'The Use and Representation of Cacao during the Classic Period at Copan, Honduras', in McNeil (ed.), *Chocolate in Mesoamerica*, 225.

69 *Popol Vuh: The Sacred Book of the Ancient Quiché Maya*, trans. Delia Goetz and Sylvanus G. Morley from the Spanish of Adrián Recinos (London: William Hodge & Co., 1951), 166.

70 Simon Martin, 'Cacao in Ancient Maya Religion', in McNeil (ed.), *Chocolate in Mesoamerica*, 155–6.

71 Cameron L. McNeil, 'Introduction', in McNeil (ed.), *Chocolate in Mesoamerica*, 15.

72 Grivetti and Shapiro (eds), *Chocolate*, 30.

73 McNeil, 'Introduction', in McNeil (ed.), *Chocolate in Mesoamerica*, 15.

74 Cabezon, Barriga and Grivetti, 'Chocolate and Sinful Behaviors', in Grivetti and Shapiro (eds), *Chocolate: History, Culture, and Heritage*, 37–48.

75 Kaufman and Justeson, 'The History of the Word for "Cacao" and Related Terms in Ancient Meso-America', 134.

76 Sophie D. Coe and Michael D. Coe, *The True History of Chocolate* (New York: Thames & Hudson, 1996), 38.

77 Fuentes (ed. and trans.), *The Conquistadors*, 174.

78 Louis Evan Grivetti and Beatriz Cabezon, 'Ancient Gods and Christian Celebrations: Chocolate and Religion', in Grivetti and Shapiro (eds), *Chocolate*, 27–36.

79 Antonio de León Pinelo, *Question moral si el chocolate quebranta el ayuno eclesiastico* [The Moral Question of Whether Chocolate Breaks the Ecclesiastical Fast] (Madrid: Viuda de Iuan Gonçalez, 1636), 101.

80 Philippe Sylvestre Dufour, *Traitez nouveaux & curieux du café, du thé et du chocolate* [*sic*]*: Ouvrage également nécessaire aux médecins, & a tous ceux qui aiment leur santé* (Lyon: Jean Girin & B. Rivière, 1685), 438. Translation by the author.

81 NcNeil, 'Introduction', in McNeil (ed.), *Chocolate in Mesoamerica*, 21.

82 Clarence-Smith, *Cocoa and Chocolate*, chs 6 and 7.

83 Marie-Catherine d'Aulnoy, *La Cour et la ville de Madrid vers la fin du XVIIe siècle* (Paris: E. Plon, 1874), https://www.gutenberg.org/cache/epub/29114/pg29114-images.html. Translation by the author.

84 Coe and Coe, *The True History of Chocolate*, 179.

85 Wolfgang Schivelbusch, *Tastes of Paradise: A Social History of Spices, Stimulants, and Intoxicants*, trans. David Jacobson (New York: Pantheon Books, 1992), 91.

86 Quoted in Mynors Bright (ed.), *The Diary of Samuel Pepys MA FRS* (London: George Bell, 1893), Vol. 1, 163n.

87 'Waked in the morning with my head in a sad taking through the last night's drink, which I am very sorry for; so rose and went out with Mr Creed to drink our morning draft, which he did give me in chocolate to settle my stomach.' 24 April 1661. *Ibid.*, 73 and 163.

88 Bertram M. Gordon, 'Commerce, Colonies, and Cacao: Chocolate in England from Introduction to Industrialization', in Grivetti and Shapiro (eds), *Chocolate*, 584.

89 Clarence-Smith, *Cocoa and Chocolate*, 9.

90 Hence the constant concern with medical endorsement, such as in this seventeenth-century tea advertisement: 'That excellent *and by all Physicians, approved*, China drink, called by the Chineans Tcha, by other nations Tay alias Tee, is sold at the Sultaness Head Coffee-House, in Sweetings Rents, by the Royal Exchange, London.' Quoted in Roy Moxham, *Tea: Addiction, Exploitation and Empire* (New York: Carroll & Graf, 2003), 18.

91 Translation by the author.

92 Louis Petit de Bachaumont, *Les Mémoires secrets pour servir à l'histoire de la République des Lettres en France depuis 1762 jusqu'à nos jours* (London: John Adamson, 1777), Vol. 6, 196–7. Translation by the author.

93 Horace Mann, letter from Florence to Sir Horace Walpole in London, 8 October 1774, in W. S. Lewis (ed.), *The Yale Edition of Horace Walpole's Correspondence* (New Haven, CT: Yale University Press, 1965), Vol. 24, 49.
94 Schivelbusch, *Tastes of Paradise*, 92.
95 See Jürgen Habermas, *The Structural Transformation of the Public Sphere: An Inquiry into a Category of Bourgeois Society*, trans. Thomas Burger, with Frederick Lawrence (Cambridge, MA: MIT Press, 1989).
96 Clarence-Smith, *Cocoa and Chocolate*, 33; G. R. Porter, *The Progress of the Nation* (London: John Murray, 1851), 552.
97 Clarence-Smith, *Cocoa and Chocolate*, 51.
98 *Ibid.*, 15.
99 Coe and Coe, *The True History of Chocolate*, 294.
100 *Ibid.*, 302.
101 Clarence-Smith, *Cocoa and Chocolate*, 52.
102 *Ibid.*, 19.
103 *Ibid.*, 55–61.
104 Clarence-Smith, *Cocoa and Chocolate*, 57.
105 N. L. Stone (ed.), *Customs Tariff of the German Customs Union* (Washington, DC: Government Printing Office, 1908).
106 Clarence-Smith, *Cocoa and Chocolate*, 65.
107 J. A. Mann and James Chapman, 'Cocoa: Its Cultivation, Manufacture and Uses; Its Advantages and Value as an Article of Food', *Journal of the Society of Arts*, Vol. 8, No. 413 (1860), 799.
108 Sylvia Moodie-Kublalsingh, *The Cocoa Panyols of Trinidad: An Oral Record* (London: I. B.Tauris, 1994), 27.
109 Clarence-Smith, *Cocoa and Chocolate*, 87.
110 *Ibid.*, 95–9.
111 *Ibid.*, 104–5.
112 *Ibid.*, 5.
113 *Ibid.*, 110–11.
114 'The cacao lands . . . were fertilized with blood,' he wrote, looking back from old age. Jorge Amado, *The Violent Land* (London: Penguin, 2013), 1.
115 Clarence-Smith, *Cocoa and Chocolate*, 158; Lowell J. Satre, *Chocolate on Trial: Slavery, Politics, and the Ethics of Business* (Athens, OH: Ohio University Press, 2005), 10.
116 Satre, *Chocolate on Trial*, 12.

117 Quoted in *ibid.*, 125.
118 Quotation is from *Modern Slavery: An Exposure of 'Red Cocoa' and the Chinese Slavery Lie*, a 1910 pamphlet published by *The World.*
119 Clarence-Smith, *Cocoa and Chocolate*, 114.
120 Quoted in Satre, *Chocolate on Trial*, 130.
121 *Ibid.*, 187.
122 'Chamber of Mines CEO Calls for Shift from Local Procurement to Local Manufacturing at MIME 2025', Ghana Chamber of Mines press release, 13 November 2025; 'Ghana's Gold Output Could Rise 6.25% to 5.1 Million Ounces in 2025', Reuters, 30 May 2025.
123 My interview with investigative journalist Kent Mensah.
124 May Angel and Maxwell Akalaare Adombila, 'Ghana to Delay More Cocoa Deliveries as Supply Crisis Worsens', Reuters, 12 June 2024.
125 Emmanuel Bruce, 'Cocobod's Contract Rollover Costs Nation $1.3 Billion', *Graphic Business*, 1 March 2025.
126 'Mining Companies Pay GHS 17.68 Billion to Government in 2024', Ghana Chamber of Mines press release, 22 July 2025; AngloGold Ashanti Annual Report 2024.
127 Edem Kojo, 'Ghana's Unemployment Rate Eases Slightly to 13.0% in 2025 Third Quarter', *Joy Online*, 19 December 2025.
128 My interview with investigative journalist Kent Mensah; see also Eromo Egbejule, 'Polluted Rivers, Uprooted Farmland and Lost Taxes: Ghana Counts Cost of Illegal Gold Mining Boom', *Guardian*, 25 November 2024.
129 Austin, 'Vent for Surplus or Productivity Breakthrough?', 1054.
130 Francis Abrokwah, Henry Dzahini-Obiatey, Isaac Galyuon, Francis Osae-Awuku and Emmanuelle Muller, 'Geographical Distribution of Cacao Swollen Shoot Virus Molecular Variability in Ghana', *Plant Disease*, Vol. 100, No. 10 (2016).
131 Figures from Cocobod 2020–1 Annual Report and US Department of Agriculture, 'Ghana: Cocoa Sector Overview, 2025', 31 March 2025.
132 Food Business Africa, 'Ghana's Cocoa Production Reaches 429K Tons, with 2023/2024 Harvest Almost Complete', 18 July 2024.
133 Louisa J. Esdaile and Justin M. Chalker, 'The Mercury Problem in Artisanal and Small-Scale Gold Mining', *Chemistry: A European Journal*, Vol. 24, No. 27 (2018), 6905.
134 BNE IntelliNews, 'EU and Japan to Test Ghana's Cocoa for Heavy Metals over Mining Contamination Fears', 28 February 2025.

135 Press release issued by the NGO WaterAid, 'WaterAid Demands Immediate Halt to Illegal Mining as Water Supply Drops 75% Due to Pollution', 21 October 2024.

136 WaterAid, cited in Shola Lawal, 'As Gold Prices Surge, Ghana Faces Looming Crisis over Illegal Mining', Al Jazeera, 22 January 2025.

137 Estimate by the journalist Kent Mensah, in conversation, November 2025.

138 Lawal, 'As Gold Prices Surge'.

139 Full text of the report republished in *Modern Ghana* under the title 'Professor Frimpong Boateng Report on Work of IMCIM and the Way Forward', 25 April 2023.

140 'Asantehene Destools Three Chiefs over Galamsey', *Graphic Online*, 28 August 2024.

141 '"I Will Never Give Up in the Fight Against Illegal Mining", President Mahama Assures', *GhanaWeb*, 10 November 2025.

142 Maxwell Akalaare Adombila and Christian Akorlie, 'At Least Seven People Killed by Army at Ghana's AngloGold Ashanti Mine', *Reuters*, 19 January 2025.

143 Goldbod, 'Ghana Sees $12 Billion a Year from Small-Scale Gold Mining', 22 May 2025.

144 E.g. 'Ghana's Gold Rush Lures Chinese with Illicit Mines', Reuters, 14 March 2011; Egbejule, 'Polluted Rivers, Uprooted Farmland and Lost Taxes'.

145 See, for instance, '100 new vehicles for Ghana police', *Graphic Online*, 27 December 2019.

CHAPTER 5: THE FUTURE

1 Scott, *The Moral Economy of the Peasant*, 11.

2 Farshad A. Araghi, 'Global Depeasantization, 1945–1990', *Sociological Quarterly*, Vol. 36, No. 2 (1995), 337–68.

3 Henry Bernstein, 'Food Sovereignty via the "Peasant Way": A Sceptical View', *Journal of Peasant Studies*, Vol. 41, No. 6 (2014), 1031–63.

4 Aslany, 'The World Needs Peasants'.

Bibliography

Abbott, Elizabeth. *Sugar: A Bittersweet History*. London: Duckworth Overlook, 2009.

Abrokwah, F., et al. 'Geographical Distribution of Cacao Swollen Shoot Virus Molecular Variability in Ghana'. *Plant Disease*, Vol. 100, No. 10 (2016).

Acero, Camilo, and Frances Thomson. '"Everything Peasants Do Is Illegal": Colombian Coca Growers' Everyday Experiences of Law Enforcement and Its Impacts on State Legitimacy'. *Third World Quarterly*, Vol. 43, No. 11 (2022), 2674–92.

Acosta, J de. *The Natural and Moral History of the Indies*, trans. E. Grimston, ed. C. R. Markham. Cambridge: Cambridge University Press, 2010.

Adams, Robert McC. 'Agriculture and Urban Life in Early Southwestern Irān'. *Science*, Vol. 136, No. 3511 (1962), 109–22.

Aguilar-Moreno, Manuel. 'The Good and Evil of Chocolate in Colonial Mexico'. In *Chocolate in Mesoamerica: A Cultural History of Cacao*, ed. Cameron L. McNeil, 273–96. Gainesville, FL: University Press of Florida, 2006.

Allman, Jean, and Victoria Tashjian. *I Will Not Eat Stone: A Women's History of Colonial Asante*. Oxford: James Currey/Portsmouth, NH: Heinemann, 2000.

Amado, Jorge. *The Violent Land*, trans. Samuel Putnam. London and New York: Penguin, 2013.

Amanor, Kojo Sebastian. 'Global Resource Grabs, Agribusiness Concentration and the Smallholder: Two West African Case Studies'. *Journal of Peasant Studies*, Vol. 39, Nos 3–4 (2012), 731–49.

Amenumey, D. E. K. *Ghana: A Concise History from Pre-Colonial Times to the 20th Century*. Accra: Woeli Publishing Services, 2008.

Amin, Shahid, 'Unequal Antagonists: Peasants and Capitalists in Eastern UP in the 1930s'. *Economic and Political Weekly*, Vol. 16, Nos 42–3 (1981), 19– 31.

Araghi, Farshad A. 'Global Depeasantization, 1945–1990'. *Sociological Quarterly*, Vol. 36, No. 2 (1995), 337–68.

Aslany, Maryam. *Contested Capital: Rural Middle Classes in India*. Cambridge: Cambridge University Press, 2020.

———. 'The World Needs Peasants'. *Aeon*, 23 September 2025.

Aslany, Maryam, and Shannon Brincat. 'Class and Climate-Change Adaptation in Rural India: Beyond Community-Based Adaptation Models'. *Sustainable Development*, Vol. 29, No. 3 (2021), 571–82.

Aslany, Maryam, and Rana Dasgupta. *Harvest: The True Cost of Cotton*. Podcast series produced by Plan B Entertainment and Amazon Audible, 2025.

Attwood, Donald W. *Raising Cane: The Political Economy of Sugar in Western India*. London: Routledge, 1992.

Austin, Gareth. 'Capitalists and Chiefs in the Cocoa Hold-Ups in South Asante, 1927–1938'. *International Journal of African Historical Studies*, Vol. 21, No. 1 (1988), 63–95.

———. 'The Emergence of Capitalist Relations in South Asante Cocoa-Farming, *c*. 1916–33'. *Journal of African History*, Vol. 28 (1987), 259–79.

———. 'Vent for Surplus or Productivity Breakthrough? The Ghanaian Cocoa Take-off, *c*. 1890–1936'. *Economic History Review*, Vol. 67, No. 4 (2014), 1035–64.

Aworawo, David. 'Bitterness on a Sugar Island: British Colonialism and the Socio-economic Development of Jamaica (1655–1750)'. *Lagos Notes and Records*, Vol. 16, No. 1 (2010), 189–214.

Barker, R. The Origin and Spread of Early-Ripening Champa Rice: Its Impact on Song Dynasty China', *Rice*, Vol. 4 (2011), 184–6.

Battuta, Ibn. *Travels in Asia and Africa*, ed. and trans. H. A. R. Gibb. London: Routledge & Kegan Paul, 1953.

Beard, George M. *American Nervousness: Its Causes and Consequences: A Supplement to Nervous Exhaustion (Neurasthenia)*. New York: Putnam, 1881.

Beckert, Sven. *Capitalism: A Global History*. New York: Penguin Press, 2025.

Berdan, Frances F., et al. *Aztec Imperial Strategies*. Washington, DC: Dumbarton Oaks, 1996.

Berger, John. *Pig Earth*. London: Pantheon, 1979.
Bernstein, Henry. 'Agrarian Political Economy and Modern World Capitalism: The Contributions of Food Regime Analysis'. *Journal of Peasant Studies*, Vol 43, No. 3 (2016), 611–47.
———. *Class Dynamics of Agrarian Change*. Sterling, VA: Kumarian Press, 2010.
———. 'Food Sovereignty via the "Peasant Way": A Sceptical View'. *Journal of Peasant Studies*, Vol 41, No. 6 (2014), 1031–63.
Bhattacharya, K. R., and S. Z. Ali. 'On Rice and the Region of Rice Civilisation'. *International Journal of Sociology and Anthropology*, Vol 8, No. 8 (2016), 65–75.
Bosma, Ulbe. *The Sugar Plantation in India and Indonesia: Industrial Production, 1770–2001*. Cambridge: Cambridge University Press, 2013.
———. *The World of Sugar: How the Sweet Stuff Transformed Our Politics, Health, and Environment over 2,000 Years*. Cambridge, MA: Belknap Press, 2023.
Bosma, Ulbe, Juan A. Giusti-Cordero and G. Roger Knight, eds. *Sugarlandia Revisited: Sugar and Colonialism in Asia and the Americas, 1800–1940*. New York: Berghahn, 2007.
Briggs, Lawrence Palmer. *The Ancient Khmer Empire*. Philadelphia, PA: American Philosophical Society, 1951.
Bright, Mynors, ed. *The Diary of Samuel Pepys MA, FRS*, Vol. 1. London: George Bell, 1893.
Brook, Timothy. *The Troubled Empire: China in the Yuan and Ming Dynasties*. Cambridge, MA: Belknap Press, 2010.
Byres, T. J. *Capitalism from Above and Capitalism from Below: An Essay in Comparative Political Economy*. London: Macmillan, 1996.
Carter, James. 'When the Yellow River Changes Course'. *China Project*, 29 June 2022.
Castillo, Cristina. 'Development of Cereal Agriculture in Prehistoric Mainland Southeast Asia'. *Man in India*, Vol. 95, No. 4 (2015), 500–17.
Cervantes de Salazar, Francisco. *Crónica de la Nueva España*. Madrid: Hispanic Society of America, 1914.
Chandler, David P. *Facing the Cambodian Past: Selected Essays, 1971–1994*. Chiang Mai: Silkworm Books, 1996.
———. *A History of Cambodia*. Boulder, CO: Westview Press, 2008.
———. *The Tragedy of Cambodian History: Politics, War, and Revolution since 1945*. New Haven, CT: Yale University Press, 1991.

———. *Voices from S-21: Terror and History in Pol Pot's Secret Prison.* Berkeley, CA: University of California Press, 2000.
Chayanov, Alexander V. *The Theory of Peasant Economy*, ed. Daniel Thorner, Basile Kerblay and R. E. F. Smith. Madison, WI: University of Wisconsin Press, 1986.
Choudhary, Radhakrishna. 'Slaves and Serfs in Medieval Cambodia (circa 400–1300 AD)'. *Proceedings of the Indian History Congress*, Vol. 28 (1966), 520–31.
Cieza de León, Pedro. *The Discovery and Conquest of Peru*, ed. and trans. Alexandra Parma Cook and Noble David Cook. Durham, NC: Duke University Press, 1998.
Civáň, Peter, et al. 'Origin of the Aromatic Group of Cultivated Rice (Oryza sativa L.) Traced to the Indian Subcontinent'. *Genome Biology and Evolution*, Vol. 11, No. 3 (2019), 832–43.
Clarence-Smith, William Gervase. *Cocoa and Chocolate, 1765–1914.* London and New York: Routledge, 2000.
Clarence-Smith, William Gervase, ed. *Cocoa Pioneer Fronts since 1800: The Role of Smallholders, Planters, and Merchants.* London and New York: St Martin's Press, 1996.
Clark, Gregory, and Anthony Clark. 'Common Rights to the Land in England, 1475–1839'. *Journal of Economic History*, Vol. 61, No. 4 (2001), 1009–36.
Cobban, Alfred. *The Social Interpretation of the French Revolution.* Cambridge: Cambridge University Press, 1999.
Cobo, Bernabé. *Inca Religion and Customs*, trans. and ed. Roland Hamilton. Austin, TX: University of Texas Press, 1990.
Coe, Michael D., and Damian Evans. *Angkor and the Khmer Civilization.* London: Thames & Hudson, 2018.
Coe, Sophie D., and Michael D. Coe. *The True History of Chocolate.* New York: Thames & Hudson, 1996.
Collins, C. W., and J. Day. 'The Demon in the Bottle'. *Everyday Life* (August 1909).
Conan Doyle, Arthur. *The Sign of Four.* London: Smith, Elder & Co., 1908.
Cooper, Frederick. *Africa since 1940: The Past of the Present.* Cambridge: Cambridge University Press, 2002.
Courtwright, David T. *Forces of Habit: Drugs and the Making of the Modern World.* Cambridge, MA: Harvard University Press, 2001.

Cramb, Rob, ed. *White Gold: The Commercialisation of Rice Farming in the Lower Mekong Basin*. Singapore: Palgrave Macmillan, 2020.

Crossley, James. *Spectres of John Ball: The Peasants' Revolt in English Political History, 1381–2020*. Sheffield: Equinox, 2022.

Daguan, Zhou. *A Record of Cambodia: The Land and Its People*, ed. and trans. Peter Harris. Chiang Mai: Silkworm Books, 2007.

Dalrymple, William. *The Golden Road: How Ancient India Transformed the World*. London: Bloomsbury, 2024.

D'Altroy, Terence N. *The Incas*. Malden, MA: Blackwell, 2003.

D'Altroy, Terence N., and Timothy K. Earle. 'Staple Finance, Wealth Finance, and Storage in the Inka Political Economy'. *Current Anthropology*, Vol. 26, No. 2 (1985), 187–206.

Dasgupta, Rana. *After Nations: The Making and Unmaking of a World Order*. London: William Collins, 2026.

Davies, R. W., and Stephen G. Wheatcroft. *The Years of Hunger: Soviet Agriculture, 1931–1933*. Basingstoke: Palgrave Macmillan, 2004.

Davis, Erik. *Deathpower: Buddhism's Ritual Imagination in Cambodia*. New York: Columbia University Press, 2015.

Davis, Mike. *Late Victorian Holocausts: El Niño Famines and the Making of the Third World*. London: Verso, 2000.

de Carné, Louis. *Voyage en Indo-Chine et dans l'empire chinois*. Paris: E. Dentu, 1872.

de Fuentes, Patricia, ed. and trans. *The Conquistadors: First-Person Accounts of the Conquest of Mexico*. Norman, OK: University of Oklahoma Press, 1993.

de León Pinelo, Antonio. *Question moral si el chocolate quebranta el ayuno eclesiastico*. Madrid, 1636.

de Sahagún, Bernardino. *The Florentine Codex: The General History of the Things of New Spain*, ed. and trans. Arthur J. O. Anderson and Charles E. Dibble. Santa Fe, NM: School of American Research/Salt Lake City, UT: University of Utah Press, 1954.

DeSilva, J. M., G. Hamilton and S. Kidder. 'Cocaine Alley Queens: Gender, Race and Drug Use in American Midwestern Cities, 1890–1920'. *Urban History* (2025), 1–34.

Desnoyers, Charles, and Kiernan B. 'The Killing Fields of Jiangnan: Genocide and China's Taiping Rebellion, 1851–1864'. In *The Cambridge World History of Genocide*. Vol. 2: *Genocide in the Indigenous, Early Modern and Imperial Worlds, from c. 1535 to World*

War One, ed. Ned Blackhawk et al., 562–84. Cambridge: Cambridge University Press, 2023.

Diepart, J. C., and Dupuis, D. 'The Peasants in Turmoil: Khmer Rouge, State Formation and the Control of Land in Northwest Cambodia'. *Journal of Peasant Studies*, Vol 41, No. 4 (2014), 445–68.

Dillehay, T. D., et al. 'Early Holocene Coca Chewing in Northern Peru'. *Antiquity*, Vol. 84, No. 326 (2010), 939–53.

Dogra, Bharat. 'Denial of the Rural'. *Down to Earth* (15 September 2008).

Dostoevsky, Fyodor. *A Writer's Diary*, trans. K. Lantz. Evanston, IL: Northwestern University Press, 1997.

Du Bois, W. E. B. 'A Cup of Cocoa and Chocolate Drops (1946)'. In *International Thought*, 215–28. Cambridge: Cambridge University Press, 2022.

Dufour, Philippe Sylvestre. *Traitez nouveaux & curieux du café, du thé et du chocolate* [*sic*]*: Ouvrage également nécessaire aux médecins, & a tous ceux qui aiment leur santé*. Lyon, 1685.

Dupuy, Roger. *La République jacobine: Terreur, guerre et gouvernement révolutionnaire, 1792–1794*. Paris: Seuil, 2005.

Dyer, Christopher. *Peasants Making History: Living in an English Region, 1200–1540*. Oxford: Oxford University Press, 2022.

Díaz del Castillo, Bernal. *The Conquest of New Spain*, trans. J. M. Cohen. London: Penguin, 1973.

Ellis, Markman, Richard Coulton, and Matthew Mauger. *Empire of Tea: The Asian Leaf That Conquered the World*. London: Reaktion, 2015.

Elvin, Mark. *The Retreat of the Elephants: An Environmental History of China*. New Haven, CT: Yale University Press, 2004.

Engelhardt, Richard A. 'Two Thousand Years of Engineering Genius on the Angkor Plain'. *Expedition*, Vol. 37, No. 3 (1995), 24–35.

Esdaile, Louisa J., and Justin M. Chalker. 'The Mercury Problem in Artisanal and Small-Scale Gold Mining'. *Chemistry: A European Journal*, Vol. 24, No. 27 (2018), 6905–16.

Evans, Damian, et al. 'A Comprehensive Archaeological Map of the World's Largest Preindustrial Settlement Complex at Angkor, Cambodia'. *Proceedings of the National Academy of Sciences*, Vol. 104, No. 36 (2007): 14277–82.

Fagan, Brian, and Nadia Durrani. 'The Secrets of Angkor Wat: How Archaeology Is Rewriting History'. *Current World Archaeology*, 2016.

Ferrando, T., and Mpofu, E. 'Peasants as "Cosmopolitan Insurgents"'. *AJIL Unbound*, Vol. 116 (2022), 96–100.

Figes, Orlando. *Natasha's Dance: A Cultural History of Russia*. London: Penguin, 2003.

Fletcher, Roland, et al. 'Angkor Wat: An Introduction'. *Antiquity*, Vol. 89, No. 348 (2015), 1388–1401.

Fletcher, Roland, et al. 'The Water Management Network of Angkor, Cambodia'. *Antiquity*, Vol. 82 (2008), 658–70.

Floor, Willem M. 'Sugar'. *Encyclopaedia Iranica*, 20 July 2009.

Frankopan, Peter. *The Earth Transformed: An Untold History.* London: Bloomsbury, 2023.

Freud, Sigmund. 'Über Coca'. *Centralblatt für die gesammte Therapie*, Vol. 2 (1884), 289–314.

Fuller, Dorian Q., and Castillo, Cristina Cobo. 'The Origins and Spread of Cereal Agriculture in Mainland Southeast Asia'. In *The Languages and Linguistics of Mainland Southeast Asia: A Comprehensive Guide*, ed. Paul Sidwell and Mathias Jenny. Berlin: De Gruyter Mouton, 2021.

Fuller, Dorian Q., Emma Harvey and Ling Qin. 'Presumed Domestication? Evidence for Wild Rice Cultivation and Domestication in the Fifth Millennium BC of the Lower Yangtze Region'. *Antiquity*, Vol. 81, No. 312 (2007), 316–31.

Gagliano, Joseph A. *Coca Prohibition in Peru: The Historical Debates.* Tucson, AZ: University of Arizona Press, 1994.

Garnier, Francis. *Voyage d'exploration en Indo-Chine.* Paris: Hachette, 1885.

Gaudes, Rüdiger. 'Kaundinya, Preah Thaong, and the "Nagi Soma": Some Aspects of a Cambodian Legend'. *Asian Folklore Studies*, Vol. 52 (1993), 333–58.

Gay, George R., et al. 'An Old Girl: Flyin' Low, Dyin' Slow, Blinded by Snow: Cocaine in Perspective'. *International Journal of the Addictions*, Vol. 8, No. 6 (1973), 1027–42.

Gifford, Paul. *Ghana's New Christianity: Pentecostalism in a Globalising African Economy*. London: Hurst, 2004.

Glaize, Maurice. *Les Monuments du groupe d'Angkor*. Paris: Jean Maisonneuve, 1993.

Glin, L. C., Peter Oosterveer and A. P. J. Mol. 'Governing the Organic Cocoa Network from Ghana'. *Journal of Agrarian Change*, Vol. 15, No. 1 (2015), 43–64.

Gootenberg, Paul. *Andean Cocaine: The Making of a Global Drug*. Chapel Hill, NC: University of North Carolina Press, 2008.
———. 'Cocaine's Long March North, 1900–2010'. *Latin American Politics and Society*, Vol. 54, No. 1 (2012), 159–80.
———. 'A Forgotten Case of "Scientific Excellence on the Periphery": The Nationalist Cocaine Science of Alfredo Bignon, 1884–1887'. *Comparative Studies in Society and History*, Vol. 49, No. 1 (2007), 202–32.
———. 'Introduction: Orphans of Development: The Unanticipated Rise of Illicit Coca in the Amazon Andes, 1950–1990'. In *The Origins of Cocaine: Colonization and Failed Development in the Amazon Andes*, ed. Paul Gootenberg and Liliana M. Dávalos, 1–26. Abingdon and New York: Routledge, 2018.
Gootenberg, Paul, and Liliana M. Dávalos, eds. *The Origins of Cocaine: Colonization and Failed Development in the Amazon Andes*. Abingdon and New York: Routledge, 2018.
Gopal, Anand. *No Good Men among the Living: America, the Taliban, and the War through Afghan Eyes*. New York: Metropolitan Books, 2014.
Gopal, Lallanji. 'Sugar-Making in Ancient India'. *Journal of the Economic and Social History of the Orient*, Vol. 7, No. 1 (1964), 57–72.
Gore, E. 'Colonial Afterlives in the Global Cocoa Supply Chain: Sharecropping, Labour Exploitation, and Gendered (Re) production'. *Review of International Political Economy*, Vol. 33, No. 1 (2026), 379–408.
Gorriti, Gustavo. *La calavera en negro: El traficante que quiso gobernar un país*. Barcelona: Planeta, 2006.
Graeber, David, and Wengrow, David. *The Dawn of Everything: A New History of Humanity*. London: Allen Lane, 2021.
Green, W. Nathan. 'Placing Cambodia's Agrarian Transition in an Emerging Chinese Food Regime'. *Journal of Peasant Studies*, Vol. 49, No. 6 (2022), 1249–72.
Grisaffi, Thomas. *Coca Yes, Cocaine No: How Bolivia's Coca Growers Reshaped Democracy*. Durham, NC: Duke University Press, 2018.
Grivetti, Louis Evan, and Howard-Yana Shapiro, eds. *Chocolate: History, Culture and Heritage*. Hoboken, NJ: Wiley, 2009.
Guérin, Mathieu. *Paysans de la forêt à l'époque coloniale: La pacification des aborigènes des hautes terres du Cambodge (1863–1940)*. Rennes: Association d'histoire des sociétés rurales, 2008.

Guha, Ranajit. *Elementary Aspects of Peasant Insurgency in Colonial India*. Durham, NC: Duke University Press, 1999.

Gyapong, A. Y. 'Land Grabs, Farmworkers, and Rural Livelihoods in West Africa: Some Silences in the Food Sovereignty Discourse'. *Globalizations*, Vol. 18, No. 3 (2021), 339–54.

Habermas, Jürgen. *The Structural Transformation of the Public Sphere: An Inquiry into a Category of Bourgeois Society*, trans. Thomas Burger, with Frederick Lawrence. Cambridge, MA: MIT Press, 1989.

Habib, Amar. *Anti-Farmer Laws*, trans. Sagar Pilare. Ambajogai: Parisar Prakashan, 2018.

Hahamovitch, Cindy, and Rick Halpern. 'Not a "Sack of Potatoes": Why Labor Historians Need to Take Agriculture Seriously'. *International Labor and Working-Class History*, No. 65 (Spring 2004), 3–10.

Hall, Kenneth R. *A History of Early Southeast Asia: Maritime Trade and Societal Development, 100–1500*. Lanham, MD: Rowman & Littlefield, 2011.

———. 'International Trade and Foreign Diplomacy in Early Medieval South India'. *Journal of the Economic and Social History of the Orient*, Vol. 21, No. 1 (1978), 75–98.

Hanna, Nelly. *Making Big Money in 1600: The Life and Times of Isma'il Abu Taqiyya, Egyptian Merchant*. Syracuse, NY: Syracuse University Press, 1998.

Harris, Ian. *Cambodian Buddhism: History and Practice*. Honolulu: University of Hawai'i Press, 2005.

Harriss-White, Barbara. *India Working: Essays on Society and Economy*. Cambridge: Cambridge University Press, 2003.

———. *Rural Commercial Capital: Agricultural Markets in West Bengal*. Delhi: Oxford University Press, 1977.

———, ed. *Agricultural Markets from Theory to Practice: Field Experience in Developing Countries*. London: Macmillan, 1995.

Harriss-White, Barbara, and S. Janakarajan, eds. *Rural India Facing the 21st Century*. London: Anthem Press, 2004.

Hartwell, Robert M. 'Markets, Technology, and the Structure of Enterprise in the Development of the Eleventh-Century Chinese Iron and Steel Industry'. *Journal of Economic History*, Vol. 26, No. 1 (1966), 29–58.

———. 'A Revolution in the Chinese Iron and Coal Industries during the Northern Sung, 960–1126 AD'. *Journal of Asian Studies*, Vol. 21, No. 2 (1962), 153–62.

Hatcher, John. *The Black Death: An Intimate History*. London: Weidenfeld & Nicolson, 2008.

Heller, Henry. *The Bourgeois Revolution in France, 1789–1815*. New York and Oxford: Berghahn, 2006.

Higham, C. F. W., and Nam C. Kim, eds. *The Oxford Handbook of Early Southeast Asia*. Oxford: Oxford University Press, 2022.

Hill, Polly. 'The Migrant Cocoa Farmers of Southern Ghana'. *Africa*, Vol. 31, No. 3 (1961), 209–30.

Hobsbawm, Eric. *The Age of Extremes: The Short Twentieth Century, 1914–1991*. London: Abacus, 1994.

———. *Primitive Rebels: Studies in Archaic Forms of Social Movement in the 19th and 20th Centuries*. Manchester: Manchester University Press, 1986.

Horn, James. 'British Diaspora: Emigration from Britain, 1680–1815'. In *The Oxford History of the British Empire*, Vol. 2, *The Eighteenth Century*, ed. P. J. Marshall, Alaine Low and Wm. Roger Louis. Oxford: Oxford University Press, 1998.

Horner, I. B., trans. *The Book of the Discipline (Vinaya-Pitaka)*, Vol. 4. Lancaster: Pali Text Society, 2007.

Iliffe, John. *Africans: The History of a Continent*. Cambridge: Cambridge University Press, 2007.

Ishii, Yoneo. *The Junk Trade from Southeast Asia: Translations from the Tosen Fusetsu-gaki, 1674–1723*. Singapore: Institute of Southeast Asian Studies, 1998.

Jones, Dan. *Summer of Blood: The Peasants' Revolt of 1381*. London: HarperPress, 2009.

Jones, Peter. 'The Peasantry of France on the Eve of the French Revolution'. *History of European Ideas*, Vol. 12, No. 3 (1990), 335–50.

Jonnes, Jill. *Hep-Cats, Narcs and Pipe Dreams: A History of America's Romance with Illegal Drugs*. New York: Scribner, 1996.

Joyce, Patrick. *Remembering Peasants*. New York: Scribner, 2024.

Julien, Catherine J. 'Coca Production on the Inca Frontier: The Yungas of Chuquioma'. *Andean Past*, Vol. 5 (1998).

Kamath, S. J. *The Political Economy of Suppressed Markets: Controls, Rent-Seeking and Interest Group Behaviour in the Indian Sugar and Cement Industries*. Delhi: Oxford University Press, 1992.

Kawano, Kenji. 'Rousseau's Position in the History of the Peasantry'. *Kyoto University Economic Review*, Vol. 23, No. 1 (1953), 46–68.

Kennedy, Joseph. *Coca Exotica: The Illustrated Story of Cocaine*. New York: Cornwall Books, 1985.

Kiernan, Ben. *How Pol Pot Came to Power: Colonialism, Nationalism, and Communism in Cambodia, 1930–1975*. New Haven, CT: Yale University Press, 2004.

———. *The Pol Pot Regime: Race, Power, and Genocide in Cambodia under the Khmer Rouge, 1975–79*. New Haven, CT: Yale University Press, 1996.

Kingston-Mann, Esther. 'Lenin and the Challenge of Peasant Militance: From Bloody Sunday, 1905 to the Dissolution of the First Duma'. *Russian Review*, Vol. 38, No. 4 (1979), 434–55.

Knapp, Arthur W. *Cocoa and Chocolate: Their History from Plantation to Consumer*. London: Chapman and Hall, 1920.

Knight, G. R. 'From Plantation to Padi-Field: The Origins of the Nineteenth Century Transformation of Java's Sugar Industry'. *Modern Asian Studies*, Vol. 14, No. 2 (1980), 177–204.

Kolavalli, Shashi, and Marcella Vigneri. *The Cocoa Coast: The Board-Managed Cocoa Sector in Ghana*. Washington, DC: International Food Policy Research Institute, 2017.

Koskella, Melanie Alexxann. *A Universal Approach to Plague Epidemics in Fifteenth Century Mamluk Egypt and Syria: Contemporary Bias, Classical Islamic Medicine, and the Voices Of The Ulamá*. PhD diss., University of Utah, 2014.

Kunnath, George J. *Rebels from the Mud Houses: Dalits and the Making of the Maoist Revolution in Bihar*. London: Routledge, 2017.

Lalvani, Mala. 'Sugar Co-operatives in Maharashtra: A Political Economy Perspective'. *Journal of Development Studies*, Vol. 44, No. 10 (2008), 1474–1505.

Lentz, Christian C. 'Cultivating Subjects: Opium and Rule in Post-Colonial Vietnam'. *Modern Asian Studies*, Vol. 51, No. 4 (2017), 879–918.

Lenin, V. I. 'The Proletariat and the Peasantry'. *Novaya Zhizn*, No. 11 (12 November 1905). Reprinted in *Collected Works*, Vol. 10, 40–3. Moscow: Progress Publishers, 1965.

———. 'Socialism and the Peasantry'. *Proletary*, No. 20 (1905).

Linebaugh, Peter. *The Magna Carta Manifesto: Liberties and Commons for All.* Berkeley, CA: University of California Press, 2008.

Lovejoy, Paul E. *Transformations in Slavery: A History of Slavery in Africa.* Cambridge: Cambridge University Press, 2011.

Lowder, S. K., J. Skoet and T. Raney. 'The Number, Size, and Distribution of Farms, Smallholder Farms, and Family Farms Worldwide'. *World Development*, Vol. 87 (2016), 16–29.

Ludlow, Helen. 'Ghana, Cocoa, Colonialism and Globalisation: Introducing Historiography'. *Yesterday & Today*, No. 8 (2012), 1–21.

Maddison, Angus. *The World Economy: A Millennial Perspective.* Paris: OECD, 2001.

Major, John S., et al., eds. *The Essential Huainanzi: Liu An, King of Huainan.* New York: Columbia University Press, 2012.

Major, R. H., ed. *Select Letters of Christopher Columbus: With Other Original Documents, Relating to His Four Voyages to the New World.* Cambridge: Cambridge University Press, 2010.

Mann, J. A., and James Chapman 'Cocoa: Its Cultivation, Manufacture and Uses; Its Advantages and Value as an Article of Food'. *Journal of the Society of Arts*, Vol. 8, No. 413 (1860), 795–804.

Mantegazza, Paolo. 'Sulle virtù igieniche e medicinali della coca e sugli alimenti nervosi in generale'. *Annali Universali di Medicina*, Vol. 167 (1859), 449–519.

Mao Zedong. *On Guerrilla Warfare.* Washington, DC: US Marine Corps, 1989.

———. 'Report on an Investigation of the Peasant Movement in Hunan'. In *Selected Works of Mao-Tse-Tung*, Vol. 1. London: Lawrence & Wishart, 1954.

Markevich, Andrei, Natalya Naumenko and Nancy Qian. 'The Political-Economic Causes of the Soviet Great Famine, 1932–33'. NBER Working Paper no. 29089 (2021).

Markoff, John. *The Abolition of Feudalism: Peasants, Lords and Legislators in the French Revolution.* University Park, PA: Pennsylvania State University Press, 1996.

Marks, Robert B. *China: An Environmental History*, 2nd edn. Lanham, MD: Rowman & Littlefield, 2017.

Marx, Karl. 'The Eighteenth Brumaire of Louis Bonaparte'. *In Karl Marx and Frederick Engels: Collected Works.* London: Lawrence & Wishart, 1979.

Marx, Karl, and Friedrich Engels. *The Communist Manifesto*, trans. Samuel Moore. London: Penguin, 2002.

Mason, T. David, and Christopher Campany. 'Guerrillas, Drugs and Peasants: The Rational Peasant and the War on Drugs in Peru'. *Terrorism and Political Violence*, Vol 7, No. 4 (1995), 140–70.

McNeil, Cameron L., ed. *Chocolate in Mesoamerica: A Cultural History of Cacao*. Gainesville, FL: University Press of Florida, 2006.

McPhee, Peter. 'A Vicious Civil War in the French Revolution: "The Vendée", 1793–1795'. In *The Cambridge World History of Genocide*, Vol. 2, ed. N. Blackhawk et al. Cambridge: Cambridge University Press, 2023.

Medelius, Mónica. 'El licenciado Cristóbal Ramírez de Cartagena: Relator, Fiscal y Oidor de la Audiencia de Lima. Su Memorial de 1591'. *Surandino Monográfico*, No. 3 (2013): 63–92.

Merlhès, Victor, ed. *Correspondance de Paul Gauguin*, Vol. 1: 1873–1888. Paris: Fondation Singer-Polignac, 1984.

Meyer, Birgit. '"Make a Complete Break with the Past": Memory and Post-Colonial Modernity in Ghanaian Pentecostalist Discourse'. *Journal of Religion in Africa*, Vol. 28, No. 3 (1998), 316–49.

———. 'Pentecostalism and Neo-Liberal Capitalism: Faith, Prosperity and Vision in African Pentecostal-Charismatic Churches'. *Journal for the Study of Religion*, Vol. 20, No. 2 (2007), 5–28.

Migdal, Joel S. *Peasants, Politics, and Revolution: Pressures toward Political and Social Change in the Third World*. Princeton, NJ: Princeton University Press, 1977.

Mikell, Gwendolyn. *Cocoa and Chaos in Ghana*. New York: Paragon House, 1989.

Mintz, Sidney. 'Labor and Sugar in Puerto Rico and in Jamaica, 1800–1850'. *Comparative Studies in Society and History*, Vol. 1, No. 3 (1959), 273–81.

———. *Sweetness and Power: The Place of Sugar in Modern History*. New York: Penguin, 1985.

Moodie-Kublalsingh, Sylvia. *The Cocoa Panyols of Trinidad: An Oral Record*. London: I. B. Tauris, 1994.

Mortimer, W. Golden. *History of Coca: 'The Divine Plant' of the Incas*. New York: J. H. Vail, 1901.

Mouhot, Henri. *Travels in the Central Parts of Indo-China (Siam), Cambodia and Laos during the Years 1858, 1859 and 1860*, Vol. 1. London: John Murray, 1864.

Moxham, Roy. *Tea: Addiction, Exploitation and Empire*. New York: Carroll & Graf, 2003.

Muojama, Olisa Godson. 'Cocoa Marketing Board and the Sustainable Cocoa Economy in Colonial Nigeria'. *African Economic History*, Vol. 47, No. 1 (2019), 1–31.

Neruda, Pablo. *The Heights of Macchu Picchu*, trans. Nathaniel Tarn. London: Jonathan Cape, 1966.

Netting, Robert McC. *Smallholders, Householders: Farm Families and the Ecology of Intensive, Sustainable Agriculture*. Stanford, CA: Stanford University Press, 1993.

Niemann, Albert. *Über eine neue organische Base in den Cocablättern.* PhD diss., University of Göttingen, 1860.

Nkrumah, Kwame. *Ghana: The Autobiography of Kwame Nkrumah.* New York: International Publishers, 1957.

North-Coombes, Daniel. 'Slavery, Emancipation and the Labour "Crisis" in the Sugar Industry of Mauritius, 1790–1842'. *Tanzania Zamani*, Vol. 3, No. 1 (1997), 16–49.

Olson, Kenneth R., and Lois Wright Morton. 'Tonle Sap Lake and River and Confluence with the Mekong River in Cambodia'. *Journal of Soil and Water Conservation*, Vol. 73, No. 3 (2018), 60A–66A.

Oppong-Boateng, Juliet. *Economic Enterprises of the Basel Mission Society in the Gold Coast: A Study of the Basel Mission Trading Company from 1859 to 1917*. MPhil thesis, University of Ghana, 2014.

Pacini, Deborah, and Christine Franquemont (eds). *Coca and Cocaine: Effects on People and Policy in Latin America.* Cambridge, MA: Cultural Survival Inc./Latin American Studies Program, Cornell University, 1986.

Page, Martin. *The First Global Village: How Portugal Changed the World.* Alfragide: Casa das Letras, 2002.

Paredes, Maritza, and Hernán Manrique. 'Ideas of Modernisation and Territorial Transformation: The Case of the Upper Huallaga Valley of Peru'. In *The Origins of Cocaine: Colonisation and Failed Development in the Amazon Andes*, ed. Paul Gootenberg and Liliana M. Dávalos. Abingdon and New York: Routledge, 2018.

———. 'The State's Developmentalist Illusion and the Origins of Illegal Coca Cultivation in Peru's Alto Huallaga Valley (1960–80)'. *Journal of Latin American Studies*, Vol. 53, No. 2 (2021), 245–67.

Paredes, Maritza, and A. Pastor. 'Illicit Crops in the Frontier Margins: Amazonian Indigenous Livelihoods and the Expansion of Coca in Peru'. *Journal of Peasant Studies*, Vol. 51, No. 4 (2024), 960–81.

Paredes Guerrero, Brenda Tatiana. *Two Quechua Protestant Villages and Terror in Huanta, Peru 1980–1991*. MA thesis, University of North Carolina at Charlotte, 2018.

Parker, Matthew. *The Sugar Barons: Family, Corruption, Empire and War in the West Indies*. New York: Walker & Co., 2011.

Parmar, Inderjeet. 'The "Big 3" Foundations and American Global Power'. *American Journal of Economics and Sociology*, Vol. 74, No. 4 (2015), 676–703.

Pawar, Sharad. *On My Terms: From the Grassroots to the Corridors of Power*. New Delhi: Speaking Tiger, 2016.

Penny, Dan, et al. 'The Environmental Impact of Cambodia's Ancient City of Mahendraparvata (Phnom Kulen)'. *PLoS One*, Vol. 9, No. 1 (2014).

Perry, Elizabeth J. *Rebels and Revolutionaries in North China, 1845–1945*. Stanford, CA: Stanford University Press, 1980.

Petit de Bachaumont, Louis. *Les Mémoires secrets pour servir à l'histoire de la République des Lettres en France depuis 1762 jusqu'à nos jours*, Vol. 6. London: John Adamson, 1777.

Pietz, David A. *The Yellow River: The Problem of Water in Modern China*. Cambridge, MA: Harvard University Press, 2015.

Pistor, Katharina. *The Code of Capital: How the Law Creates Wealth and Inequality*. Princeton, NJ: Princeton University Press, 2019.

Pliny the Elder. *Natural History: A Selection*, ed. and trans. John Healey. London: Penguin, 2004.

Polo, Marco. *The Travels*, ed. and trans. Nigel Cliff. London: Penguin, 2016.

Ponting, Clive. *World History: A New Perspective*. London: Pimlico, 2001.

Poole, Colin. *Tonle Sap: The Heart of Cambodia's Natural Heritage*. Bangkok: River Books, 2006.

Popkin, Samuel L. *The Rational Peasant: The Political Economy of Rural Society in Vietnam*. Berkeley, CA: University of California Press, 1979.

Popol Vuh: The Sacred Book of the Ancient Quiché Maya, trans. Delia Goetz and Sylvanus G. Morley. London: William Hodge & Co., 1951.

Prabhupāda, A. C. Bhaktivedanta Swami (trans.). *Śrīmad Bhāgavatam.* Los Angeles: Bhaktivedanta Book Trust, 1976.

Presilla, Maricel E. *The New Taste of Chocolate: A Cultural and Natural History of Cacao with Recipes*, rev. edn. Berkeley, CA: Ten Speed Press, 2009.

Preschez, Philippe. 'Le Cambodge depuis 1941: État des travaux'. *Revue française de science politique*, Vol. 11, No. 4 (1961), 906–35.

Quiroga de San Antonio, Friar Gabriel. *Brève et véridique relation des événements du Cambodge*, trans. Antoine Cabaton. Paris: Ernest Leroux, 1914.

Ramírez, María Clemencia. *Between the Guerrillas and the State: The Cocalero Movement, Citizenship, and Identity in the Colombian Amazon*, trans. Andy Klatt. Durham, NC: Duke University Press, 2011.

Ramseyer, Friedrich A., and Johannes Kühne. *Four Years in Ashantee.* London: James Nisbet & Co., 1875.

Rappaport, Erika. *A Thirst for Empire: How Tea Shaped the Modern World.* Princeton, NJ: Princeton University Press, 2017.

Rezakhani, Khodadad. 'Continuity and Change in Late Antique Irān: An Economic View of the Sasanians'. *International Journal of the Society of Iranian Archaeologists*, Vol. 1, No. 2 (2015), 93–106.

Rice, Stian, and James Tyner. 'The Rice Cities of the Khmer Rouge: An Urban Political Ecology of Rural Mass Violence'. *Transactions of the Institute of British Geographers*, Vol. 42, No. 4 (2017), 589–602.

Rojas Herrera, Itayosara, and Joost Dessein. '"We Are Not Drug Traffickers, We Are Colombian Peasants": The Voices and History of Cocaleros in the Substitution Programme of Illicit Crops in Colombia'. *Geoforum*, Vol. 141 (2023).

Rivera Cusicanqui, Silvia. '/Coca: An Indigenous Commodity and Its Paradoxes'. *ReVista. Harvard Review of Latin America*, Vol. 11, No. 1 (2011).

Root, Hilton L. *The Fountain of Privilege: Political Foundations of Markets in Old Regime France and England.* Berkeley, CA: University of California Press, 1994.

———. *Peasants and King in Burgundy: Agrarian Foundations of French Absolutism.* Berkeley, CA: University of California Press, 1987.

Roper, Lyndal. *Summer of Fire and Blood: The German Peasants' War.* London: Basic Books, 2025.

Rosen, Stanley. 'The Chinese Communist Party and Chinese Society: Popular Attitudes toward Party Membership and the Party's Image'. *Australian Journal of Chinese Affairs*, Vol. 24 (1990), 51–92.

Rostworowski de Diez Canseco, María. *Pachacamac y el Señor de los Milagros: Una trayectoria milenaria*. Lima: Instituto de Estudios Peruanos, 2002.

Rothschild, V. 'State Repression and Selective Expression: Communal Canteens and the "Collective" Memory of China's Great Leap Famine'. *China Quarterly*, Vol. 265 (2025), 146–64.

Ryan, Órla. *Chocolate Nations: Living and Dying for Cocoa in West Africa*. London: Zed Books, 2011.

Sáenz Rovner, Eduardo. *The Cuban Connection: Drug Trafficking, Smuggling and Gambling in Cuba from the 1920s to the Revolution*. Chapel Hill, NC: University of North Carolina Press, 2008.

Saignes, Thierry. 'Capoche, Potosí y la Coca: El Consumo Popular de Estimulantes en el Siglo XVII'. *Revista de Indias*, Vol. 48, Nos 182–3 (1988), 207–35.

Samanez, Cecillia Tovar. 'Being a Church in a Time of Violence: Peruvian Church during the Armed Internal Conflict 1980 to 2000'. *Religions*, Vol. 11, No. 11 (2020).

Sancho de la Hoz, Pedro. 'Relación para Su Majestad de lo sucedido en la conquista y pacificación de estas provincias de la Nueva Castilla (1534)'. In *Los Cronistas de la Conquista*, ed. Horacio H. Urteaga. Paris: Desclée de Brouwer, 1938.

Sato, Tsugitaka. *Sugar in the Social Life of Medieval Islam*. Leiden: Brill, 2014.

Satre, Lowell J. *Chocolate on Trial: Slavery, Politics, and the Ethics of Business*. Athens, OH: Ohio University Press, 2005.

Savage, Susannah. 'Chocolate Cartels: The Rise of Cocoa Smuggling'. *Financial Times*, 1 August 2025.

Schama, Simon. *Citizens: A Chronicle of the French Revolution*. New York: Knopf, 1989.

Scheppegrell, William. 'The Abuse and Dangers of Cocaine'. *Medical News*, Vol. 73, No. 14 (1898), 417–22.

Schivelbusch, Wolfgang. *Tastes of Paradise: A Social History of Spices, Stimulants, and Intoxicants*. trans. David Jacobson. New York: Pantheon, 1992.

Scott, James C. *Against the Grain: A Deep History of the Earliest States*. New Haven, CT: Yale University Press, 2017.

———. *The Art of Not Being Governed: An Anarchist History of Upland Southeast Asia*. New Haven, CT: Yale University Press, 2009.
———. *Comparative Political Corruption*. Englewood Cliffs, NJ: Prentice-Hall, 1972.
———. *Decoding Subaltern Politics: Ideology, Disguise, and Resistance in Agrarian Politics*. London: Routledge, 2012.
———. *Domination and the Arts of Resistance: Hidden Transcripts*. New Haven, CT: Yale University Press, 1990.
———. *In Praise of Floods: The Untamed River and the Life It Brings*. New Haven, CT: Yale University Press, 2025.
———. *The Moral Economy of the Peasant: Rebellion and Subsistence in Southeast Asia*. New Haven, CT: Yale University Press, 1976.
———. *Political Ideology in Malaysia: Reality and the Beliefs of an Elite*. New Haven, CT: Yale University Press, 1968.
———. *Seeing Like a State: How Certain Schemes to Improve the Human Condition Have Failed*. New Haven, CT: Yale University Press, 1998.
———. *Weapons of the Weak: Everyday Forms of Peasant Resistance*. New Haven, CT: Yale University Press, 1985.
Shanin, Teodor. *The Awkward Class: Political Sociology of Peasantry in a Developing Society: Russia 1910–1925*. Oxford: Clarendon Press, 1972.
———, ed. *Peasants and Peasant Societies*. Harmondsworth: Penguin, 1971.
Shehadeh, N. 'The Climate of Jordan in the Past and Present'. *Studies in the History and Archaeology of Jordan*, Vol. 2 (1985), 25–37.
Sheridan, Richard B. *Sugar and Slavery: An Economic History of the British West Indies, 1623–1775*. Baltimore, MD: Johns Hopkins University Press, 1974.
Siaw, Daniel, George Ofosu and David Sarpong. 'Cocoa Production, Farmlands, and the Galamsey: Examining Current and Emerging Trends in the ASM–Agriculture Nexus'. *Journal of Rural Studies* 99 (2023), 103001.
Silva, Fabio, Alison et al. 'A Tale of Two Rice Varieties: Modelling the Prehistoric Dispersals of Japonica and Proto-Indica Rices'. *The Holocene*, Vol. 28, No. 11 (2018), 1745–58.
Southall, Roger J. 'Farmers, Traders and Brokers in the Gold Coast Cocoa Economy'. *Canadian Journal of African Studies/Revue Canadienne des Études Africaines*, Vol. 12, No. 2 (1978), 185–211.

Spicer, Joaneath. 'The Abduction of Helen: A Monumental Series Celebrating the Wedding of Caterina Corner in 1468'. *Journal of the Walters Art Museum*, Vol. 74 (2019).

Stobart, Jon. *Sugar and Spice: Grocers and Groceries in Provincial England, 1650–1830*. Oxford: Oxford University Press, 2013.

Stokes, Eric. *The Peasant and the Raj: Studies in Agrarian Society and Peasant Rebellion in Colonial India*. Cambridge: Cambridge University Press, 1978.

Stone, N. L., ed. *Customs Tariff of the German Customs Union*. Washington, DC: Government Printing Office, 1908.

Swift, Peter. 'Changing Ethnic Identities among the Kuy in Cambodia: Assimilation, Reassertion and the Making of Indigenous Identity'. *Asia Pacific Viewpoint*, Vol. 54, No. 3 (2013), 296–308.

Szamuely, Tibor. *The Russian Tradition*. London: Fontana, 1974.

Tackett, Timothy. *The Coming of the Terror in the French Revolution*. Cambridge, MA: Belknap Press, 2015.

Tena, Esayas, et al. 'Sugarcane Production under Smallholder Farming Systems: Farmers Preferred Traits, Constraints and Genetic Resources'. *Cogent Food & Agriculture*, Vol. 2, No. 1 (2016).

Thomson, Frances. 'Escaping Capitalist Market Imperatives: Commercial Coca Cultivation in the Colombian Amazon'. *Journal of Peasant Studies*, Vol. 51, No. 4 (2024), 826–60.

Thomson, Frances, Patrick Meehan and Jonathan Goodhand. 'The Political Economy of Illicit Drug Crops: Forum Introduction'. *Journal of Peasant Studies*, Vol. 51, No. 4 (2024), 763–800.

Thomson, Sinclair. *We Alone Will Rule: Native Andean Politics in the Age of Insurgency*. Madison, WI: University of Wisconsin Press, 2002.

Tomich, Dale W. *Slavery in the Circuit of Sugar: Martinique and the World-Economy, 1830–1848*. Albany, NY: State University of New York Press, 2016.

Topik, Steven, Carlos Marichal and Zephyr Frank, eds. *From Silver to Cocaine: Latin American Commodity Chains and the Building of the World Economy, 1500–2000*. Durham, NC: Duke University Press, 2006.

Tyner, James A. *From Rice Fields to Killing Fields*. Syracuse, NY: Syracuse University Press, 2017.

Ukpabi, S. C. 'The British Colonial Office Approach to the Ashanti War of 1900'. *African Studies Review*, Vol. 13, No. 3 (1970), 363–80.

Valdez, Lidio M., Juan Taboada and J. Ernesto Valdez. 'Ancient Use of Coca Leaves in the Peruvian Central Highlands'. *Journal of Anthropological Research*, Vol. 71, No. 2 (2015), 231–58.
Van de Ven, Hans. *China at War: Triumph and Tragedy in the Emergence of the New China*. Cambridge, MA: Harvard University Press, 2018.
Van der Ploeg, Jan Douwe. *The New Peasantries: Struggles for Autonomy and Sustainability in an Era of Empire and Globalization*. London: Earthscan, 2008.
van Dun, Mirella. 'Cocaine Flows and the State in Peru's Amazonian Borderlands'. *Journal of Latin American Studies*, Vol. 48, No. 3 (2016), 509–35.
Vanhaute, Eric. *Peasants in World History*. London: Routledge, 2021.
Vargas Llosa, Mario. *Death in the Andes*, trans. Edith Grossman. London: Faber & Faber, 1996.
Vickery, Michael. *Cambodia 1975–1982*. Boston: South End Press, 1984.
———. *Kampuchea: Politics, Economics and Society*. London: Frances Pinter, 1986.
———. *Society, Economics, and Politics in Pre-Angkor Cambodia: The 7th–8th Centuries*. Tokyo: Centre for East Asian Cultural Studies for UNESCO and the Toyo Bunko, 1998.
Vogel, Hans Ulrich. 'Gas: Exploitation and Use of Natural Gas in Premodern China'. In *Encyclopaedia of the History of Science, Technology, and Medicine in Non-Western Cultures*, ed. Helaine Selin, 963–5. Dordrecht: Kluwer Academic, 1997.
Voltaire. 'Essai sur les moeurs et l'esprit des nations'. In *OEuvres complètes de Voltaire*, Vol. 11. Paris: Garnier Frères, 1963.
Vries, Peer. *State, Economy and the Great Divergence: Great Britain and China, 1680s–1850s*. London: Bloomsbury, 2015.
Wagner, Donald B. 'The Administration of the Iron Industry in Eleventh-Century China'. *Journal of the Economic and Social History of the Orient*, Vol. 44, No. 2 (2001), 175–97.
Walker, Bethany J. 'Mamluk Investment in Transjordan: A "Boom and Bust" Economy'. *Mamluk Studies Review*, Vol. 8, No. 2 (2004), 119–47.
Walsingham, Thomas. *The Chronica Maiora of Thomas Walsingham, 1376–1422*, trans. David Preest. Woodbridge: Boydell Press, 2005.
Walvin, James. *Sugar: The World Corrupted: From Slavery to Obesity*. New York: Pegasus, 2018.

Wang, Liyao, et al. 'Insights into the Environmental–Economic Sustainability of Rice Production in China'. *Journal of Cleaner Production*, Vol. 498 (2025).

Weber, Eugen. *Peasants into Frenchmen: The Modernization of Rural France, 1870–1914*. Stanford, CA: Stanford University Press, 1976.

Wilson, H. H. *Rig-Veda Sanhitá: A Collection of Ancient Hindu Hymns*, Vol. 1. London: Trübner, 1866.

Winstanley, Gerrard. 'A Declaration to the Powers of England'. In *The Complete Works of Gerrard Winstanley*, Vol. 2, ed. Thomas N. Corns, Ann Hughes and David Loewenstein. Oxford: Oxford University Press, 2009.

Wolf, Eric R. *Peasants*. Englewood Cliffs, NJ: Prentice-Hall, 1966.

———. *Peasant Wars of the Twentieth Century*. New York: Harper & Row, 1969.

Wong, R. Bin. 'China before Capitalism'. In *The Cambridge History of Capitalism*, vol. 1, *The Rise of Capitalism: From Ancient Origins to 1848*, ed. L. Neal and J. G. Williamson, 125–64. Cambridge: Cambridge University Press, 2014.

Wood, Michael. *The Story of China: A Portrait of a Civilisation and Its People*. London: Simon & Schuster, 2020.

Wyngaard, Amy S. *From Savage to Citizen: The Invention of the Peasant in the French Enlightenment*. Newark, DE: University of Delaware Press, 2004.

Yang Jing Qing and Maman Lesmana. 'Hindu-Buddhist Influence on the Myths of Rice Gods in Southeast Asia and Its Role in Modern Agriculture Development'. *International Journal of Research and Innovation in Social Science*, Vol. 6, No. 3 (2022), 589–97.

Young, Allen M. *The Chocolate Tree: A Natural History of Cacao*. Gainesville, FL: University Press of Florida, 2007.

Zech, Steven T. *Between Two Fires: Civilian Resistance during Internal Armed Conflict in Peru*. PhD dissertation, University of Washington, 2016.

Index

Illustrations have page no. in *italics*. Footnotes have suffix 'n'. Figures are given in *italics*.

Image Credits

Integrated images

p. 49: Willoughby Wallace Hooper / Bridgeman Images
p. 51: CPA Media Pte Ltd / Alamy
p. 76: INTERFOTO / Alamy
p. 81: Carlo Bollo / Alamy
p. 112: Map by Martin Lubikowski
p. 114: Author's own photograph
p. 124: Glyn Thomas / Alamy
p. 136: Photo 12 / Alamy
p. 137: Wendy Kay / Alamy
p. 172: Ivy Close Images / Alamy
p. 174: World History Archive / Alamy
p. 176: © The Advertising Archives / Bridgeman Images
p. 177: courtesy of Vladan Kzmvić, licensed under a Creative Commons Attribution CC0
p. 219: courtesy of Jack Bornholm, licensed under a Creative Commons Attribution CC0
p. 237: courtesy of Michel Chauvet, licensed under a Creative Commons Attribution CC0
p. 239: Penta Springs Limited / Alamy
p. 241: World History Archive / Alamy

Plate section

Image 1: Svintage Archive / Alamy
Image 2: © Look and Learn
Image 3: Gem Archive / Alamy
Image 4: Heritage Images / Hulton Archive / Getty Images
Image 5: Skimage / Alamy
Image 6: © Fine Art Images / Heritage Images / Heritage Image Partnership Ltd / Alamy
Image 7: Heritage Images / Heritage Image Partnership Ltd / Alamy
Image 8: Photo 12 / Universal Images Group / Getty Images
Image 9: Kate Kimber / Alamy
Image 10: Art Collection 2 / Alamy
Image 11: The Picture Art Collection / Alamy
Image 12: Volgi archive / Alamy
Image 13: courtesy of xennex, licensed under a Creative Commons Attribution
Image 14: Well / BOT / Alamy
Image 15: EMU history / Alamy
Image 16: Heritage Images / Hulton Archive / Getty Images
Image 17: Helene Rogers / Art Directors & TRIP / Alamy
Image 18: EMU history / Alamy
Image 19: D. Evans, R. Fletcher, 'The landscape of Angkor Wat redefined', *Antiquity*, Vol. 89, No. 348 (2015), 1402–1419. Copyright © Antiquity Publications Ltd, 2015.
Image 20: CPA Media Pte Ltd / Alamy
Image 21: Sendero Luminoso courtesy of Mr Publius, licensed under a Creative Commons Attribution CC0
Image 22: Museo Larco, Lima – Peru. ML001059, ML100723
Image 23: 'Coca Aperitif Drinks Poster Paris 1899' by M. G. Whittingham
Image 24: vellum / Bridgeman Images
Image 25: Museum of London / Heritage Images / Getty Images
Image 26: courtesy of Mr Nostalgic, licensed under a Creative Commons Attribution CC0 1.0

Acknowledgements

During my research for *Peasants*, many farmers in India, Cambodia, Peru and Ghana welcomed me into their villages, fields and homes. They offered me their hospitality, their stories, their ideas and their friendship. This book owes more to them than I can express.

A great many others offered guidance and generosity along the way. My thanks go to all of them; what follows is only a partial list.

In India: Professor Rajas Parchure, Anil Ghanwat, Amar Habib and Pankaj Mahale; my local guide and interpreter Sameer Sudhakar Rasekar; my translator and transcriber Mansoor Amlani; journalists Dattatray Jadhav and P. Sainath; my local associates Vaibhav Pandit, Bhushan Unde, and Mangesh Dahiwale; and GramHeet farmer organisation.

In Cambodia: Professor Sok Kimchhin and Professor Samnang Nguon at the Royal University of Agriculture in Phnom Penh; Sopheak Youk for wonderfully informative conversations; and Heum Sarin for translation and local assistance.

In Peru: Dan Collyns; Gustavo Gorriti and Romina Hella at IDL-Reporteros, whose guidance and introductions made this fieldwork possible; my local associate Edison Salvador Huaman Ccapchi; Marleny Salazar at DEVIDA; Anderson, for translation; and Willy, for practical arrangements.

In Ghana: my associate Ewoade Doreen Dziedzorm Abra, whose translations and trusted introductions to local communities were invaluable; journalist Kent Mensah for his masterful analysis of the complex landscape of rural Ghana and illegal gold mining; and Ebenezar and Resford for logistical support.

I wrote this book across several academic institutions. First and foremost, I am grateful to the African Studies Centre at the University of Oxford for its hospitality throughout the course of this book. Conversations with fellows and colleagues there greatly enriched the comparative and interdisciplinary dimensions of this project. I am especially thankful to Professor Miles Tendi for his mentorship and support.

Wolfson College, Oxford, was where I first began thinking seriously about many of the questions that eventually became this book and much of the research, reflection and writing took shape there.

At Yale University's Program in Agrarian Studies, I thank Professor Kalyanakrishnan Sivaramakrishnan, Professor Elisabeth Wood and my other colleagues. At Ca' Foscari University of Venice, I am thankful to Professor Monica Billio and the Department of Economics. Here I spent my Marie Skłodowska-Curie Fellowship, funded by the European Commission's Horizon Europe programme, whose support for my academic work I gratefully acknowledge.

My lifelong mentors, Professor Barbara Harriss-White and Professor Christophe Jaffrelot, have influenced this work profoundly. In writing a book that moves across several regions and histories, I relied on the advice and scholarship of other academic friends and colleagues. I would like to thank especially Dr Hugo Rojas-Corral, Professor David Wengrow, William Dalrymple, Dr Jack Turner, Dr Christopher Sponsel, Dr Muhammad Ali Jan, Professor Jens Lerche, Orlando Mostyn-Owen, Dr Ionut Moise and Dr Tone Sommerfelt. Particular thanks to Professor Jørgen Carling at the Peace Research Institute Oslo for first introducing me to Ghana.

For reading drafts and offering thoughtful feedback, I thank Professor Michael Odijie, Professor Lucia Dammert, Dr Andrés Ajens, Dr Enrique Morales, Beltran Calveyra and colleagues at the Yale University's Agrarian Studies seminar series.

Enormous gratitude to David Godwin at David Godwin Associates and to Jennifer Joel and Karolina Sutton at Creative Artists Agency. And to my ever-inspiring editors, Alexis Kirschbaum at Bloomsbury, Hilary Redmon and Daniel Halpern at Knopf – whose belief in this project sustained it from its earliest days.

Thank you to friends who encouraged me throughout – Steffi, Rutger, Umar and Kaveh. To my parents, whose enthusiasm for this project from afar carried me through. And to my late grandparents, with remembrance. Especially my grandfather, who took me on journeys from Iran's Alborz mountains to the rice fields along the Caspian, who showed me the qanats and pomegranate orchards of Yazd and who introduced me to the lore of the rural landscape and our place within it. I hope he would appreciate my attempts to honour what he taught me.

My deepest debt is to Rana, to whom I dedicate this book.

A Note on the Author

Maryam Aslany's work focuses on the crisis of the global countryside. Over the last fourteen years, she has carried out field research among agricultural societies in some of the most remote landscapes of Asia, Africa and Latin America.

She is currently a Marie Skłodowska-Curie Fellow at Ca' Foscari University of Venice and a Research Associate at the African Studies Centre at the University of Oxford. She was previously a Junior Research Fellow at Wolfson College, Oxford, and a Research Fellow at the Peace Research Institute Oslo.

She is the author of *Contested Capital* and *Harvest*, an Audible podcast series.